The Old Republicans

The Old Republicans

SOUTHERN CONSERVATISM

IN THE

AGE OF JEFFERSON

Norman K. Risjord

COLUMBIA UNIVERSITY PRESS

New York and London 1965

Copyright © 1965 Columbia University Press
Library of Congress Catalog Card Number: 65–17642
Printed in the United States of America

For Connie, Mark, and Eric

Acknowledgments

Professor Bernard Mayo of the University of Virginia, who guided this project from term paper to doctoral dissertation, has given me constant encouragement in the preparation of this book. His careful scholarship and perceptive thought have been a continuing source of inspiration. Professors Thomas Perkins Abernethy and Dumas Malone, who have read portions of the manuscript, have also given me much valuable criticism. Two of my former colleagues at DePauw University, Clifton Phillips and James Findlay, offered a number of worthwhile suggestions concerning style and interpretation.

The Institute of Early American History and Culture, Williamsburg, Virginia, has kindly permitted me to use, in Chapter V, portions of my article, "1812: Conservatives, War Hawks, and the Nation's Honor," *William and Mary Quarterly*, 3rd series, XVIII (1961), 196–210. I must also express my gratitude to the many librarians whose kind assistance eased the labors of research. Finally, I should like to thank my wife, who accompanied me through the joy and the pain of producing a book.

Norman K. Risjord

Madison, Wisconsin
September, 1964

Contents

The Old Republicans

Introduction

Jeffersonian Democracy was a political movement that may be described as liberal but not necessarily progressive. Carried to its logical conclusions, it was essentially negative. Fundamental to the political thought of the Jeffersonians was the compact theory of government with its corollaries of economy, simplicity, and severe limitations on the power of the central government. Though Jefferson's own faith in human nature lent an air of optimistic democracy to these ideas, in the hands of some of his followers these doctrines became powerful engines of conservatism.

The Old Republicans appeared as a reaction to the surge of nationalism that followed the War of 1812, but this group had ties, in personnel and in political principle, with both earlier and later conservative movements within the Republican party. This is a study of the conservative wing of Jefferson's Republican party, the men who took deeply to heart the compact theory of government and carried it to its logical conclusions. Since the Old Republicans were mostly Southerners, this study includes also the development of Southern conservative thought into a self-conscious sectionalism. The Old Republicans are thus the missing link in the conservative tradition between the Antifederalists of 1788 and the states' rights Southerners of the Jacksonian era.

The conservative tradition in America itself is a puzzling one.

Scholars who attempt to define American conservatism in terms of the ideas of Edmund Burke are confounded by the fact that America never had an effective feudal aristocracy and abandoned the monarchy and the established Church in the Revolution. Instead, as Louis Hartz so well demonstrates, the American political tradition was founded on a bourgeois Puritan and Lockean Liberalism.[1] Yet within the Liberal tradition it is still possible to progress or stand still. As a working definition of American conservatism for the purposes of historical evaluation I would suggest the following: a psychological resistance to change; a reluctance to adapt political programs to the felt needs of the times. To be sure, such a definition is pragmatic and relative and depends largely on the subjective evaluation of the historian. But it avoids the theoretical vagaries and confusion stemming from the effort to link conservatism with Burke or Medieval Feudalism, and it is no more subjective than the Populist interpretation of American history popularized by such facile writers as Charles Beard or Vernon Louis Parrington.

There are, it is true, many similarities between the thought of the Old Republicans and the philosophy of Edmund Burke, and John Randolph himself once acknowledged Burke to be the most important influence on his thought.[2] Like Burke, the Southern conservatives based their political philosophy on a desire to preserve the traditions and supremacy of a whiggish squire-archy, and they shared with him a reverence for traditional institutions, an opposition to "King Whirl," a distrust of human nature, and a pessimism toward the future that is characteristic of all conservatives. But in Burke these predilections reinforced his veneration for the Establishment; in the Old Republicans they fathered an Antifederalist distrust of power.

The Old Republicans were Liberals in the classic sense of the term—liberty *from* government, freedom of the individual. Burke flirted for a time with Liberalism (e.g., reform of the royal household), but his preference for an organic state and established institutions won out and, in Lord Acton's phrase, "made the first of Liberals the first of Conservatives." The Burke to whom Randolph bore tribute was the Burke who defended Dunning's resolution, not the Burke of the *Reflections*. Significantly the Old Republicans voiced no criticism of France until 1806 when it became evident that Napoleon had perverted the idealism of the French Revolution to serve the ends of French imperialism. In the 1790s, Randolph, like many young Republicans, used the French calendar, signed his letters "Citizen," and approved of the writings of Tom Paine. The Old Republicans were the heirs not of Edmund Burke but of the philosophes and the Enlightenment. They broke with Jefferson, not because he was a Liberal but because he was not Liberal enough.

It is nevertheless possible to characterize the Old Republicans as conservatives, even while denying their connection with Edmund Burke. They were conservative because they sought to apply the doctrines of the physiocrats long after they had become obsolete. They founded their philosophy on the assumption that agriculture was the only secure economic basis for society. They would have solved the problem of marketing farm products by relying on foreign merchants or at most tolerating the "direct trade"—the export of surplus staples. Ideally, society for them was a tempered feudalism, a hierarchical structure of mutual obligations and responsibilities in which the ownership of land was a prerequisite for political or social position. Politically, they accepted the physiocratic doctrines that agriculture was the cornerstone of freedom and that a free society could flourish only in a small state. They agreed with the dictum of the Virginian George Mason that there "never was a government over a very extensive country without destroying the liberties of the people."

These physiocratic assumptions were reinforced by the Antifederalist legacy of states' rights as a weapon for preserving local powers and personal liberties. The smaller the unit of government the less the possibility of usurpation and the less harm that

could be wrought by an occasional usurper. But this Antifederalist fear of power—healthy when applied to the defense of
a liberal republic against tyranny—led them to oppose all positive action by the central government. Liberalism was to become
the predominant intellectual current in the nineteenth century.
In the hands of the Jacksonians it was even progressive, but the
Old Republicans used it to defend an eighteenth-century society
and a colonial, agrarian economy in an age that was witnessing
the dawn of the industrial revolution.

The Old Republicans can be identified as conservatives on
other grounds as well. Because they favored government by
landed gentlemen, they opposed any extension of the franchise
to the propertyless and any effort to give more political weight
to the populous West. John Taylor of Caroline based his whole
philosophic edifice on a landowning gentry. Randolph, Littleton Waller Tazewell, and Benjamin Watkins Leigh led the fight
against ballot-box democracy in the Virginia constitutional convention of 1829. Nathaniel Macon silently opposed the suffrage
movement in North Carolina that culminated in the constitutional convention of 1835.

The Old Republicans were conservative, finally, because they
failed to recognize the importance of the force of nationalism
and its impact on the American people. Nationalism had a profound influence on the foreign policy of Jefferson and Madison
—in the Louisiana Purchase, the West Florida controversy, and
the War of 1812. After the war it was the biggest single factor
in shaping domestic programs. The Old Republicans at first
ignored the phenomenon and then tried to obstruct its influence.

Identifying the Old Republicans as conservatives does not
imply that they were the only conservatives in the period. There
are as many varieties of conservatism as there are sets of values
worth conserving. But there are essential differences between the
conservatism of John Taylor of Caroline and that of a Fisher
Ames, a George Cabot, or a Chancellor Kent. The Federalists
preferred a strong central government as the best agency for

defending the values they held sacred—security of property, political stability, respect for religion. The Southern conservatives were convinced that a consolidated political state would be manipulated in undesirable directions by a majoritarian democracy. They felt that the best defense against the threat of a nationalist, industrialized democracy was to retain a decentralized government in which their way of life could be defended from local bastions of gentlemanly rule.

The Federalist system thus represented a neomercantilist threat to American Liberalism. In its foreign policy and measures of domestic repression it represented an early phase of the conservative reaction engendered in the Western world by the Jacobinical tendencies of the French Revolution—a reaction characterized after 1815 as "the age of Metternich." In opposition to this system the Republican party developed its basic tenets—preoccupation with executive discretion, the size of government, taxes, armies, and navies—the "principles of 1798," to which the Old Republicans adhered throughout their history.

The election of Jefferson in 1800 brought a fresh breath of Liberalism to the United States. Jefferson provided a new direction in the fiscal system of the government, a democratic attitude toward the press and the judiciary, and the first steps toward separation of business and government. But to the Southern conservatives within his own party he did not carry his program far enough. He neither sought constitutional amendments to prevent a future sedition law nor did he instigate a direct attack on the symbol of the Federalist system, the Bank of the United States. In short, the nationalism of the Federalists was assimilated by Jefferson and Madison and given only a new direction, resulting in the purchase of Louisiana, the acquisition of West Florida, and the War of 1812.

The enthusiastic support Republicans gave to the Louisiana Purchase stands in sharp contrast to the explosion that resulted from the effort to obtain West Florida in 1806. Southern conservatives were willing to cooperate in legitimate expansion, particularly when it served their agrarian society, but they developed a puritanical aversion to the seamy side of nationalist expansion. John Randolph's schism, to be sure, was largely a personal vendetta, dictated by his personal revulsion against the Yazoo frauds and a nearly irrational fear of Madison's influence in the administration. But Randolph hoped for open support from the conservative wing and was bitterly disappointed when he failed to get it. Despite its failure (due in part to Randolph's own eccentricities), the Quid schism was the manifestation of conservative discontent.

Although the Quids were an ineffectual and hopelessly outnumbered faction, their defection throws considerable light on the later history of the Republican party. John Randolph in the West Florida controversy was the first prominent Republican to criticize Napoleon openly, the first to realize clearly the extent to which in France the sense of republican destiny had degenerated into rank chauvinism. This suspicion of the motives of France tended to reinforce their skepticism of the Jeffersonian policy of commercial retaliation against England. More concerned than Jefferson for the economic interests of the South, the Quids refused to sacrifice the export trade in Southern staples on the altar of national honor. Just as the Southern conservatives passed on the torch of states' rights to John C. Calhoun a quarter of a century later, the arguments of the Quids against the nonintercourse acts and the embargo laid the theoretical foundations for the long period of mutual friendship between the Southern planter and the British manufacturer.

After the humiliating defeat of James Monroe in the presidential election of 1808 demonstrated the weakness of the Quids, the nature of Southern conservatism underwent a subtle change. The Randolph schism actually embarrassed most Southern conservatives, for it brought all critics under suspicion and placed a premium on party regularity. After the election Southern conservatives eagerly returned to the fold leaving Randolph in virtual isolation. After 1808, therefore, opposition to the administration is no longer a satisfactory criterion for conservatism. It must be defined instead as a refusal to respond positively to the needs of the nation, a definition which included, for a time, President Madison himself.

A rapid series of events marked the deterioration of relations with England. The *Chesapeake* affair, the repudiation of Erskine, and the mission of "Copenhagen" Jackson piled humiliation upon injury, fed the spirit of American nationalism, and fostered a growing demand for war. Unable to adjust their philosophy to this rapidly changing situation the Republican conservatives, a majority of the party till 1811, continued to approach the great problems, foreign and domestic, that faced the nation, within the doctrinal framework of strict construction and pacifism created by the Republican party in the 1790s. They cooperated with John Randolph's efforts to emasculate the army and navy in 1810, they adhered to the policy of commercial retaliation long after its futility had been demonstrated, and they permitted the Bank of the United States to expire in 1811 despite its obvious usefulness.

The election of the War Hawks, nationalists determined to redeem the self-respect of the nation, was the measure of the extent to which the conservatives had failed to respond to the times. The record of the Twelfth Congress is largely the story of the efforts of the War Hawks to convert Republican conservatives from a Jeffersonian pacifism to the necessity for war. John Randolph remained obdurate, but almost completely alone, in his refusal to compromise the "principles of '98" or become a virtual satellite of the French empire. Most other conservatives supported the declaration of war, largely for lack of an acceptable alternative, but they did so with many misgivings for the future of the Liberal republic.

Despite the reluctance with which they approached the conflict, the Southern conservatives gave loyal support to the war effort and the Madison Administration. They balked only on an occasional issue that involved too radical a departure from

Old Republican doctrine. Even in the critical year 1814, when a British force burned Washington and British armies descended on the New England frontier and New Orleans, the conservatives blocked a proposed conscript law, postponed the establishment of a second Bank of the United States, and opposed a program of naval construction. When news of peace arrived early in 1815 they led a nearly successful effort to slash the army to a mere six thousand men.

The first few years following the war were again a period of transition for the Southern conservatives. The "Young Republicans" were in solid control of Congress and the spirit of nationalism was in vogue. Only ten Old Republicans voted against all three key measures of the "new nationalism"—the bank, the tariff, and internal improvements. The conservative reaction against the postwar nationalism appeared not in Congress but in Virginia, and it was a delayed reaction that did not materialize until 1817. A variety of factors caused the revival of Southern conservatism in 1817. By then the dimensions of the new nationalism had become clear, particularly with the threat of a nationwide network of roads and canals that would open up the new lands of the West. This threat coincided with an agricultural depression in the upper South which drained off population to the virgin lands of Alabama and Mississippi. The depression produced dissatisfaction with the protective tariff, as it did in South Carolina a decade later, and a battle with the Supreme Court over the right of appeal from state courts brought home to Virginians the scope of the nationalist threat to states' rights.

Interestingly enough, many of the Old Republicans who appeared in 1817 were not old at all. The leadership of the faction fell upon relatively young men, such as Philip Pendleton Barbour, elected as a War Hawk in 1813, and John Tyler, who entered Congress in 1816 after serving several terms in the Virginia House of Delegates. Many of the conservatives of the prewar period had either died or retired from politics. Only Randolph and Macon had witnessed the political battles of the 1790s. Yet in the reaction of 1817 they gained new friends among men who had been loyal supporters of Jefferson and Madison and who had stood firm in support of the war—men such as Thomas Ritchie, editor of the influential Richmond *Enquirer*. The conservatism of the Old Republicans after the war was partly a response to the shift of popular sentiment in Virginia and partly a matter of age and a temperamental inability to adjust to the times. The result, in any case, was a conservative reaction in the upper South that had repercussions in Tennessee and Georgia. During the first administration of James Monroe, the Old Republicans, numbering about thirty in Congress, managed to stymie a federal program of internal improvements, conducted a major attack on the Second Bank of the United States, reduced taxes, and maintained a running criticism of the conduct of the War Department. Any positive activity on the part of the federal government was virtually impossible.

The conjunction of the economic depression and the Missouri debate in 1819–20 marked the climax and, ironically, the death knell of the Old Republican movement, for after 1820 the South began to develop a self-conscious sectionalism. The doctrines and slogans of Old Republicanism were adopted by the new Southern sectionalists for their own purposes, while the membership was absorbed into the political movement in behalf of the presidential aspirations of William Harris Crawford.

After the election of 1824 the Old Republicans were guided by Martin Van Buren into the presidential camp of Andrew Jackson. To Southern conservatives the basic appeal of Jacksonian Democracy was its Liberalism—its demand for simplicity and purity in government and its opposition to government-chartered monopolies. But it soon became apparent that Jacksonian Liberalism was more commercial than agrarian, that it was oriented toward popular democracy rather than the preservation of the Southern gentry. The patronage policies of the

President and the nullification controversy alienated a few, including Randolph and Tyler, but others, such as Macon and Ritchie, remained loyal to Jackson.

The division of the Old Republicans on the issues posed by Jacksonian Democracy symbolizes their dual legacy. They kept alive the torch of states' rights and passed it on to the lower South, until it was carried into the Civil War and expired. But, ironically enough, they also provided the concepts and the slogans for the new industrial Liberalism, which triumphed in the Civil War. The duality of this heritage persists even into the twentieth century. The agrarian sentiments of the Old Republicans were revived not long ago by the group of Southern intellectuals who combined to produce *I'll Take My Stand* (1930) and *Who Owns America?* (1936). The preservation of a particularist localism, on the other hand, continues to be an important obstacle to change, both in the defense of racial inequality and the protection of property interests. It remains an important feature of modern conservative thought in its continuing battle against a consolidated government controlled by a mass democracy.

Prelude: 1798

Almost as if he were remembering the details of a nightmare, Thomas Jefferson at the end of his life could still recall vividly the peril in which the Republican party—indeed the Constitution itself—stood in that terrible spring of 1798. The Federalist usurpations, he wrote,

and violations of the Constitution at that period, and their majority in both Houses of Congress, were so great, so decided, and so daring, that, after combating their aggressions inch by inch without being able in the least to check their career, the Republican leaders thought it would be best for them to give up their useless efforts there, go home, get into their respective Legislatures, embody whatever of resistance they could be formed into, and if ineffectual, to perish there as in the last ditch. All therefore retired, leaving Mr. Gallatin alone in the House of Representatives and myself in the Senate, where I then presided as Vice President. . . . No one who was not a witness of the scenes of that gloomy period can form any idea of the afflicting persecutions and personal indignities we had to brook.[1]

For nearly seven years the three great Virginians—Jefferson, Madison, and Monroe—had been slowly building up an opposition political party, a party that in domestic affairs fought Hamilton's funding system, the Bank of the United States, and the excise taxes and in foreign affairs demanded a neutrality that was at least sympathetic toward the French Republic. Yet after nearly a decade they had had only limited success in appealing to the people for support. Hamilton's fiscal system was too complex and too successful to serve as a text for popular appeals. And despite the unpopularity of the Jay Treaty in the South and West and its effect on the evolution of political parties, foreign affairs proved disappointing as a source of political issues. The temporary *rapprochement* with England following the Jay Treaty, the tendency of the French to interfere in American affairs, and the obvious need for neutrality prevented the Republicans from exploiting the field.

In the spring of 1798 their situation was particularly desperate. The publication in March of the dispatches relating to the XYZ Affair produced a tremendous popular reaction against France, and the Federalist administration of John Adams basked in a newfound popularity. On March 19 the President sent to Congress a message that hinted at the possibility of war with France and asked Congress to make preparations for that eventuality. The Federalist Congress responded with alacrity, passing laws to suspend commerce with France, to authorize the seizure of French merchant vessels, to increase the size of the army, and to make additional naval preparations. Confronted by the popular clamor for war, the Republicans hesitated to oppose the preparations and confined themselves to delaying tactics, hoping to avoid war until the furor subsided. "At this moment all the passions are boiling over," wrote Jefferson, "and one who keeps himself cool and clear of the contagion is so far below the point of ordinary conversation that he finds himself insulated in every society." [2]

As the military preparedness bills came before Congress during April and May the small band of Republicans fought a rearguard action by attacking every detail. A bill to add sixteen vessels to the navy to furnish greater protection to American commerce was opposed by John Williams of New York on the ground that it would entail an enormous expense, which the Federalists proposed to meet by levying a federal property tax. "If the landed interest," averred Williams, "was to be called upon for three or four millions of dollars a year to protect com-

merce, the country had better have no commerce at all." Another bill to create a separate Department of the Navy with a
secretary of cabinet rank was opposed by the Republicans on the
ground that the War Department was perfectly competent to
administer the navy and the creation of a new department would
merely extend the bureaucratic complexity of the government
and the patronage power of the President. It might even further
embroil us with France. "Whenever an office was established,"
noted Williams, "something was always found for it to do. Soon
after the War Department was established, we had an Indian
War. . . ." He did not carry the comparison through, but the
implication was obvious. Both navy bills passed, however, the
first by 42–26 and the second 47–41.[3]

A bill authorizing the President to raise a provisional army of
20,000 men was attacked by Republicans for many reasons.
Albert Gallatin pointed out that the bill, by delegating to the
President the power to raise the additional troops whenever he
thought them needed, in effect abandoned the constitutional provision that only Congress could "raise and support armies."
Nathaniel Macon, North Carolina planter, maintained that the
militia was perfectly competent to defend the nation from invasion. Macon thought it

wonderful that gentlemen should persist in bringing troops into the
Southern states against their will. If members from that quarter were
of the opinion that their militia was sufficient defense, why will
gentlemen be so over civil as to force troops upon them?

Could it be that the additional military forces were intended for
something other than defense against foreign invasion? Gallatin,
whose western Pennsylvania constituents had been prominent in
the Whisky Rebellion four years before, charged that the bill

contemplated the erection of a standing military force of the very
worst kind . . . a plan to arm one description of men exclusively of
others, and give them to the President of the United States to be
used as he pleased; and what security had they that they would not
be used for dangerous purposes?

As a result of this Republican criticism the bill was altered to reduce the discretion of the President and the number of men to
be raised was halved, but the bill passed anyway 51–40.[4]

The Republican opposition to the extension of the powers of
the central government in 1798 was not exclusively political.
Dr. Thomas Cooper, a disciple of the English Radical Joseph
Priestley and a friend of Jefferson's, published a pamphlet that
explained the Republican stand in economic terms. The dispute
with France, Cooper argued, involved fundamentally not the
question of diplomatic representation but our foreign trade and
rights as neutrals. And any attempt to defend this trade by military action was basically uneconomic because the cost of maintaining a large navy was greater that the profits derived from the
trade. Moreover, the preparations for war would inevitably result in heavy taxes on the people for the benefit only of the pro-
British merchants in the commercial cities.[5]

Cooper's fears that in the end someone would have to pay the
bill were borne out in May when the Federalists introduced a
measure to raise additional money by a direct tax on houses,
land, and slaves to be apportioned among the states. Despite
Republican allegations that this method of taxation would operate inequitably against landowners, the bill was passed over the
objections of a dwindling minority, 69–19. The purpose of the
tax was to furnish security for a new treasury loan, and a few
days later a bill authorizing the President to borrow up to $5
million passed the House with similar ease.[6] In the Senate, where
the Republicans could muster only the Virginians Henry Tazewell and Stevens Thompson Mason, Timothy Bloodworth of
North Carolina, Andrew Jackson and Joseph Anderson of Tennessee, John Brown of Georgia, and John Langdon of New
Hampshire, these measures of military preparation were passed
by even more lopsided majorities.

John Taylor of Caroline, whose *Enquiry into the Principles
and Tendency of Certain Public Measures* published in 1794 accused Hamilton of creating with his funding system an "aris-

tocracy of paper and patronage," thought that the Federalists of 1798, by vastly extending the power and patronage of the Executive and by greatly increasing the military strength of the government, were trying to change the very nature of the federal system. In a letter to Jefferson, Taylor suggested that a separation of the union was the only way to end the conflict. Jefferson, though seriously alarmed, was not yet ready to contemplate disunion and urged Taylor to be patient, for the "reign of witches" was bound to pass over.[7]

The worst was yet to come, however. In May the Federalists introduced a series of bills placing stringent regulations on foreigners. One bill extended from five to fourteen years the waiting period required for an alien to become a citizen. A second provided for the deportation of aliens of a hostile nation, while a third authorized the President to expel any alien whom he judged dangerous to the peace and safety of the nation. In June they brought in a bill to punish as seditious anyone who published criticism of the administration or the government. The Alien bills, in the discretion they left to the President, were at least of questionable legality; the Sedition bill, a direct violation of the First Amendment, was patently unconstitutional.[8]

The Republicans fought the bills through a month of debate. Edward Livingston of New York in opposing the Enemy Alien bill said, "If we are ready to violate the Constitution, will the people submit to our unauthorized acts? Sir, they ought not to submit; they would deserve the chains that our measures are forging for them, if they did not resist." A few days later when the House was debating the Sedition bill the Federalists accused Edward Livingston of sedition by his veiled threat of popular rebellion. They disclaimed any desire to silence members of the House, but they thought such speeches should not be printed and circulated publicly. Gallatin, however, came to the aid of Livingston and endorsed his concept of resistance to unconstitutional measures. Gallatin believed "that doctrine to be strictly correct and neither seditious nor treasonable." The Republican protests were to no avail: the Enemy Alien bill passed 46–40 and the Sedition bill 44–41.[9]

Perhaps Gallatin and Livingston had conferred with Jefferson, for these remarks seemed to set the tone for the Republican protest. In the summer of 1798 Jefferson drafted a series of resolutions which were given to John Breckinridge of Kentucky to be introduced into the Kentucky legislature. Reflecting the old Antifederalist fear that the extension of governmental power was necessarily a threat to the liberties of the citizens, Jefferson wrote: "Free government is founded in jealousy, and not in confidence. . . . In questions of power, then, let no more be said of confidence in man, but bind him down from mischief, by the chains of the Constitution." Jefferson felt that the Constitution, honestly interpreted, left the essential powers of government with the sovereign states, who, being closer to the people, were more likely to observe their rights. In an effort to generalize this assumption into a philosophy he formulated in his resolutions the defensive doctrine that the union was a compact among the states with certain limited powers assigned to a central government. Since each state had voluntarily joined the compact, each, logically, retained the right "to judge for itself of infractions [of the compact and of] the mode and measure of redress." Thus, "where powers are assumed which have not been delegated, a nullification of the act is the right remedy; that every State has a natural right in cases not within the compact . . . to nullify of their own authority all assumptions of power. . . ." The resolutions then demonstrated the unconstitutionality of the Alien and Sedition Acts and invited the legislatures of the other states to "concur in declaring these acts void and of no force." [10] The Kentucky legislature toned down slightly Jefferson's language and passed the resolutions in the autumn of 1798.

Other resolutions drawn up by Madison and submitted to the Virginia Assembly were more mild. But they also adopted the compact theory, asserting "that in the case of a deliberate, palpable, and dangerous exercise of other powers not granted by the said compact, the States, who are parties thereto, have the right, and are in duty bound to interpose for arresting the progress of the evil and for maintaining . . . the authorities, rights, and liberties appertaining to them." [11]

At last the Republican leaders had an issue on which they could appeal to the electorate. Though the reception of the Virginia and Kentucky resolutions by the other state legislatures was generally hostile, they were endorsed by popular meetings all over the South and West and contributed materially to the election victory in 1800.[12] The resistance to the Federalist war measures in the spring of 1798 had given the Republicans a specific program of opposition to all forms of centralized power. The Virginia and Kentucky resolutions had generalized that program into a philosophy. But it had been a traumatic experience, and those who had participated would not soon forget it.

The Conservative Wing

Few elections in American history have been more bitterly contested than the election of 1800. In a period when the terms *faction* and *party* were still epithets, when the experiment in representative government was still toddling on its newfound legs, differences in political viewpoint were easily exaggerated into a conflict of principle that seemed to involve the very security of the Republican system. To the Republican party it was a victory for the representatives of the people over a faction that had resorted to a standing army, a malicious credit system, and the use of extraconstitutional means of silencing popular criticism to maintain itself in power. The victory of Mr. Jefferson, wrote one jubilant Virginian, was "the Triumph of the democratic Representatives in Congress over the tools of the Anglo-monarchico Aristocratic faction: the Triumph of the sovereign people over their rebellious servants, and of Human Nature or of Humanity over the accursed Persecutors of the Human Race." [1]

To many Republicans the victory in 1800 involved more than a mere change in personnel. It was the signal for a drastic change that would limit the power and activities of government and usher in a new age of freedom for the individual. Expressing this view was another Virginian who had been prominent in the Republican opposition: "In this quarter, we think the great work is only begun; and that without a *substantial reform*, we shall have little reason to congratulate ourselves on the mere change of men." [2]

The Republican platform in 1800 was largely a negative one, a crystallization of nearly ten years' opposition to the administrations of Washington and Adams. The general principles of the party were best expressed some years later by John Randolph of Roanoke when he found it necessary to remind the House of Representatives of the basic principles that had brought the Republican party into power. "What are they?" asked Randolph:

Love of peace, hatred of offensive war, jealousy of the State governments towards the General Government and of the influence of the Executive over the coordinate branches of the Government; a dread of standing armies; a loathing of public debt, taxes, and excises; tenderness for the liberty of the citizen; jealousy, Argus-eyed jealousy of the patronage of the President.[3]

A catalogue, in short, of the basic features of nineteenth-century American Liberalism.

Despite Republican accusations, the Federalists had laid the foundations for a stable government, and President Jefferson found himself at the head of a successful organization which had been built up slowly over the previous twelve years. As a practical politician he was willing to compromise with circumstance, and as a realistic statesman he saw that a moderate policy was best calculated to secure the future of the republic. Confident of the strength of his ideas, Jefferson saw that a Republican victory had reduced the threat of governmental power, and he refrained from resurrecting obsolete issues such as the Alien and Sedition Acts, which had expired quietly in 1800. He realized, moreover, that to attack Hamilton's system would precipitate a bitter struggle and perhaps drive moderates from the Republican ranks.[4] His accomplishments over the next four years were real enough. The system of internal taxes was abolished and provision was made for the gradual retirement of the national debt; the army and navy budgets and ranks were slashed, the Judiciary Act of 1801 was repealed, and the naturalization law was revised.

But at best these measures only trimmed the edges of the Federalist system.

The President's inaugural address was moderate enough to win the approval even of Alexander Hamilton, who regarded it "as virtually a candid retraction of past misapprehensions, and a pledge to the community that the new President will not lend himself to dangerous innovations, but in essential points tread in the steps of his predecessors." [5] The phrase "we are all republicans, we are all federalists," which symbolized the President's conciliatory attitude, struck the flinty core of the conservative group within his party and sent a shower of rumors through the Republican ranks. Even some of the moderate Republicans showed concern over the President's attitude. John Dawson, a close friend of Secretary of State Madison, wrote to James Monroe early in 1801, "Some of our . . . republicans express great uneasiness at rumors which are in circulation—it is said the President intends to adopt the system of accomodation, to endeavor by favors to draw over those, who have been his opponents—if he does he will certainly loose his best interest. . . . " Monroe thought enough of reports such as this to warn Jefferson to proceed cautiously.[6]

The President, in truth, never considered the leadership of the Federalist party as capable of conciliation, but he hoped to draw away the rank and file of the party by a moderate policy. Although he confided to intimates that Republicans would be given a proportionate share of offices, his public statements left the distinct impression that Federalist officeholders would not be discharged for their political views.[7] This alarmed many Republicans who feared the Republican program might be undermined by Federalist clerks in the government. The demands for patronage forced Jefferson shortly to declare that Republicans would be appointed to all vacant posts and that delinquent officials, the "midnight appointments" of John Adams, and Federalist attorneys and marshals would be removed. Even so, this policy was implemented very slowly. After two years in power Republicans were in possession of only a little more than half the principal federal offices. As late as 1803 Nathaniel Macon of North Carolina was complaining that not a single Federalist had been removed from office in his state.[8] The early ambiguity in the President's attitude toward Federalist officeholders and the caution with which he displaced them planted the first seed of suspicion in the minds of some of the more ardent Republicans.

There was more, however, than conciliation in Jefferson's conduct through the first four years of his administration. The responsibilities of power forced him to temper much of his early idealism, and he found himself forced to adapt many of his old policies to the exigencies of domestic politics and to the stresses of foreign relations in a world that respected only power and money. Although the Republican party had originated in a reaction against the neomercantilism of the Federalists, the Jeffersonians found themselves after 1800 unable to sever completely the ties between business and government and unable to abandon completely the nationalism of the Federalist system.

The victory of the Republicans in 1800 brought a fresh breath of Liberalism to American politics. Liberal thought was not anticapitalist, but it did demand an end to the alliance between business and government symbolized by the Bank of the United States and the Hamiltonian funding system. Jefferson himself was not opposed to all banks, as his agency in the founding of the Bank of Virginia in 1793 suggests. After he became President, he was concerned only that the bankers might become a suspicious, fearful, discontented segment of society. This, no doubt, is what he had in mind when he wrote to Gallatin, "I am decidedly in favor of making all the banks Republican." [9]

The Republicans in power had important commercial affiliations, and while they initiated a program to pay off the national debt as quickly as possible they never attacked directly the other symbol of Federalism, the Bank of the United States. Jefferson, moreover, was not wholly averse to using the government as a positive agency for the development of agriculture and commerce. In 1806 the President and his Secretary of the Treasury worked out a plan for a nationwide system of roads and canals that would not only aid the development of the economy but dispose of an anticipated surplus in the treasury. In 1808 Jefferson even asked Gallatin to draft a bill placing protective duties on certain manufactured products.[10] The vestiges of mercantilism and the commercial flavor of Jeffersonian Liberalism tended to breed suspicions in the less flexible, agrarian wing of the Republican party.

The conduct of foreign affairs after 1800 proved equally frustrating to the Republican conservatives. The nationalism that had characterized Federalist domestic policy was assimilated by Jefferson and Madison and given a new direction. Within two months after his inauguration Jefferson found himself in an undeclared war with the pirates of the Barbary Coast. Jefferson accepted the challenge and employed the Federalist-created navy in a successful effort to terminate the humiliating tribute exacted by the pirates in the Mediterranean. The defense of American prestige proved expensive, however, and threatened the whole system of retrenchment. Among the first to see this effect was John Randolph, head of the House Committee on Ways and Means and floor leader for the administration in Congress. "This Tripolitan War is utterly incompatible with the repeal of the internal taxes and the payment of the debt within the time contemplated by Mr. Gallatin," he complained in January, 1802.[11]

The purchase of Louisiana, a vast extension of national boundaries, also represented an increase in government centralization. Though certainly popular in the South and West, the purchase forced the President to hedge on the principle of strict construction. Persuaded by his friends not to seek an amendment to the Constitution granting him power to purchase foreign territory, Jefferson was eventually able to reconcile his assumption of power with his former views by the doctrine of the *salus populi*. In 1810, though still admitting the purchase was extra-legal, he defended the right of the President to act on "superior ground," a right he never would have conceded John Adams.[12] While the Louisiana Purchase met the uniform approval of Republicans, who realized that it would ensure an essentially rural society in America for the foreseeable future, it nevertheless was clear evidence of Jefferson's embrace of nationalism.

Nationalism is the basic thread of continuity that ties together the Federalist and Republican systems. It was born in the Revolution, possibly even before—in the "revolution in the minds and hearts of the people" observed by John Adams.[13] It may well have been the most important psychological factor in the formation of the Constitution, and it was at the heart of the Hamiltonian system. It can even be detected in Federalist foreign policy, in the policy of neutrality toward the war in Europe and in the Federalist response to the XYZ Affair. Although Jefferson and Madison eschewed domestic nationalism, they actively pursued a nationalistic foreign policy, evidenced by the acquisition of Louisiana and West Florida and by the war with England.

Nationalism in early nineteenth-century America may be defined as a combination of domestic centralization and a foreign policy that involved an active pursuit of national interests, the expansion of national boundaries, and a sensitivity to national prestige. The two features of nationalism were frequently intertwined. The intrigues of Jefferson and Madison to acquire West Florida were administration policy in which the Executive held the initiative. Congress and the people were expected only to be cooperative bystanders. The War of 1812, initially a nationalistic response to humiliations suffered at the hands of England, resulted in a domestic program of neomercantilism reminiscent of the Hamiltonian system.

The impact of nationalism, unfortunately, is almost impossible to document. The term itself is a modern one, and the phenomenon is relatively recent, born, it is generally conceded, in "the age of democratic revolution" at the end of the eighteenth century.[14] In this period, therefore, the force was only vaguely felt and seldom expressed. It can be detected only in the actions of its disciples and in the apprehensions of those whom it failed to touch.

The suspicion of nationalism evident in the conservative wing of the Republican party after 1801 was part of the legacy of Antifederalism. This is not to say that the Republican conservatives had any direct connection with the Antifederalists of 1788. In an era when the average life expectancy was less than forty years, rare was the man who participated actively in politics for as long as twenty years. In the decade and a half since the Constitution was ratified a new generation of political figures had come to maturity. The Republican conservatives nevertheless shared the Antifederalist fear of authority and suspicion of centralization. These were the roots of their discontent with the Jeffersonian compromises.

It was evident early in Jefferson's Administration that not all the Republicans acquiesced in the President's disposition to let the burning issues of 1798 fade peacefully into obscurity. "I am fully convinced of the danger of the republican cause at this time. We are too idle. I almost fear our administration are too good for human nature. . . ," wrote John Taylor of Caroline in 1802.[15] Behind Taylor's apprehension was the old Antifederalist fear of governmental power. In October of 1801 Taylor's uncle and former guardian, Edmund Pendleton, had written a pamphlet entitled *The Danger Not Over*, which was a critique of the Constitution that proposed a series of amendments restricting the powers of the government in regard to the army, the navy, finances, and the making of treaties. Though a supporter of the Constitution in 1788, Pendleton had approved the document with reservations and had desired amendments at the time. His experience with Federalism had no doubt reinforced his fears.

The Virginia House of Delegates in the 1801–2 session passed a list of seven amendments similar to those suggested by Pendleton, but the state Senate postponed action on them. Taylor sought the endorsement of the administration for the amendments and suggested to Wilson Cary Nicholas that the President present them to Congress. When Nicholas informed him that the President lacked the power to make such recommendations, Taylor acidly replied that in that case the only safeguard for the liberties of the people was for Jefferson to remain in office permanently.[16]

Failing in their attempt to secure Constitutional amendments and ignored by a victorious party, the Republican conservatives gradually drew together in a vaguely discontented, though usually silent, faction within the party. Writing to his friend James Monroe some years later, John Taylor disagreed with Monroe's theory that the party had split over Jefferson's system of commercial retaliation. Describing the gradual division of the Republican party, Taylor wrote:

I think that the republican minority originated at a much earlier period than you state, and upon very different grounds. There were a number of people who soon thought and said to one another, that Mr. Jefferson did many good things, but neglected some better things; and who now view his policy as very like a compromise with Mr. Hamilton's. . . . Federalism, indeed, having been defeated, has gained a new footing by being taken into partnership with republicanism. It was this project which divided the republican party.[17]

During the administration of Jefferson this group of malcontents was never very numerous—indeed, a mere handful of men, mostly Virginians—but their political influence gave them an importance that was out of proportion to their numbers. In Virginia the conservatives seem to have been confined largely to the middle Tidewater and the district south of the James River, areas which had furnished the core of Antifederalist sentiment in Virginia since the Revolution.[18] Where the rest of eastern Virginia was more progressive agriculturally and had shifted largely to the production of wheat and other grains, the middle Tidewater, central Piedmont, and Southside were still growing tobacco on rapidly depleting soils.

The dominant figure in the middle Tidewater was Taylor,

agrarian conservative who had opposed the Constitution in 1788 and who represented an interesting combination of agricultural progressivism and political conservatism. Having made his plantation—"Hazelwood"—on the Rappahannock River a model of diversified agriculture, Taylor was to devote a lifetime to persuading his fellow planters of the benefits of soil conservation through crop rotation and fertilizing. But Taylor's crusade for progressive farming methods was more than an economic program; it had important political purposes. "The significant thing about Taylor's program," suggests Avery Craven, "was the effort to give a firm and enduring economic foundation from which the farmer might wage his battle for the preservation of the country gentleman ideal." [19] Significantly, tobacco and wheat, alone among the great Southern export staples, could be grown as efficiently on small farms as on large plantations. Taylor's economic system thus complemented his agrarian political philosophy. Most of the Virginia conservatives, to be sure, were wealthy, slave-owning planters like Taylor, but they tended to sneer at the cotton and rice barons of the lower South and kept the independent yeoman farmer at the base of their philosophical pyramid.[20]

James M. Garnett, a neighbor of Taylor, represented a similar combination of progressive agriculture and conservative politics.[21] More interested in organizations that would spread their doctrines, Garnett was later instrumental in the founding of the Virginia Agricultural Society and served as the perennial president of the Fredericksburg Agricultural Society. Garnett represented the middle Tidewater district in Congress during Jefferson's Administration, and the neighboring district in the central Piedmont was represented by the equally conservative Philip R. Thompson of Culpeper. The area south of the James produced no theoretician of the stature of Taylor, but it consistently elected to Congress during Jefferson's presidency the conservatives John Randolph of Roanoke, Christopher Clark of Lynchburg, and Edwin Gray of Portsmouth and Nansemond

County. Representing the mountainous southwest corner of the state was Abram Trigg, general of militia in the Revolution and Antifederalist delegate to the Virginia convention of 1788. Trigg had been a member of Congress since 1797 and was an intimate associate of Randolph until his retirement in 1809.

The extent of conservative opinion in these areas of Virginia is impossible to determine, for these same districts produced men of equal stature in the Republican party who consistently supported Jefferson and Madison—men such as Wilson Cary Nicholas, John Wayles Eppes, and James Barbour. It would be erroneous to assume that the election of a number of conservatives to the General Assembly and to the House of Representatives indicated a strong current of conservative opinion among the "Gentlemen Freeholders." The Virginia gentry were selected for political office largely on the basis of their local standing and influence. Candidates usually contented themselves with a vague statement of attachment to Republican principles and seldom approached the voters with specific programs of political action. Inadequate communications and apathetic voters permitted the gentleman politician a certain amount of independence of thought and action, and his opinions on specific issues normally resulted from personal predilections and friendships. Conservatism in Virginia thus was largely confined to certain members of the ruling circle, and their ideas were seldom made public. Indeed, the failure of John Randolph to attract any support for his opposition to the administration in 1806 and the colossal failure of Monroe's candidacy against Madison in the election of 1808 suggest that conservatism had scant public support in Virginia, particularly when it clashed with the party leadership.

Besides planters of the middle Tidewater and the Southside, the conservative wing in Virginia included a number of lawyers, pre-eminent among whom was Judge Spencer Roane. A son-in-law and protégé of Patrick Henry, Roane had served on the Supreme Court of Appeals since 1794. His political influence stemmed from his membership in the "Richmond Junto," which dominated the central committee of the Republican party in Virginia.[22] Another lawyer of considerable local influence was Littleton Waller Tazewell of Norfolk. Except for a brief term in Congress in 1800, Tazewell held no political office until he was elected to the Senate in 1824, but he was a close friend and confidant of both Randolph and Monroe. Benjamin Watkins Leigh, a lawyer of Petersburg, was also a close friend of John Randolph and performed valuable services in maintaining contacts between the conservatives in Congress and those in Virginia. Like Tazewell, he held no political office until his election to the Senate in 1834, except for a brief tour in the House of Delegates in 1811–13.

Rounding out this group was Randolph's stepfather, St. George Tucker. Though a man of limited political influence, Tucker had a wide circle of acquaintances throughout the state and was a highly respected professor of law at the College of William and Mary. As a teacher, Tucker was able to imbue a whole generation of future lawyer-planters with the doctrines of strict construction and states' rights. A radical on the subject, Tucker regarded the federal government as little more than "the organ through which the united republics communicate with foreign nations, and with each other."[23] Though these men were leading lights of the bar, one should not assume that the legal profession in Virginia was exclusively committed to the doctrines of a particularist agrarianism. The wide influence of commercial nationalists like John Marshall and the consistent support given to Jefferson and Madison by prominent lawyers like Philip Norborne Nicholas and William Wirt suggest again that political opinions were more a matter of individual predilection than professional or economic interest.

This was also true of the conservative wing in North Carolina, which was centered in the valley of the Roanoke River in the north-central part of the state. The fertile soil of this beautiful valley was peculiarly suited to the cultivation of the bright yellow tobacco, and landholding was concentrated in the hands of great planters to a degree exceeded only in the rice and sugar country of the lower South. Besides the profitable bright, the soil of this valley seems to have nurtured a provincial conservatism, for this was the home of the Antifederalist leader Willie Jones, who, more than any other man, was responsible for the initial failure of North Carolina to ratify the federal Constitution. Though Jones lived on till 1801, the leadership of his political organization was assumed during the 1790s by his young disciple Nathaniel Macon of Warren County. Also an opponent of the Constitution, Macon had first entered Congress in 1791 where he quickly associated himself with the Republican opposition. From "Buck Spring," his plantation on the Roanoke River, Macon directed the "Warren Junto," a nickname given by contemporaries to his circle of powerful friends.[24]

Associated with Macon in the "Warren Junto" were David Stone of Wake County near Raleigh and James Turner of Warren County, who served alternately as senators and governors of North Carolina during the administrations of Jefferson and Madison. While Macon represented the Warren district in Congress, the neighboring Raleigh-Durham district was represented by Richard Stanford, member of the House since 1797 and a man whose political career was dominated by his personal attachment to John Randolph. It is likely that Stanford's district as a whole was less conservative than Macon's; he was kept in office by the votes of the sizable Federalist minority in the Raleigh area which appreciated his persistent opposition to the Republican administrations. As in Virginia, Republican conservatism in North Carolina was related more to the social and political views of individuals than to broad economic patterns.

Maryland and South Carolina were still in a period of transition from Federalist to Republican domination. Faced with strong Federalist opposition, Republicans in both states were inclined toward moderation and gave wholehearted support to the Republican administration. Such dissent as there was within Republican ranks resulted from personal attachment rather than sectional-economic forces. Joseph H. Nicholson, who had married into the wealthy and influential Lloyd family of the Eastern Shore of Maryland, entered the House of Representatives in 1799 and remained a close personal friend of John Randolph until his retirement in 1806. In South Carolina the up-country planter David Rogerson Williams represented the northern Piedmont in Congress from 1805 to 1809. Though he was later to return to Congress a strong nationalist, Williams in his earlier stint was almost completely under the personal sway of John Randolph. Another up-country planter and friend of Randolph was Thomas Sumter, partisan hero of the Revolution in South Carolina, who served as a senator from South Carolina under Jefferson and Madison. An Antifederalist who had voted against the Constitution, Sumter had also been one of the early opponents of the Hamiltonian system in the first and second Congresses.

Republican conservatism in Georgia is difficult to assess because of the divisions in the party created by the Yazoo scandal. The Republican leader of Georgia at this time was Senator James Jackson, who had ridden to power in 1796 on the strength of his opposition to the Yazoo frauds. Like most Georgians he had supported the Constitution in 1788, but when elected to the first Congress in 1789 the "leather-lunged Jackson" caught the full significance of the nationalistic program of the Federalists long "before it dawned on Jefferson and Madison." [25] After the Yazoo scandals he served a term as governor and then was elected to the Senate in 1801.

In the mid-1790s Georgia had shifted to the Republican camp in disappointment over Washington's Indian policy, and by 1800 the only Federalist strength was among the comparatively poor cattle raisers of the frontier. Jackson's Republican organization found its major support among the wealthy seaboard planters who grew rice or sea-island cotton and among the cotton planters who had emigrated from Virginia and the Carolinas into east-central Georgia. Though Jackson might loosely be described as a Republican conservative, his only major disagreement with Jefferson concerned the Yazoo compromise. His personality was very similar to that of John Randolph—they shared a certain irascible honesty—and the two were close friends. Indeed, Randolph was reported to have said once that he had modeled his life after Jackson's. But the Georgian never shared Randolph's discontent with the administration of Jefferson.[26]

After Jackson's death in 1806 the mantle of Republican leadership in Georgia fell upon William Harris Crawford, a former schoolteacher and lawyer who had emigrated from Virginia as a boy. Crawford had made his political debut as the first public opponent of the Yazoo land sales of 1795, and Jackson had taken him under his wing to increase his strength in central Georgia.[27] Another protégé of Jackson's was George M. Troup, who contested Crawford for the leadership of the party in Georgia after 1806, though the two seldom differed significantly in political views. When both were elected to Congress in 1807—Crawford in the Senate and Troup in the House—Randolph saw in them potential allies in his opposition to the Yazoo compromise. The Georgians apparently gave him a good deal of sympathy, but only on the Yazoo issue was their support visible. On the other hand, Joseph Bryan and Thomas Spalding, less influential congressmen from eastern Georgia, were more under the personal influence of John Randolph and joined his opposition to President Jefferson. In general, however, there was no significant conservative sentiment in Georgia until the Indian-removal question produced a states' rights reaction in the mid-1820s.

Bound together by a loose set of ideas, the "principles of 1798," the Southern conservatives demanded a return to the agrarian-centered policies that characterized the Republican party while in opposition. Jefferson had not really abandoned these ideas. The differences that split his party were less a conflict of principle than the application of principle to the every-day management of the government. Jefferson was inclined to temporize, while the conservatives were not. Even so, the disa-greement was not violent enough to cause an open rupture in the party, and throughout his first term the President was able to maintain at least the appearance of complete party unity.

The revolt of the Southern conservatives, when it came at last in 1805 and 1806, was only one of a number of fissures that destroyed the unity of the Republican party during Jefferson's second term in office. In the tangled web of New York politics Vice-President Aaron Burr had become progressively isolated from the Jefferson Administration. Mistrusting Burr because of his actions in the election of 1800, the administration had chan-neled its patronage favors through the Clinton-Livingston fac-tion in New York. In a desperate effort to retrieve his political fortunes, Burr made a bid for the governorship in 1804 with Federalist support. He was defeated by the Clinton-Livingston alliance, which succeeded in electing its candidate with the tacit support of the administration.[28]

A parallel schism developed within the Republican party in Pennsylvania. Originating in an effort to purge the state judiciary of Federalists, the feud soon degenerated into a battle of person-alities and a struggle for control of the party machinery in the state. The more ardent Republicans who initiated the assault on the judiciary were led by Senator Michael Leib and William Duane, editor of the influential Philadelphia *Aurora*. Governor Thomas McKean, who intervened to save the judiciary, headed a moderate faction of Republicans who were dubbed the *Tertium Quids*, indicating a "third something" between the Federal-ists and Republicans. The President retained the devotion of both factions, although the Duane-Leib group was openly criti-cal of Madison and Gallatin. By avoiding any commitment to either side Jefferson managed to keep the feud localized, and it had little impact on national politics.[29]

Although the Southern conservatives shared some of the views of the extremists in Pennsylvania, there was never any direct connection between the two. Jefferson feared such an alliance and took steps to prevent it, but the Southerners showed little interest in the Pennsylvania schism. Both Randolph and Nathaniel Macon felt that the Pennsylvania feud might do great damage to the party and would aid only the Federalists, while John Taylor of Caroline considered Duane's disaffection a result of his desire for more political power and patronage in Pennsylvania.[30]

When the party split in Pennsylvania appeared, the Southern conservatives were not yet ready to rebel against the leadership of Jefferson. Indeed, in 1804, John Taylor wrote an election manifesto entitled *A Defense of the Measures of the Administration of Thomas Jefferson*, though it was his last public support for Jefferson's compromises. Nor is it likely that there would ever have been an open rebellion against the administration but for the character of one man—Randolph of Roanoke, Republican floor leader in the House.

The causes of Randolph's break with the administration have long interested historians. One explanation, offered originally by Jefferson's private secretary, William A. Burwell, was Randolph's desire to be sole government leader in Congress. As early as 1803 he had complained to Jefferson that his position as floor leader was being damaged because Thomas Mann Randolph and John Wayles Eppes, Jefferson's sons-in-law, were introducing administration measures. This sore was reopened in the early spring of 1806, thought Burwell, when the administration began depending more and more on a Massachusetts Republican, Barnabas Bidwell, to carry its measures through Congress.[31]

At the same time the administration was contemplating the appointment of a special commissioner to aid James Monroe, the American minister in London, in negotiating a treaty with England. Randolph fully expected to receive this appointment, but the administration ignored him for reasons that have been suggested by the historian George Tucker, who was a personal friend of Jefferson:

They [Jefferson and Madison] had seen enough of Mr. Randolph to know that his defects of temper rendered him unfit for such a situation—that he could neither be expected to yield implicit obedience to the views of those who employed him, nor be capable of the address, or patient research, or temperate logic for effecting them.[32]

Disappointed in failing to receive an appointment he had expected and enraged over the undermining of his position in the House, Randolph presumably began attacking the administration in revenge.

Neither factor can be considered a prime cause of the schism, however, for both imply some previous experience with Randolph's temperament that had rendered his standing with the administration somewhat precarious. Each incident was a result of the schism, and each in turn added fuel to the fire.

A recent biographer of Madison, Irving Brant, delves somewhat deeper into the mystery. Viewing it almost entirely through Randolph's almost irrational hatred of Madison, Brant suggests that Randolph was governed by jealousy of the ruling group, a jealousy that was perforce directed at Madison since Jefferson was impregnable and Monroe and Gallatin kept up a correspondence with him. "Madison, having no public or social motive for frequent contact, sought none. That was enough to make Randolph his enemy. . . . Monroe and Gallatin, giving minor satisfaction to Randolph's ego, were rewarded with a temporary fealty disproportionate to any effort they made to win it." [33]

Important as the psychological and physiological factors were in determining Randolph's conduct, I feel that to dismiss the schism as "neurotic jealousy" is to miss the significance of the split in the party. More important, Brant fails to explain the whole conservative opposition to Madison, whose name was associated with nationalism and mercantilism. It was Madison, many recalled, who had led the fight for the Constitution and who had supported in 1789 a protective tariff and a navigation act that would subsidize the shipping interest. "The book called the federalist," wrote John Taylor remembering Madison's essays in support of the Constitution, "is full of federalism, if I understand what federalism is." And to Taylor it too nearly resembled the "obnoxious doctrines in John Adams's book." [34] Of this latent distrust for Madison, John Randolph was the most vocal and dramatic exponent. He rebelled against the administration with the tacit sympathy of the conservative wing, though he quickly alienated that sympathy through his own excesses and eccentricities. John Randolph's schism, of fleeting importance in itself, reflected the deeper core of conservative discontent.

It had long been clear, at least to his personal friends, that Randolph was no party hack content to follow every twist and turn of the administration. Nurtured on the idealism that attended the birth of the republic, Randolph received his political instruction from men whose greatest fear was arbitrary power in the hands of a single man. Even in 1800 it was by no means certain that the American experiment would be able to endure, and the collapse of the republican government in France in 1799 only reminded the fearful of the usual fate of republics. We thus find Randolph writing his friend Joseph H. Nicholson of Maryland in December, 1800, "I need not say how much I would prefer J[efferson] to B[urr]. But I cannot like some of our party who are as much devoted to him as the fed[eralist]s were to Gen. Washington. . . . If our salvation depends on a single man 'tis not worth our attention." Two weeks later he wrote Nicholson along the same vein:

'Tis true that I have observed, with a disgust, which I have been at no pains to conceal, a spirit of *personal* attachment evinced by some of the supporters of Mr. J[efferson] whose republicanism has not been the most unequivocal. . . . There are those men who support republicanism from *monarchical* principles—and if the head of that very great and truly good and wise man can be turned with adulatory nonsense, they will endeavor to persuade him that our salvation depends on an individual. This is the essence of monarchy—and with this doctrine I have been, am, and ever will be at issue.[35]

Evident in this letter is a moral overtone that reveals a good deal of Randolph's character. Politics to him was a religion; upon every issue hung the fate of the republic. To compromise the self-evident principles upon which a free government is based would be to compromise the whole structure. Randolph was never able to compromise or to tolerate those who disagreed with him. Had his insistence on principle been based solely on the Antifederalist fear of strong government, one might be more disposed to respect his uncompromising stand, but scattered among his "principles" was an agrarian bias that was determined by his background as a Virginia planter. This was unfortunate in one who aspired to leadership in the party, for the balance of power in both the party and the country lay with the moderate Republicans, most of whom were from the Middle Atlantic states, an area on the threshold of the Industrial Revolution. Not two months after the opening of the first Republican Congress Randolph was recording his distrust of the moderates in a letter to his stepfather:

Parties here consist of the old Federalists courting popularity—they are a small minority. The same kind of characters republicanized and luke-warm republicans, who added to the former will perhaps constitute a bare majority of the house;—and republicans who hold the same principles now that they professed under adverse fortunes— and who *if they were all here* might amount to above 80 members. These are determined to pay the debt off, to repeal . . . unnecessary expenses, military, naval, civil, to enforce economy as well upon men calling themselves republican as upon federalists, and to punish delinquents without respect to their *political professions.*[36]

By 1803 Randolph was blaming the Tripolitan war on the Federalists and those "soi-disant republicans who pant for military command and the emoluments of office." [37] Randolph, however, was expressing no more than the general sentiments of the conservative wing of the party. That he was the most critical and outspoken member of that group cannot be doubted, nor is one surprised to find him assuming the leadership of the revolt.

In the election of 1804 Jefferson carried every state except Connecticut and Delaware, winning 162 out of 176 electoral votes. The Republican party by that year was a motley coalition that included the small farmers of upper New England, the commercial interests of New York, the manufacturers of New Jersey and Pennsylvania, and the planters of the South. Jefferson was leaning more and more on the Northern Republicans for support, this the Southern leaders resented. The party was held together by a personal loyalty to Jefferson and by the success of the administration in its economic reforms and in a foreign policy that had succeeded in doubling the size of the country. The Federalist Judiciary Act of 1801 had been repealed, and all direct taxes except the salt tax had been abolished. Gallatin's policy of economic retrenchment had reduced the costs of the government and the size of the army and navy, and great strides had been taken toward extinguishing the national debt.

Yet the conservatives were not satisfied. Nothing had been done to ravel the threads of alliance between business and government woven by Hamilton's funding system and national bank. The Alien and Sedition Acts had been allowed to expire peacefully and still formed a dangerous precedent for any future despot. Though the President had voluntarily reduced the size of the government, no legal limitation had been placed on the appointive power, and nothing prevented the future abuse of executive patronage. John Taylor of Caroline thought the whole Republican program of 1798 should have been engraved permanently on the Constitution by amendments. The purpose of the Republican system was to create a pure and disinterested government, and unless its principles were written into the Constitution there was no way to prevent special interests from warping the government to their own ends. "Are not the paper systems," Taylor wondered, "the Sedition and Alien law precedents, the executive patronage, and the influence of Congress by contracts capable of affecting our policy? If not why did we complain of them. If so, why do we neglect to provide against them?" [38] Taylor was not simply musing; most of his questions became realities within a decade. Had Jefferson and the ruling circle paid more heed to Taylor they would have found themselves in a better position fifteen years later when they finally recognized the danger to their agrarian society.

By 1804 the conservatives had begun to court James Monroe, then minister to France, as the most desirable successor to President Jefferson in 1808. In contrast to Madison, Monroe had been an Antifederalist who voted against the Constitution in the Virginia ratifying convention. After Madison's break with Federalism, Monroe had become one of his chief lieutenants, active in the formation of the Republican party in Virginia. From the conservative standpoint, his political career was free of taint, and he stood in easy contrast to the apparent inconsistencies of Madison. "My inclination towards Col. Monroe's election," explained John Taylor in 1808, "turned upon the supposition, that his principles differed from those in the Federalist, which I thought wrong." [39]

Beginning in 1803 Monroe received a series of letters from Randolph, Taylor, and Macon that offered friendship and spoke vaguely of the need for "principle" in the Republican party.[40] Monroe received similar letters from some of his old friends in Virginia, such as Littleton Waller Tazewell of Norfolk. Writing to Monroe some years later Tazewell described the purposes of the conservatives. Fearing that to oppose the administration openly would split the party and bring the Federalists back into power, they felt it best to "permit the present administration to pass away unnoticed" and concentrate instead on electing a successor who would adhere more closely to Republican principles. "Long before your return to America your friends had decided to put you in nomination for the Presidency. . . . The work was going on slowly, though safely, when the disastrous measures pursued by the Administration brought on the open rupture between the Republicans." [41]

These "disastrous measures," which brought Randolph and his friends into open rebellion with the sympathy, if not the active support, of the rest of the Southern conservatives, were the Yazoo compromise and the administration's policy in regard to West Florida.

The Quid Schism[1]

The first fissure in the Republican party in Congress appeared after the contest over the Yazoo compromise in 1804. The Yazoo issue was a hangover from the Federalist era when the Georgia legislature had been bribed to sell for a nominal sum thirty-five million acres of Indian land in present-day Alabama and Mississippi. The fraud in the bargain was soon exposed, and in 1796 a reform legislature rescinded the contract. But in the meantime the land companies had resold the land to speculators throughout the Union, many of whom were unaware of the original fraud. When Georgia ceded her western land claims to the federal government in 1802, the treaty of cession contained a provision for a compromise with the Yazoo claimants. President Jefferson appointed a cabinet-level commission, consisting of Madison, Gallatin, and Levi Lincoln, to work out a settlement. On February 14, 1803, the commissioners recommended that, in the interest of fairness, five million acres of public land in the Southwest be set aside for the innocent claimants.[2]

The recommended compromise was not popular among the more ardent Republicans. The original Yazoo fraud was reminiscent of the sort of stockjobbing that had taken place under the Federalist system. Republicans had been horrified by the speculation engendered by Hamilton's funding system, and Old Republicans would not soon forget the experience. As late as 1814 John Taylor of Caroline could be found fulminating against the subversion of the republic by "paper and patronage." John Randolph was particularly exercised about the commissioners' report. He had been visiting with his friend Joseph Bryan in Georgia in 1796, and the popular clamor against the fraud had no doubt excited his sympathy. He considered the Yazoo sale an outrage on decency, and any attempt to compromise with those who had profited by it was tainted with the original dishonesty. Ever ready to suspect the existence of an insidious conspiracy, he felt that the administration was too closely involved in the settlement, and his suspicions seemed confirmed when Postmaster General Gideon Granger appeared on the floor of Congress to lobby for the claimants.

When the commissioners' report came before the House in the spring of 1804, Randolph made his first public break with administration policy by submitting a series of declaratory resolves criticizing the compromise. Randolph's resolutions affirmed the power of the sovereign state of Georgia to rescind a fraudulent contract and sought to prevent the settlement of any claims.[3] Although a final decision was temporarily postponed, it was evident from the debate that the Yazoo issue had become a symbol of Jeffersonian compromise.

The issue came to a head in the spring of 1805 when the commissioners' report again came before Congress. The House indulged in a lengthy and bitter debate, during which Randolph accused Postmaster General Granger of bringing administration pressure to bear on Congress. To Randolph the involvement of the administration was clear evidence that the Republican party was abandoning the standards of virtue it had set up while in opposition. At last, on February 2, 1805, the House passed by a vote of 63–58 a resolution authorizing the commission to settle the Yazoo claims. Voting with Randolph in the minority were seventeen members of the Virginia delegation, including the President's sons-in-law. The only Virginia Republicans who supported the compromise were John G. Jackson, Madison's brother-in-law, and John Dawson, a personal friend of Madison's.[4] The victory for the administration turned out to be only temporary, for a bill embodying the resolution was again postponed indefinitely. This was the climax but by no means the end of the Yazoo drama. Bills providing for the settlement of the claims were introduced annually thereafter, but a compromise was not reached until 1814 when Randolph, defeated for his opposition to the war, was missing from his usual seat.

In the debate Randolph had carefully absolved the commissioners from blame, thereby leaving open an avenue for reconciliation with the administration. He was as yet unwilling to enter open rebellion, and he needed the united support of the party in the impeachment proceedings of Justice Samuel Chase. In 1804, the House of Representatives had voted in favor of impeaching Chase, and the trial before the Senate began on February 9, 1805, a week after the end of the Yazoo debate. Randolph was chosen to head the prosecution, but he had expended all his energy and time in the Yazoo debate.

The Senate vote on March 1 failing to convict Chase on any one of the six articles of impeachment was a serious blow to Randolph's influence in the party. His mismanagement and ill-preparedness disgusted the Northern Republicans and deepened the distrust of Jefferson and Madison. The failure also embittered Randolph, for he was convinced that Madison's disapproval of the proceedings was responsible for the acquittal. This presumption was unfair, however, for though Madison was highly amused at the embarrassment of the prosecutors, he was not sufficiently interested in the outcome of the trial to attempt to influence it one way or another. For that matter, even Randolph's close friend Nathaniel Macon had doubts about the advisability of impeaching Chase.[5] Just or not in his conclusions, Randolph returned home at the end of the session disillusioned with his party and the administration. To Nicholson he wrote, "Everything and everybody seem to be jumbled out of place, except a few men who are steeped in supine indiffernce, whilst meddling fools and designing knaves are governing the country. . . ."[6]

Jefferson's decision in the summer of 1805 to retire after the end of his second term added to Randolph's anxieties, for it made Madison a candidate for the presidency in 1808 and the probable choice by both the President and the party as Jefferson's successor. Randolph wrote to Gallatin in October regretting Jefferson's resolution to retire and adding, "If I were sure that Monroe would succeed him, my regret would be very much diminished." [7]

The opposition of Randolph and the conservatives to Madison came to a head in the West Florida controversy in the winter of 1805–6. This issue arose out of the administration's attempts to procure West Florida from Spain. Since 1803 the policy of Jefferson and Madison had been to insist that West Florida was included in the Louisiana Purchase, a contention that was based on the Treaty of San Ildefonso of 1800, by which Louisiana had been transferred from Spain to France. That treaty described the territory of Louisiana as "the same extent it had when France possessed it." Under French possession prior to 1763 Louisiana had embraced the entire Mississippi valley, from the Appalachians to the Rockies.

West Florida was a strip of territory along the Gulf of Mexico bounded on the north by the 31st parallel (the southern boundary of the United States by treaties of 1783 and 1795), on the west by the Mississippi River and on the east by the Perdido River, which flows into the Gulf near Pensacola. This territory France had ceded to Britain by the Treaty of Paris of 1763, at the same time that she had ceded Louisiana west of the Mississippi to Spain. By this same treaty Britain had obtained Florida from Spain and had subsequently combined East and West Florida for administrative purposes. At the end of the American Revolution Britain had been forced to cede both the Floridas to Spain. Since West Florida had once been part of French Louisiana, the possibility arose that it was included in the Spanish cession of 1800.

This small strip of land was of vital importance to the United States. Through it flowed the major rivers of the Southwest, and it contained the finest natural harbor on the Gulf coast, Mobile Bay. In 1802 the American minister to France, Robert R. Livingston, was instructed to purchase it along with the "island" of New Orleans. In the treaty of sale in 1803 Livingston and Monroe accepted Louisiana just as it had been defined in the Treaty of San Ildefonso, and the status of West Florida was left in deliberate uncertainty by Talleyrand. The United States subsequently claimed that Louisiana included West Florida as far as the Perdido River. Not until 1804 did France clarify her position by denying that West Florida had ever been claimed by France as part of Louisiana, but by then it was clear that Napoleon was maneuvering to dominate the bargaining between the United States and Spain.[8]

In the fall of 1804 Monroe journeyed from Paris to Madrid to negotiate for recognition of the American claim to West Florida. The mission failed because Monroe had made no effort to reach a prior agreement with France. In December, 1804, the American minister to France, John Armstrong, who had succeeded Monroe, wrote to Madison that France "has determined to convert the [Florida] negotiations into a job and draw from it advantages to herself, or in other language, to her agents." [9] It was thus clear that France would be the major factor in the Florida negotiations.

By the summer of 1805 Jefferson was toying with the idea of a military occupation of both Florida and Texas, but he was dissuaded from this by Gallatin, who pointed out that if Napoleon came to the aid of Spain, the United States would be thrown into the arms of England and embroiled in the European war.[10] News received in October, 1805, of the formation of Pitt's Third Coalition against France seemed to provide a new opportunity. Napoleon would now be too preoccupied to risk an extension of the war to the New World, and he might be more amenable to a settlement of the Florida question. Accordingly a cabinet meeting held on November 12 approved an overture to Spain, in which Spain would be offered $5 million for the Floridas on the understanding that she would pay back $4 million in spoliation claims.[11]

A few days later dispatches arrived from Armstrong in Paris outlining a proposition which Talleyrand had made to him through the intermediary of an "unknown gentleman." France, Talleyrand suggested, would be willing to see to it that Spain settled the Florida question and the related issue of the boundary between Louisiana and Texas for $10 million. It was evident that France expected a share of the money as part of the annual subsidy from Spain and that both Talleyrand and his intermediary expected to profit from the transaction. Jefferson promptly summoned another cabinet meeting, at which it was decided to accept the proposal, though the price was kept at $5 million.[12] That this sort of proposition suggested too much the XYZ Affair and might therefore raise objections from the conservative wing of the party seems never to have occurred to Jefferson or the Cabinet.

The President's annual message, sent to Congress on December, 3, 1805, was extremely belligerent in tone. He dwelt at some length on the troubles with Spain, took note of Spanish provocations on the Southwest frontier, and informed Congress that he had ordered the army to "repel by arms any similar aggressions in the future." It is evident that Jefferson had not completely rejected the possibility of using force against Spain, and he no doubt felt that a warlike attitude might soften Spanish obstinacy on the Florida question. The message also included, at the suggestion of Madison, a rehearsal of the difficulties with England stemming from a reversal in British maritime policy. He concluded by issuing a call for defense measures, an expansion of the army, and an increase in the navy, including the construction of some seventy-fours.[13]

Three days later he sent to Congress a secret message on the subject of the Spanish problem. To the amazement of Congress he retreated from his belligerent stance and suggested that the Florida question could be settled by negotiation. Instead of informing Congress of the French proposal and the cabinet decisions, he contented himself with the vague suggestion that the means for negotiation rested with Congress.[14] Clearly, he intended the Republican leadership to call on him for specific instructions, a procedure that was becoming routine. Jefferson habitually worked closely with the party leadership in Congress, communicating his views and occasionally drafting legislation. Jefferson, concludes a modern scholar, "was a strong executive who, directly and through his Cabinet, exercised great influence over Congress." [15] Yet it was just this sort of procedure that aroused the opposition of the conservatives. Though exercised subtly, it nevertheless was too reminiscent of the political theories of John Adams. On the day before the President sent his confidential message to Congress John Randolph wrote to his friend Monroe:

It is certainly a melancholy truth that . . . the only question which the major part of [the House of Representatives] inquires into is "what is the wish of the Executive?" and an intimation of the pleasure of that branch of the government is of equal force with law. There is a proneness to seek office and favors among us which is truly mortifying and distressing to the true republicans, the number of whom, it is to be feared, diminishes every day.[16]

When he called on the President, Randolph was dismayed to discover that an appropriation of $2 million was wanted for the purchase of West Florida. In an interview with Madison he was informed that the only alternative was a war with both France and Spain. Realizing that the money would end up in the coffers of France, he flatly refused to participate in an effort to bribe one nation to deprive another of its possessions. The most disgraceful feature of the proposal, he felt, was that the administration concocted the policy and then shifted to Congress the public responsibility for resorting to bribery instead of manly force. He too, he informed the President, "had a character to support and principles to maintain." [17]

To Randolph the whole affair betrayed the lingering odor of Federalist corruption and typified the gradual subversion of pure Republicanism. By exposing it he would kill two birds with one stone. He would acquaint the public with the hidden dangers in the growth of executive power and, at the same time, expose a Machiavellian intrigue that was clearly the product of the Federalist mentality of James Madison. Randolph incorrectly assumed that Madison had originated the entire scheme. By exposing him Randolph hoped to end the Secretary's political career and pave the way for the presidential succession of the less nationalistic Monroe.

Speaker of the House Nathaniel Macon referred the messages of the President to a select committee of John Randolph, Joseph H. Nicholson of Maryland, David Rogerson Williams of South Carolina, Gordon Mumford of New York, Barnabas Bidwell of Massachusetts, Robert Brown of Pennsylvania, and John Cotton Smith of Connecticut. Whether from the intention of the Speaker, the Republicans upon whom the administration could count, Bidwell and Brown, were a minority of the committee. Nicholson and Williams were personal friends of Randolph, while the Federalists Smith and Mumford could be expected to oppose any plan sponsored by the administration. Given the President's vagueness and a committee majority, Randolph was quick to seize the opportunity to embarrass the administration. A letter to George Hay, Monroe's son-in-law, reveals his disgust with the party at this time: "The Administration may do as it pleases. It favors federal principles, and, with the exception of a few great rival characters, federal men. . . . The old republican party is already ruined, past redemption. New men and new maxims are the order of the day. . . ." [18]

Neglecting to disclose to his committee his conversations with the President and Secretary of State concerning the Florida appropriation, Randolph maintained the fiction that the President's warlike words called for measures to defend the Southwest frontier. He thus hoped to commit Congress to the more honorable policy of belligerence toward Spain. This would force the President to ask for an appropriation publicly, thereby exposing the whole sordid attempt at bribery.

Disenchanted with Randolph the President sought out Barnabas Bidwell and communicated his request for a $2 million appropriation. This move excited Randolph's jealousy and precipitated a struggle for party leadership in Congress. It seemed to confirm his fears of executive influence, and his suspicions were enhanced by the fact that Bidwell was a Massachusetts Republican and a newcomer to party councils. The Randolph majority on the committee quickly rejected a series of resolutions drawn up by the President and a motion by Bidwell for a $2 million appropriation.[19]

The committee report, submitted to the House on January 3, recommended that troops be raised for the defense of the southern frontier. Bidwell immediately countered with a resolution to appropriate a sum of money for the "extraordinary expenses" of the administration in its diplomatic negotiations. The House debated the resolutions behind closed doors for the next week, while Randolph struggled hopelessly against the phalanx of administration Republicans. On January 11 the House rejected the report of Randolph's committee, and three days later it adopted, by a vote of 77–54, Bidwell's motion for an appropriation of $2 million. Voting with Randolph in the minority were the Federalists and twenty-seven Republicans. The Virginia delegation divided twelve to ten against the administration, which at least was a personal victory for Randolph. More significant, for the first time on an issue vital to the President more than half the majority consisted of Northern men.[20]

On the day after the House passed the "Two Million Act" the administration sent to Congress dispatches from Monroe in

London. These dispatches, written in October, advocated that the Floridas be seized by force. Though they had arrived in Washington in the middle of December, they were held by the Secretary of State until the Florida purchase bill passed the House. Monroe's position seemed to back Randolph's demand for troops in the Southwest, and Randolph later accused the Secretary of State of deliberately concealing the dispatches. Had the dispatches been given to Congress as soon as they arrived, Randolph wrote to Monroe, Congress would never have consented to the disgraceful means of acquiring Florida by bribing France. Though there is reason to believe that if Monroe was willing to acquire the Floridas by force he would also agree to acquiring them by bribery, Randolph assumed that Monroe would disapprove of the administration's policy. To attract Monroe to his side he left the minister with the impression that the Secretary of State had deliberately ignored Monroe's suggestions in pursuing a policy of his own, an implication that was not far from the truth.[21]

These letters from Monroe also furnished Randolph a pretext upon which to invite the support of Gallatin. Randolph had been aware of the dispatches as early as December 21, for he had received a personal letter from Monroe on the same packet. In a conversation with Gallatin that day, however, he discovered that the Secretary of the Treasury was ignorant of the contents of the dispatches. This gave Randolph an opportunity to accuse the administration of withholding information from cabinet members as well as from Congress.[22]

Gallatin, though sympathizing generally with the conservatives, remained loyal to the administration. Monroe in London remained an enigma to both the President and the Randolphites. By the end of January, 1806, the Republican insurgents consisted only of the small group in the House that had voted with Randolph against the Florida appropriation. It yet remained to be seen whether the party schism would be permanent and

whether Randolph in his personal vendetta against the Secretary
of State could attract the general support of the conservative
wing of the party.

That he would get little aid from the Senate was soon evident.
The "Two Million Act" passed the Senate early in February
with only four Republicans voting with the Federalists in opposition.[23] The Quaker pacifist George Logan and three other
Republicans absented themselves rather than vote against the
administration. Logan sympathized with the objectives of the
insurgents in the House, but rather than enter open rebellion
he preferred to express his views privately in a letter to Jefferson.

Your errors in conducting the exterior relations of our country
oppress the minds of your best friends with the most anxious solici-
tude—You may yet retrieve your character & preserve the confidence of your fellow citizens. Call together your too long neglected
Council, take the state of the Union into consideration, submit every
subject with frankness to discussion, & united with them, determine
on such measures as may preserve the peace and honor of our
Country.

Your own reputation imperiously demands that you should recede
from pretensions and projects which are demonstrably groundless &
unjust.

Jefferson answered by inviting Logan to an interview to discuss
the situation.[24]

At the end of February, 1806, Jefferson nominated John Armstrong commissioner plenipotentiary to settle the disputes with
Spain. Armstrong was to be armed with the $2 million appropri-
ation, but the delays caused by Randolph, the publicity given
the act, and Napoleon's preoccupation with the war in Europe
foredoomed the negotiation.

The implications of the party schism did not remain uncertain for long. Foreign policy was still the weak spot of the
Jefferson Administration, primarily because it presented the best
springboard for an attack on Jefferson's probable successor,

Secretary of State Madison. The administration was still reeling from the attack on its Spanish policy when the House of Representatives took up the subject of relations with England.

The problems that complicated Anglo-American relations dated back to 1793 and stemmed directly from the struggle between England and France. The war had been very profitable to American merchants. With the merchant fleets of France and Spain held in port by British cruisers and the West Indian colonies of those countries virtually cut off from Europe, American merchants had taken over much of this carrying trade, supplying the West Indies with American foodstuffs and carrying the products of the colonies to the European continent.

The success of Yankee skippers, who could offer lower rates and more efficient service, aroused the jealousy of the British shipping interest, which had long regarded the carrying trade as its own. Prodded by the shipping interest in Parliament, England had attempted to halt this trade as soon as the war began by invoking her old "rule of 1756," by which a trade closed in time of peace was also illegal in time of war. Ironically England thereby used her navy to enforce the French and Spanish navigation systems. Though the United States never recognized the validity of the "rule of 1756," she was helpless against the British Navy. American merchant captains chose instead to circumvent the British rule by bringing their West Indian cargoes to an American port, paying the customs duties, and transshipping them to European markets. Held legal by a British court in 1800, this practice was successful until 1805 when the British court reversed itself in the *Essex* case and held the indirect trade to be illegal under the "rule of 1756." This decision made the whole American carrying trade fair game for British men-of-war, and the number of seizures of American ships greatly increased in the second half of 1805.

Another issue that troubled Anglo-American relations was the impressment of American seamen. A sizable portion of the American merchant fleet was manned by deserters from British warships. Faced with a shortage of sailors to man her vessels and receiving little aid from the American government, Britain was impelled to recover her deserters by force. This practice had serious implications, for the waylaying of American vessels on the high seas was a trespass on America's national sovereignty. And, the immediate judgment of citizenship by British captains interested in filling out their crews lent itself to abuse and injustice; many native-born as well as naturalized Americans were forced into the British Navy.

Faced with these provocations, Jefferson felt that some sort of American response was essential. To Dr. Thomas Cooper he wrote:

The love of peace which we sincerely feel & profess, has begun to produce an opinion in Europe that our government is entirely in Quaker principles, & will turn the left cheek when the right has been smitten. This opinion must be corrected when just occasion arises, or we shall become the plunder of all nations.[25]

Submission was thus out of the question, but a declaration of war did not seem justified without a further effort at negotiation. The negotiation could safely be entrusted to Monroe, in London, but his position had to be strengthened to avoid the trap that had ruined Jay a decade before. The obvious bargaining lever to provide Monroe was the threat of commercial retaliation. An ancient American policy born in the pre-Revolutionary struggle with England, the idea of commercial restrictions had been revived by Madison in 1793 as an alternative to war. The concept was thus engrained within the principles of the Republican party and had the advantage of being an honorable response to British provocations short of war. By early 1806 the President and his Secretary of State were privately informing members of Congress of this new direction in policy.[26]

The section of the President's annual message that dealt with the British depredations on American commerce had been referred in the House to the powerful Committee on Ways and

Means. When on January 17 the President sent to the House dispatches from Monroe and a renewed plea for measures against Britain, this too was referred to the Ways and Means Committee. On the committee with John Randolph were Joseph H. Nicholson of Maryland, Joseph Clay of Pennsylvania, Josiah Quincy of Massachusetts, David Meriwether of Georgia, William Dickson of Tennessee, and Jonathan O. Mosely of Connecticut.[27] Randolph dominated the Ways and Means Committee even more completely than he had controlled the special committee on Florida. Nicholson and Clay were members of the conservative group and personal friends of Randolph. David Meriwether was one of several Georgia Republicans who sympathized with the conservatives. He had voted against the administration on both the Yazoo compromise and the "Two Million Act." The Federalists Quincy and Mosely could be expected to oppose any measure suggested by the administration. The only member of the committee on whom the administration could depend was the Republican Dickson of Tennessee. Given this majority of opponents of any strong measures against Britain, the Ways and Means Committee sat on the problem for two months.

In the meantime Jefferson and Madison decided to emphasize the importance of the negotiations in London by appointing a special commissioner to join Monroe. Several prominent Republicans expected to receive the honor of an appointment, among them John Randolph and Senator Smith of Maryland. Christopher Clark of Virginia even made a special appeal to Madison in behalf of Randolph, but he was not successful. When the administration announced the appointment of William Pinkney, a Baltimore lawyer who had had some diplomatic experience in London, the disappointment of Randolph and Smith was sharpened into bitterness by the knowledge that they had been passed over in favor of a prominent Federalist. Nathaniel Macon expressed the feelings of the conservatives when he wrote, "W[illiam] P[inkney] of Baltimore is nominated Minister extra-to London. He must therefore be a good republican, or we are all federalists and all republicans; or have the times changed." [28]

After two months of futile waiting for action from Ways and Means, the House moved to bypass the committee and take up the subject of America's relations with England. On January 29 Andrew Gregg of Pennsylvania, after reviewing the insults and injuries received at the hands of Great Britain, offered a resolution that no product grown or manufactured in Great Britain ought to be imported into the United States. A week later Joseph Clay of Pennsylvania, conservative friend of John Randolph, spoke in favor of a mild but permanent system of commercial restrictions. Clay offered as an alternative to the Gregg resolution a series of resolutions designed to prohibit all trade "not permanently permitted by the laws or regulations of the European powers," which would in effect have been a submission to the *Essex* decision. He felt that the Gregg resolution was so sweeping that it would do as much harm to the United States as to Britain and that it could not be enforced for any length of time.[29] Clay's resolutions were directed at the core of the problem, the West Indies carrying trade, and would thus do less damage to the direct trade—the exchange of American farm staples for European manufactured goods.

On February 10 Nicholson introduced another resolution designed to coerce Great Britain by restricting American imports. Less sweeping than Gregg's resolution, Nicholson's proposal was to exclude only such goods as we "can supply ourselves with our own industry, or obtain from other countries." Noting that the object of nonintercourse was to force Britain into making concessions without injuring ourselves, Nicholson offered a specific list of manufactured goods the importation of which could be restricted without damaging our own economy.[30]

It is interesting that the two proposals to the Gregg resolution were introduced by members of the Republican conservative wing. First it must be noted that Clay and Nicholson were the only members of the conservative group in the House who were not Southern planters and hence were less compelled to support the idea of free trade. Clay no doubt shared with his fellow delegates from Pennsylvania the feeling that some sort of retaliatory measure was mandatory, but as the representative of the commercial city of Philadelphia he was no doubt interested in seeing that whatever system was adopted would be as mild as possible. The Nicholson resolution, on the other hand, was an administration measure. Drawn up originally by Senator Samuel Smith with suggestions from Madison, it also had the support of Gallatin as being less harmful to the treasury income than Gregg's resolution. Gallatin most probably handed it to his brother-in-law, Nicholson, for presentation to Congress.[31]

To Randolph the nonimportation resolutions were akin to the West Florida crisis. It was evident that the policy had originated with the administration, and Congress was again expected to cooperate meekly. This was final evidence of the growing power of the Executive and its subtle subversion of the prerogatives of Congress. It was obviously a cabinet policy, he shrilled to the House during the debate on the Gregg resolution, "not of an open declared cabinet; but of an invisible, inscrutable, unconstitutional cabinet, unknown to the Constitution. I speak of backstairs influence—of men who bring messages to this House, which, although they do not appear on the journals, govern its decisions." [32]

The policy of commercial retaliation, moreover, was a policy of nationalism that seemed to benefit only the Northern merchants. Ignoring the problems of impressment and blockade, Randolph concentrated on the West Indies carrying trade as the immediate cause of Anglo-American friction. Resting his arguments on the physiocratic assumptions that agriculture was the only true foundation for a nation and that the only purpose of commerce was to carry farm surpluses to market, Randolph asserted that the measure jeopardized the economic interests of the whole nation for the benefit of a few merchants. The direct

trade with Europe, the necessary outlet for the agricultural products of the nation, Randolph argued, was being sacrificed for
a "circuitous commerce, for the fraudulent protection of belligerent property under your neutral flag." That the administration
could abandon "the great agricultural interest" in order to protect a dubious carrying trade was final proof to Randolph that
it had abandoned its old Republican principles and was being
controlled by Northern merchants.

Randolph also pointed out that a policy of retaliation against
England would throw the United States into the arms of France.
The practical effect of the policy of commercial restrictions
would be to extend Napoleon's "Continental System" to the
North American continent. Napoleon had sealed off the markets
of Europe from English traders, and America was now cooperating with the Emperor by closing American markets as well.
France admittedly was the traditional ally of the United States,
but France was no longer a republic. We were now cooperating
with a military despot, charged Randolph.

Gentlemen talk of 1793. They might as well go back to the Trojan
War. What was your situation then? Then every heart beat high
with sympathy for France, for *republican France!* . . . Because she
was fighting the battles of the human race against the combined enemies of liberty; because she was performing the part which Great
Britain now, in fact, sustains, forming the only bulwark against
universal dominion.

This was the first public announcement of the Republicans'
fear of Napoleonic France. But it was more than that. It was an
indication that the conservative wing of the party was leaning
more and more toward a policy of amity with Great Britain, a
policy founded less on a fear of France than on the economic
interest of the South. The direct trade, for which Randolph
contended, was the direct exchange of Southern agricultural
staples for the manufactured products of Great Britain, a trade
that would have been severely damaged by the proposed exclusion of British goods. Randolph's arguments here foreshadowed

the Southern opposition to the protective tariff two decades later.

Had Randolph stopped at this point he might have erected a stable platform for conservative discontent. He had succeeded in giving voice to many of the fears that had disturbed Southern conservatives for several years. But Randolph was never capable of moderation. He sealed his political fate by provoking an open break with the administration. Revealing the political motives behind his stand, he turned his abuse directly on the Secretary of State. Picking up a copy of a pamphlet Madison had written in defense of America's neutral rights, he read several passages, ridiculed the points made, and then threw the book on the floor. This was the first open attack on the Secretary of State and the object of it was clear. Expressed by one neutral observer, British minister Anthony Merry, Randolph's purpose was "to lower . . . [Madison's] political character and estimation in order that Mr. Monroe . . . might be the only person looked up to as proper to succeed to the Presidency." [33]

Not content with attacking the administration, Randolph turned his abuse on the whole House of Representatives. His own proposal was an embargo on American shipping, which at least "would have got our property home, and our adversary's into our power." But would the House undertake anything really constructive? No, "like true political quacks, you deal only in handbills and nostrums." How could Congress achieve anything constructive, concluded Randolph, when the affairs of the nation, instead of being in the hands of responsible men, had been "committed to Tom, Dick, and Harry, the refuse of the retail trade of politics. . . ."

Oratorical excesses such as this eliminated his following in Congress and prevented Randolph from obtaining any influence among Southern conservatives. More than one observer felt Randolph had gone too far. Noted Senator Plumer, Federalist from New Hampshire, "The severe philippic that John Randolph pronounced ag[ains]t this resolution—ag[ains]t the President &

Mr. Madison, has bro't some members in favor of the measure, who, I believe, would otherwise been opposed to it." Senator Smith of Maryland agreed that Randolph's abuse of the House and of the administration had lost him many friends, but Smith thought Randolph had made a worse mistake in defending the tactics of England. "If Randolph had maintained the ground of neutral rights and fought Grigg's [*sic*] Resolution on its merits, he would have put down the President and Madison," Smith observed. "Indeed I fear he will do it yet, for nobody will defend them." Smith was a nationalist who evidently favored stronger measures than any yet proposed, and his judgment of the administration was no doubt affected by his bitterness over the Pinkney appointment.[34]

The conservative wing of the party was a very fluid group. There were no doubt many Republicans who sympathized generally with its principles, but who hesitated to oppose the administration. It was the support of these, both in and out of Congress, that Randolph needed. But when he labeled the proposals of Clay and Nicholson, members of his own following, "handbills and nostrums," he did much to alienate the wavering. Indeed, many who voted with Randolph against the Gregg resolution voted in favor of the milder Nicholson resolution when it came before the House a week later.

Despite Randolph's excesses, his tiny band of personal friends remained loyal. On March 8 David Rogerson Williams of South Carolina took up the assault on the Gregg resolution. Nicknamed "Thunder and Lightning Williams" from the emotional quality of his oratory, Williams five years later was among Henry Clay's band of War Hawks. Yet in 1806 he was a staunch conservative who had supported Randolph on the Yazoo and West Florida issues. Like Randolph, he was independent, candid to a fault, and frequently voted on moral criteria.[35]

The carrying trade, Williams pointed out, echoing Randolph, was not a right but a temporary wartime advantage, an advantage American merchants had only as long as the French and

Spanish merchant fleets remained bottled up in their harbors. This trade, moreover, was carried on by a small minority of the community, and Congress was being asked to place restrictions on the whole community for the benefit of a few merchants. The proposed restrictions would do more than damage the trade of the rest of the nation; they would reduce the customs duties of the treasury, which would have to be compensated for by taxes on the rest of the country. Even this might be bearable if the merchants themselves had demanded protection, but none of the memorials from the commercial cities suggested a policy of retaliation against England. Baltimore suggested a policy of obtaining redress through "amicable explanations," while the city of Boston requested a "special mission" to England. From these petitions it was clear, concluded Williams, that the people most affected by the British depredations did not want a policy of retaliation.[36]

Two days later Christopher Clark, representative from the Lynchburg district of southside Virginia, carried the conservative case a little further. Iterating the remarks of Randolph and Williams that the carrying trade was not worth the sacrifice to the nation, Clark asserted that the Gregg resolution was unconstitutional because it was designed to promote the interests of the few under the guise of protecting the "general welfare." Then, enlarging upon Randolph's defense of England, Clark told the House that Great Britain was "fighting our battles and those of the world" by opposing the military despotism of France. America, should she attempt to hinder the British war effort, would be damaging her own interests. Instead of passing hostile measures the United States ought to console itself with the thought that "in a state of war neutral powers must suffer some injury."[37] This was the broadest apology for Britain in the debate, and it showed just how far the conservatives had moved from the traditional Republican position on foreign policy.

Christopher Clark was followed shortly by Nicholson, whose

resolution was still pending before the House. Nicholson nevertheless followed the Randolph line and pounded away at the
distinction between the direct trade involving our own agricultural products and the carrying trade which had caused all the
trouble. Nathaniel Macon, following Nicholson on the floor,
built his opposition to the resolution on the traditional Republican fear of war and the conservatives' distaste for nationalist
policies. Observing that the whole purpose of retaliation was to
uphold the national honor, Macon referred to a remark by Representative Smilie of Pennsylvania that he would rather have
war than loss of national honor. "This thing called national
honor," asserted Macon, "has ruined more than half the people
in the world, and has almost banished liberty and happiness
from Europe." Whatever the cost in national honor, Macon felt,
"we shall not be degraded by living at peace with the world."
Appealing to history for support he asked, "What destroyed the
prosperity and liberty of Venice, of Genoa, and of Holland?
Wars, and wars, too, generally undertaken to protect the carrying trade." [38]

On March 13, after the administration Republicans had defeated a motion to discharge the Gregg resolution altogether,
John Smilie of Pennsylvania moved that the House take up the
consideration of the Nicholson resolution. The milder Nicholson
resolution had the backing of the administration, and it had a
better chance of receiving the unanimous support of the Republican party. Perhaps also the administration Republicans hoped
to split the conservative group and isolate John Randolph.

After frustrating several moves by the conservatives to postpone action, the House on March 17 approved the Nicholson
resolution 87–35, with the Federalists and only nine Republicans voting in the minority. Randolph withdrew from the House
before the question was put, and Clark, Williams, and Clay
joined Nicholson in voting for the resolution. Jefferson, who
on the previous day predicted to Monroe that only fifteen Republicans would oppose the measure, was delighted with this

showing of party unity. Considering it a repudiation of Randolph, he wrote Monroe, "I have never seen a H[ouse] of Representatives more solidly united in doing what they believe to be the best for the public interest. There can be no better proof than the fact that so eminent a leader should be at once and almost unanimously abandoned."[39]

In the Senate the conservative George Logan tried without success to get the bill postponed on the ground that it would hinder an accommodation with England. In the end a number of Federalists voted with the Republican majority to pass the bill 19–9. Voting with Logan in the minority were the same Republicans who had opposed the West Florida appropriation—Adair of Kentucky, Stone of North Carolina, and Sumter of South Carolina.[40] George Logan of Pennsylvania was one of the very few Republican conservatives in the North. A Quaker pacifist, he had become famous for his unauthorized mission to France in 1798 in an effort to prevent war. Though not a member of the inner circle of admirers around John Randolph, he was a true Republican of '98.

Adair was a political maverick who remained on the fringes of the conservative movement. Though his political career was temporarily ended in 1806 when he fell victim to the charm of Aaron Burr, he returned to politics in the early 1820s to serve as governor of Kentucky and leader of the antibank relief party. Stone was a friend of Nathaniel Macon who left the Senate in 1807 to become governor of North Carolina. He returned to the Senate in 1813, but was forced by the legislature to resign the following year for his opposition to the war effort of the Madison administration.[41]

Thomas Sumter, on the other hand, reflected the thinking of John Randolph. Revolutionary war hero and opponent of the Constitution, he was one of the few Antifederalists to be elected to the first Congress in 1789. His first vote to be recorded opposed the erection of a federal judiciary system on the ground that it "was hostile to [popular] liberties and dangerous in the extreme," and he was one of the first to join Madison in opposition to Hamilton's fiscal system. He was elected to the Senate in 1801, served until his resignation in 1810, and remained a staunch friend of John Randolph, who once said of him: "Were I allowed to vote by proxy, and on that vote depended the welfare of the Republic, I would make Thomas Sumter my proxy."[42]

In the House the five Republicans who voted with John Randolph against the Nonimportation Act fairly well defined the hard core of the conservative group in that body. Three were Randolph's colleagues from Virginia—James M. Garnett, Philip R. Thompson, and Abram Trigg. The other two were Richard Stanford, a friend of Nathaniel Macon from North Carolina, and Thomas Spalding of Georgia. Included among the conservatives also were Williams, Clay, Clark, and Edwin Gray, whose political sympathies were evident, even though they voted for the Nicholson resolution and the Nonimportation Act. One other representative must also be included in this group, though he was forced to resign his seat for personal reasons a few weeks before the Nonimportation Act was passed—Joseph Bryan of Georgia, who was Randolph's companion and roommate while the two were studying law under Edmund Randolph in Philadelphia in 1793.[43] These, together with the three leaders, Randolph, Macon, and Nicholson, made a total of thirteen Quids in the House of Representatives, a surprisingly small number considering the furor their opposition had aroused.

Several factors account for the importance of this group, an importance that was all out of proportion to its size. Their mere opposition, for one thing, as a departure from the almost absolute unity of the party that characterized Jefferson's first term, attracted attention. Then, too, the group included some of the most talented members of the Republican party. Randolph was one of the ablest parliamentarians, and by far the best orator in the House, while Macon and Nicholson were held in

high regard by members of the party. Nor did this group silently cast its votes in opposition. The oratory of Randolph and
the arguments of Williams, Clay, and Nicholson in explaining the
conservative position occupied much of the time of the House.
Moreover, the faction was able to influence the decisions of the
House through its control of key committees, aided no doubt
by the appointive power of Speaker Macon.

The number of members who voted consistently with John
Randolph is not a fair indication of the extent of conservative
feeling in the House. Though many of the Republicans who
voted against the administration did so on their personal eval-
uations of the issues themselves without regard to the views of
Randolph and his friends, a sizable portion of the party—over
twenty members—voted with the Quids on more than one of
the great issues that split the party. Many of these no doubt
sympathized with the Quids, but hesitated to vote against the
administration. As Randolph later wrote, "if all, who *talked*
with us by the fireside, had supported their own opinions, our
numbers would have been very different." [44]

The Quids, after all, were only reminding the party of its old
out-of-power principles, and the conflict between principle and
political expediency showed itself in the voting of more than
one Republican. The President's son-in-law, John Wayles Eppes,
for example, had publicly endorsed Edmund Pendleton's proposed amendments in 1802 and opposed the Yazoo compromise,
but he voted for the "Two Million Act" and then supported
Randolph's motion to remove the secrecy from the Florida proceedings. He opposed the Gregg resolution, but voted for the
Nonimportation Act and then abstained from voting on the embargo in December, 1807. Despite the apparent confusion, voting such as this gave the conservatives considerable strength and
enabled them, with the support of 27 Federalist votes, to cause
the administration some embarrassment on several crucial issues.
All in all, 72 of the 115 Republicans in the House opposed the

administration on at least one of the three major issues that divided the party—the Yazoo compromise, the "Two Million Act," and the Nonimportation Act.

Amid the confused voting, however, one trend is significant. Thirteen Republicans, including three Northerners (Thomas Sammons of New York and John Rea and Samuel Smith of Pennsylvania), voted with the thirteen Quids on every issue except the Nonimportation Act. Though this reveals the widespread hostility to the British policy and the feeling that some sort of retaliation was in order, it also suggests that Jefferson's efforts to reunite his party were having some effect. The mild Nicholson resolution, insofar as it tended to split the conservatives, was a political coup for the administration. Jefferson was quick to exploit this confusion with attempts to conciliate the conservative leaders, and he accompanied these moves with political pressure in the local districts. The President turned first to Monroe, who was already the conservatives' candidate for 1808. "Some of your new friends are attacking your old ones out of friendship to you, but in a way to render you great injury. In a few weeks I shall be able to write you less enigmatically. In the meantime be cautious what and to whom you write, that you may not be allied to operations of which you are not informed." [45]

Jefferson's next problem was to avert an alliance between the Quids in Congress and the Pennsylvania schismatics, who for two years had been sniping at the President's Cabinet, particularly at Madison and Gallatin, in the name of pure Republicanism. A week after his letter to Monroe he wrote a conciliatory note to William Duane assuring him that the administration was united and that Randolph had little support in Congress or in the country.[46]

Dr. Thomas Cooper, since 1800 a state judge in Pennsylvania, also had to be kept in line. Consistent with his opposition to the Federalist measures of 1798, Cooper was inclined to oppose as unduly expensive any measures to protect the carrying trade.

But Jefferson managed to persuade him that the federal government must move to protect foreign commerce, like any other legitimate enterprise, or the United States would be plundered by all nations.[47]

The President then turned to the Quid leaders in Congress. Nicholson was offered a seat on the bench of the Sixth Federal District in Maryland. Nicholson throughout the session had been torn by conflicting sympathies. A warm friend of Randolph and Macon, he shared their dislike of Madison. But he was also the brother-in-law of Gallatin and had willingly introduced Gallatin's nonimportation measure into the House. Since he was also a poor man with a large family, he accepted Jefferson's appointment and resigned his seat in the House at the end of March. Randolph thus lost his best friend in Congress, but Nicholson retained his conservative principles, for Randolph noted happily a few months later, "Nicholson is fast in the faith and quite zealous. . . ."[48]

Though Jefferson was inclined to overawe Monroe and had rid himself of Nicholson with mutual benefit, he realized that Speaker Macon could be neither overawed nor bought out. Instead he wrote Macon a conciliatory note similar to the one he had written George Logan. "Some enemy whom we know not, is sowing tares among us. Between you and myself nothing but opportunities of explanation can be necessary to defeat those endeavors. At least on my part my confidence in you is so unqualified that nothing further is necessary for my satisfaction. I must therefore ask a conversation with you." [49]

Unfortunately the President's confidence in Macon was less in doubt than Macon's confidence in Jefferson. Macon, however, never considered himself in opposition to the administration. He voted in honest accord with his own views on the merits of each issue. His opposition to the administration resulted from his own independence and from his differences with the President over the application of the party program, not from any ulterior motives. When in the following session of

Congress Randolph opposed measures merely to embarrass the administration, Macon did not hesitate to support the President. It is unlikely, therefore, that he was impressed one way or another by the President's plea for party unity.

Jefferson had even less success with David R. Williams. To a dinner invitation, Williams once coldly replied that he had always regarded Adams's social affairs "as decoys to the representatives in Congress. . . ." And, since he had always reprobated this practice, consistency induced him to decline the President's invitation.[50]

Randolph's behavior in the House aided Jefferson to win back the wavering. The excesses of his speeches infuriated the Northerners, and his domineering attitude taxed even his friends. Even the mild-mannered Nathaniel Macon complained to Nicholson, "When going to the House I am sure I look like one going to jail, and when returning look [like] one going to the gallows." The strains of the party conflict were felt even in Virginia where John Taylor of Caroline wrote, "We are writhing in these parts under political torture, and stare like a man in a dark room. For my own part, were I inclined to move, the fear of breaking my shinns [sic] would keep me still." In his second speech on the Gregg resolution Randolph had declared that he was no longer a Republican but a member of a third party called "Quiddists" or "Quids." On April 7 he declared a formal opposition to the administration, a move which, Jefferson felt at least, lost him several adherents who had thought his opposition only temporary.[51]

Pressure on the Randolphites was being exerted from more directions than the President. As early as the middle of December newspapers had reported that Randolph, Macon, and Nicholson were in opposition to the President over the administration's Spanish policy, but since the debates were secret the reports only aroused the public curiosity. The Quids had to take the issue to the nation both to expose the chicanery of the administration and to clear themselves. Wrote Randolph's friend

Joseph Bryan from Georgia: "The people want your motives. They are at a loss to understand how you could oppose Madison and in some measure the President without swerving from your former opinions." [52]

The obvious solution was to make public the documents relative to West Florida and expose the administration's whole Spanish policy. When the debate on the Gregg resolution opened Randolph seized the opportunity to link nonintercourse with the attempt to purchase West Florida. "Let them take off the injunction of secrecy. They dare not. . . . They dare not come out and tell the nation what they have done." Thinly veiled allusions such as this again aroused the public curiosity and forced the House to reconsider the injunction of secrecy that covered the Florida proceedings. Reopening his attack on Madison, Randolph told the House that "most of the evils which the United States now suffered proceeded from the measures of the Executive—and from the weak and pusillanimous spirit of the keeper of the Cabinet—the Secretary of State." [53]

Though the obvious purpose was to discredit Madison by exposing his foreign policy, Randolph grossly overestimated the potential indignation. When on March 31 a combination of Quids and Federalists, together with Republicans who felt the administration had nothing to hide, voted to remove the injunction of secrecy, the publication of the documents caused scarcely a ripple of public excitement. There is little doubt that the vast majority of the American people, barring the Federalist parts of New England, approved the purchase of Florida, and few had any qualms of conscience over how it might be effected.

Frustrated in their attempt to excite popular indignation, the Quids in Congress shifted to a new tactic of embarrassing the administration by reminding it of its old out-of-power principles. Any measure which was ostensibly based on the principles of pure Republicanism was sure to attract considerable support in the party, and the Quids had no trouble conceiving measures to purify the government. In February Randolph had offered a set of three resolutions designed to implement the constitutional provision that no person holding office under the United States shall be a member of either House of Congress. The first resolution stated that a government contractor should be considered an officer of the United States within the meaning of the Constitution and therefore barred from a seat in Congress. The second denounced the union of civil and military power in a single individual, and the third recommended that a law be passed barring any officer of the army or navy from holding civil office under the government. Randolph explained that the purpose of the constitutional prohibition was to prevent one branch of government from influencing another and that his resolutions were designed to ensure the independence of the legislature by keeping out "placemen and pensioners." [54]

The resolutions were based on the traditions of English Whiggery and the early principles of the Republican party. But they embarrassed the administration, whose appointees in Louisiana held civil as well as military authority, and they embarrassed certain members of the House who held mail or army contracts. The first resolution, probably because it directly affected members of the House, was voted down by a large majority, but the second and third caused more trouble. There is some indication that these latter resolutions were directed primarily against General James Wilkinson, newly appointed governor of Louisiana. When Wilkinson's appointment had come before the Senate for confirmation in January, 1806, some of the Republican senators had voiced doubts about the union of civil and military authority in one person. Wilkinson reportedly was confirmed only with Federalist support. In his arguments in favor of the resolutions on April 1 Joseph Clay cited Wilkinson as an example of a dangerous plurality of offices, and Randolph, following him on the floor, expressly stated that he thought the Executive was wrong in making the appointment. It is possible that the allusion to Wilkinson had some effect, for the House agreed to the third resolution on the following day. Randolph accordingly brought in a bill to effect the resolution, and it was passed on April 11.[55]

That same day Randolph as chairman of the Ways and Means committee reported a bill appropriating money for the navy. Appropriation bills were normally passed early in the congressional session, but Randolph's committee had managed to sit on the navy bill for five months. The Republican party had never given more than halfhearted support to the navy, and the agrarian-minded conservatives had no use for it at all. The navy, moreover, was an excellent channel through which the Quids could harass the administration.

As soon as Randolph introduced the bill David Rogerson Williams was on his feet objecting to an item appropriating half a million dollars for "contingent expenses." Williams thought catchall funds were dangerous and requested an itemizing of expenses. Williams, of course, was on good Republican ground, for Gallatin's insistence on itemized appropriations in the federal budget beginning in 1795 was one of the solid achievements of the Republican party while in opposition. Randolph answered Williams explaining that when he drew up that section of the bill he felt that it did not matter what sum was appropriated or how it was listed. The Executive would spend as much as it pleased, and the next Congress would make up the difference without question.[56]

Undaunted by this exchange the House easily defeated Williams' motion, and a few days later it took up the other part of the naval appropriation—a bill supplying funds for the fortification of ports and harbors and to build gunboats. Williams and Clay attempted to delete the provision for ports and harbors, but they were quickly voted down by the House. The appropriation bill finally passed by a vote of 58–28, carried almost entirely by Northern Republicans and Federalists.[57] Tactics such as these, however, were irresponsible and self-defeating. After denouncing the Nonimportation Act as a "milk and water bill" and criticizing the Executive for a "weak and pusillanimous" policy, the Quids inconsistently opposed all measures to improve the national defense.

On the last day of the session, April 21, 1806, James Sloan of New Jersey, whose amendments to the Gregg resolution Randolph had derided as "Sloan's Vegetable Specific," offered a resolution that all standing committees be elected by the House, instead of being appointed by the Speaker. Accusing Randolph of having undermined the Executive by delaying appropriations for the army and navy until the end of the session, Sloan expressed the growing dissatisfaction of the Northern Republicans with the control of key committees by the conservative minority. He then denounced Randolph for his vindictive attacks on members of the House and promised to call up his resolution on the first day of the next session.[58]

There is little doubt that Randolph's tactics and personal abuse of members of the House as well as the administration cost him the support of many otherwise sympathetic conservatives. The attempts to embarrass the Executive, even in the name of principle, were transparent enough to cause John Taylor of Caroline to lament the spirit of faction within the party. "But when I see republicans," he wrote to Wilson Cary Nicholas, "in whose purity I equally confided, dividing and accusing each other, it persuades me that principle is a phantom under our form of government. . . ."

Taylor nevertheless was inclined to place responsibility for the schism on the administration, which had failed to place itself squarely on a foundation of pure Republicanism. "Had the present administration done something for principle," he continued,

by overturning the sedition law construction of the constitution— or by shortening the Senate's tenure—or diminishing the president's patronage—or making that office rotatory, it would have invigorated principle to struggle for honest government, far beyond the exploits of diminishing the public debt, and coextensively increasing it by purchasing Louisiana;—for brilliant as they are, the counting-house duskishness of the subjects will rapidly consign them to oblivion; whilst the fame of ingrafting some principle into our policy, capable of redeeming and preserving its purity, would live forever.[59]

On the other hand, it was this very pragmatic approach, of which Taylor complained, that enabled Jefferson to hold his party together. The party was too diversified, represented too many conflicting economic interests, for the administration to cater exclusively to the demands of the Southern agrarians, however attractive their appeal to principle might seem.

By the end of this extraordinary session of Congress the Quid schism had all but destroyed the conservative wing of the party. Randolph was ruined politically, Nicholson was on the bench, and Nathaniel Macon, who was to be driven from the Speakership in the next Congress, never completely recovered his influence. Those conservatives, on the other hand, who refused to follow the eccentric leadership of John Randolph, tended to submit more readily to administration leadership than they had before.

By going into opposition the Quids lost any chance they might have had for influencing the Republican party, while the excesses and eccentricities of John Randolph prevented them from gaining enough support to form a third party. Though Randolph had declared his permanent opposition to the administration, neither he nor his followers ever considered themselves anything but Republicans. After 1806 the Quids were nothing more than a vociferous but small and ineffective protest group within the Republican party.

IV

Isolation and Defeat,
1806–1808

John Randolph's schism in Congress was acutely embarrassing
to most of the Republican conservatives. Not only did it expose
the division within the party but it forced the administration
Republicans to close ranks against the dissidents. President Jefferson begged his friend Wilson Cary Nicholas to enter Congress and assume a position of leadership. Senator William
Branch Giles sparked a move to induce Creed Taylor to run
for Congress against Randolph. And in the election of 1806 the
Quid Philip R. Thompson of Culpeper was defeated in a bid
for re-election, no doubt owing to the influence of Madison in
the district.[1] The schism thus placed a premium on party regularity and actually hindered the effort to prevent Madison from
becoming Jefferson's successor. Anyone who criticized the policy of the administration risked being branded a factious schis-
matic and losing all influence in the party. Randolph, moreover,
was never accepted as leader of the conservatives in Virginia,
largely because of his excesses and his declaration of total opposition to the administration. Most of the conservatives preferred to pursue their aims from within, while maintaining a
semblance of party unity. They remained completely loyal to
Jefferson, even while criticizing some of his policies, and ab-
horred Randolph's personal attacks on the President.

The Quids appeared to gain a temporary victory when the Virginia legislature chose William H. Cabell governor in 1806. Although Cabell received the support of the Quids in the Assembly, he owed his election to the votes of twenty Federalists. Interestingly enough, his opponent, Alexander McRae, was a personal friend of Monroe and supported him against Madison in 1808. Neither candidate had the support of the regular party organization. The election evidently turned on personalities, however, and bore little relation to the conservative movement. The Quids never effected any formal party organization in Virginia and never succeeded in gaining control of the legislature. They remained a tiny minority increasingly isolated from the rest of the Republican conservatives.[2]

Though Randolph made little effort at this time to organize the conservatives in Virginia, he did attempt to secure some newspaper support. To counter the pressure of party discipline and the effect of political rumor he felt he had to take his story to the people, and the most effective way was through the newspapers. In June he informed Garnett that he was working on a defense to be printed over the pseudonym "Decius," but the press in Virginia, he complained, "is under a virtual imprimatur, so that I shall hardly find a vent for my productions, in case they should ever reach maturity." On a trip to Richmond in May he made an effort to explain his position to Thomas Ritchie, editor of the *Enquirer*. Ritchie seemed conciliatory, disposed to mediate the schism, and agreeably printed Randolph's version of the conflict. He soon abandoned his neutrality, however, and answered the "Decius" letters himself with an editorial defense of the administration's foreign policy.[3]

Another possible outlet for the Quids was the *Aurora* in Philadelphia whose editor, William Duane, had been attacking Madison and Gallatin for two years. Duane's ardent Republicanism was akin to that of Randolph, and Joseph Clay, an intimate friend of both, provided a personal connection. For a time there had seemed a chance that Duane would lend his support to Randolph. Ignorant of the nature of the dispute over West Florida, Duane had incautiously defended Randolph and flayed his opponents as enemies of the administration. He had been silenced, however, by a warning from his political ally, Senator Michael Leib, conveyed through the Delaware Republican Caesar A. Rodney. Leib, a strong nationalist, approved of the administration's moves in West Florida and assumed that Duane, properly informed, would also. The hopes of the Virginians were dashed in the late spring when Nicholson journeyed to Philadelphia to see Duane and reported that "the *Aurora* refuses to give circulation to anything against the powers that be, & that until October, the period of their elections, it will preserve a guarded neutrality." [4] The Pennsylvania schism had originated in state politics, and Duane remained more interested in the state gubernatorial election than in political alliances on a national scale. The Virginia Quids thus remained without newspaper backing until the Richmond *Spirit of '76* appeared on the eve of the election in September, 1808.

The summer of 1806 also saw an intensification of the struggle between the Quids and the President for the loyalty of Monroe. In May Nicholson wrote to the minister to sympathize with him over the implied rebuke of the Pinkney mission:

I do not feel myself as too rigid to conceal from you that Mr. [William] Pinkney's appointment has not given universal satisfaction to the real friends of the present administration. Those are not wanting who believe that no such appointment was necessary under the circumstances, and an opinion is entertained that it was intended to take from you the credit of settling our differences with England. [5]

Nicholson's barb hit a tender spot, for in Monroe's next letter to the President he told Jefferson bluntly that his position in England had been "much weakened" by the appointment of a special commissioner, and he warned the President against appointing Federalists to foreign posts. This letter, however, was never mailed. Instead Monroe contented himself with a firm but polite refusal of the President's offer of a governorship in Orleans or Louisiana, which Monroe evidently suspected was an attempt to get him out of the way.[6]

The Old Republicans outside the Randolph circle also kept pressuring Monroe. Although they lacked sympathy for Randolph's personal vendetta, they remained deeply concerned over Madison's reputation as a "trimmer." In July aged John Beckley, who had been instrumental in organizing the Republican party in Pennsylvania in the 1790s, wrote to Monroe: "Madison, is deemed by many, too timid and indecisive as a statesman, and too liable to a conduct of forbearance to the federal party, which may endanger our harmony and political safety." [7]

It was soon evident that Monroe had accepted the advice of both Jefferson and Randolph to communicate his feelings to no one. His next letter to Randolph was a formal, noncommittal outline of his political ideas and handwritten by an embassy clerk. Referring to Randolph's pledge of support in the presidential contest, Monroe wrote, "My own sentiment is this, that the idea had better be relinquished. . . . There are older men, whom I have long been accustomed to consider, as having higher pretensions to the trust than myself, whose claims it would be painful to me to see rejected, and . . . the person, who seems to be contemplated by others is in that class." [8] Clearly Monroe had no objections to Madison on principle, and he was willing to wait his turn for the rewards of office. This must have been a bitter dose for Randolph, but he no doubt dismissed it as the product of Monroe's caution. For the time being, Monroe remained aloof from the party struggle.

When Congress reconvened on December 1, 1806, Sloan of New Jersey renewed his motion to appoint the standing committees by ballot. The motion was voted down, however, with the Federalists joining the Republican conservatives in opposing it. Randolph, who had arrived twenty minutes late, missed the vote, and Speaker Macon felt that he could not appoint an absent member to a committee. For the first time in five years

Randolph's name was missing from the Ways and Means committee. Though he felt badly about bypassing Randolph, the Speaker still managed to load the committee with conservatives. Joseph Clay was appointed to Randolph's place, Williams and Meriwether were retained from the previous session, and the only consistent supporter of the administration was Roger Nelson of Maryland. A few days later Garnett asked to be excused from service on the committee, and the Speaker appointed Randolph in his place. Joseph Clay, who had been named first, would ordinarily have been chairman, but he declined the position, and the committee met and elected Randolph chairman.[9]

In general the activities of this lameduck session seemed to be a vindication of the stand taken by the Quids the previous spring. The President's annual message, read to the House on December 2, 1806, all but ignored the aspects of foreign affairs that had agitated the House a few months before. Relations with England were omitted entirely, pending the Monroe-Pinkney negotiations, and in regard to Spain the President recommended only the raising of troops for the defense of the Southern frontier, a project that Randolph had sponsored the previous year. Indeed, the President seemed most concerned with the threatened surplus in the treasury, for he recommended the repeal of the salt tax (the only remaining excise), and he outlined a broad plan for internal improvements in the nation. Randolph described the message as "wormwood to certain gentry," and indeed many a supporter of the administration might have asked himself what all the excitement had been about in the previous session.[10]

In response to the pacific tone of the President's message Randolph introduced a bill to suspend the Nonimportation Act, which had not yet gone into effect. The House agreeably voted 101–5 to suspend the act until the following July. Early in January the House, by a similar vote, passed a bill to repeal the salt tax in accordance with the President's recommendation. Pleased with this virtual surrender to the conservative position, Speaker Macon wrote to Nicholson, "The doings here will hereby convince every candid man in the world that the Republicans of the *old school* were not wrong last winter." [11]

There is some indication that the administration's disposition to bury old issues was accompanied by efforts to conciliate the Quids. Randolph reported to Nicholson the increasing friendliness of the Northern Republicans toward him and concluded that they were "well disposed towards a truce. The higher powers are in the same goodly temper, as I am informed." Only the character of John Randolph kept the schism alive. Outside Congress the attitude of most conservatives was aptly expressed by John Taylor of Caroline, who wrote to Wilson Cary Nicholas, "Although I wish a few of Mr. Madison's opinions were different from what I suppose them to be, yet . . . nothing would give me so much political pleasure . . . as to see the schisms of the republicans squashed . . . by kindness and forbearance." [12] Kindness and forbearance the administration was certainly willing to extend, and it required of Randolph only that he subject himself to a minimum of party discipline, moderate his extreme adherence to principle, and accept Madison as Jefferson's successor to the presidency.

Randolph, of course, could not accept even these conditions, and his continued intractability served only to isolate him from the majority of conservatives as well as the administration. Left with only a handful of devoted followers in Congress—Williams, Stanford, Garnett, Clay, Trigg, and Gray—Randolph's opposition tended more and more to become a personal vendetta against Jefferson and Madison under the guise of conservative principles, but without the support of the conservative wing. With the possible exception of Randolph, no conservative ever considered himself outside the Republican party. The conservatives represented instead one flank of a heterogeneous organization, and in the absence of any divisive issue most of them were willing to cooperate with the administration. Thus Randolph's continued criticism of the Executive left him virtually isolated. Jefferson in February told Wilson Cary Nicholas that "the little band of schismatics" was down to three or four. He admitted, however, that Randolph's ability enabled him to dominate the House and his continued opposition left the administration forces without effective leadership.[13]

Caught unaware by the administration's attempt at conciliation, Randolph had to do some backing and filling to find new grounds for opposition. When the President reversed himself on Spanish policy and called for troops to defend the frontier instead of money to purchase Florida, Randolph also reversed himself and opposed the demand for troops on the ground that they were no longer needed. When the annual bill to appropriate funds for the navy and coastal defense came before the House, Randolph saw another opportunity for opposition. The gunboats were a favorite project of Jefferson's for coastal defense, and they had been generally accepted by the Republican party as an inexpensive alternative to an ocean-going navy. Randolph opposed them on the rather reasonable ground that they were useless and ineffective, but his refusal to appropriate money for more effective ships indicated that there was nothing constructive in his opposition. He was also unwilling to finance fortifications around the nation's ports and harbors. Not only was there no need for defensive measures, he told the House, but the problem was so vast that all the resources of the nation would not be able to handle it adequately and partial measures were worthless.[14]

Only one opportunity for embarrassing the administration was presented Randolph, and he was quick to seize it. The President in his annual message had alluded to expeditions against the Spanish territories in the Southwest, and by January the air was filled with rumors of Burr's conspiracy. On January 16 Randolph, referring to the President's message, called for information on the conspiracy. The President, with no proof of a conspiracy and only General Wilkinson's vague reports on Burr's activities as evidence, was forced into evasions and double-talk by Randolph's move. When the administration's bill to suspend the habeas corpus, aimed primarily at Burr's accomplices, Justus Erich Bollman and Samuel Swartwout, reached the House, Randolph was horrified not only at the subversion of a basic concept of the common law but at the haste with which the Senate passed the bill. He was delighted when the House rejected the bill and then voted to publish the debate on it.[15] Had the House proved as docile to the wishes of the administration as the Senate, Randolph might have had his issue.

Without an issue, however, Randolph's opposition throughout this session seemed to have little point, and it caused some soul-searching among more than one conservative. "Lately a suspicion has crossed my brain," wrote John Taylor the following summer, "that the minority as they are called, have a party enmity to the president, instead of having only honorably differed from him in opinion as I supposed." [16] It was clear that many conservatives were becoming disillusioned with Randolph's representation of their position. Many were also becoming increasingly concerned with the divisions in the party—led by DeWitt Clinton in New York, Duane in Pennsylvania, and Randolph in Washington—and fearful lest the factions harm the party in the approaching presidential election. Their distrust was only deepened by Randolph's seemingly irresponsible conduct in the next session of Congress when the country was on the verge of war with England.

The attack on the *Chesapeake* by the British frigate *Leopard* in June, 1807, threw a new issue onto the complex American political scene, and it dealt a severe blow to the pro-English sentiment of the Republican conservatives. Randolph favored immediate retaliation. He told Garnett that although he had previously favored moderation toward England, "*now that the rupture has taken place*, I would act with the most determined spirit against the *enemy*, for so I consider England at this moment." He later criticized the President for failing to summon

Congress immediately after the incident to prepare for war. Randolph was for attacking Canada and descending on Jamaica if Britain refused redress. Nicholson, even more warlike, would not even accept an offer of redress from Great Britain. "There are insults and injuries for which neither individual nor nation can accept apology," he wrote to Gallatin. Macon, on the other hand, was more moderate. If Jefferson could prevent war and still uphold the nation's honor, Macon felt, it would "add as much to his reputation as the purchase of Louisiana." [17] The sudden revival of the dispute with England at least assured an exciting session as Congress assembled in Washington on October 26, 1807—a month earlier than usual.

The House was reorganized in accordance with what Randolph had two years before called "the new order of things." Joseph B. Varnum was elected Speaker, and he put reliable administration Republicans on all the standing committees. Randolph was removed from the Ways and Means committee in favor of George Washington Campbell of Tennessee. Annoying as Randolph's antics had been at times, his abilities, particularly in finance, would be sorely missed by the House. Gallatin expressed his disappointment to his wife: "Varnum has, much against my wishes, removed Randolph from the Ways and Means Committee and appointed Campbell of Tennessee. It was improper as it related to the public business, and it will give me additional labor." [18]

The size of the conservative group was increased slightly by the elections of 1806–7. Georgia sent a moderately conservative delegation—William Wyatt Bibb, Howell Cobb, and George M. Troup. Randolph thought Bibb was "a most valuable acquisition to our party." [19] Cobb and Troup voted less consistently with Randolph, but both were supporters of Monroe and both spoke frequently on the conservative side. To the Senate the Georgia legislature sent William Harris Crawford, who supplanted the retired George Logan as the main voice of the conservative wing in the upper House. A young Virginian who had migrated to Georgia, Crawford had risen rapidly in Georgia politics as a protégé of Georgia's Republican Senator James Jackson. Jackson's main support was among the seaboard aristocracy, and Crawford brought into the coalition the interior counties, settled largely by migrants from Virginia and North Carolina. After the death of Jackson in 1806, Crawford took his seat in the Senate, and Troup assumed the leadership of the seaboard aristocracy. Though Jackson remained loyal to the Jefferson administration in all but the Yazoo issue, he succeeded in placing the stamp of conservatism on the Republican party in Georgia, and his followers began their congressional careers in the conservative wing.[20]

The President's seventh annual message, read to Congress on October 27, reviewed the difficulties with Great Britain and called on Congress for measures of defense. As usual, the President left all the specific proposals up to his floor leaders in Congress. The first important measure to come before the House was a bill to strengthen the fortifications around the nation's ports and to build additional gunboats. This year the fortifications bill passed without opposition, but the provision for gunboats ran into trouble. The conservatives with the help of the Senate defeated a similar bill in the previous session, and in spite of the apparent imminence of war with England they prepared to fight the measure again. Jefferson reported that about twenty of them had held a caucus to organize opposition to the bill, but he predicted that their efforts would be defeated.[21]

The gunboat bill came before the House early in December. The Republicans had always opposed a large navy, and the questionable usefulness of Jefferson's gunboats gave the opposition additional ammunition. Randolph, leading the assault, ridiculed the whole bill as an effort to provide gunboats to defend the harbors and forts to defend the gunboats. He thought the nation should be preparing to defend itself against attack. Further, he criticized the Executive for wasting money on gunboats which had not even been able to enforce the President's Proclamation, issued after the *Chesapeake* outrage, and keep British ships out of American territorial waters. The proper course, thought Randolph, was not to add to the navy, but to follow the example of France and build up our strength on land. Nathaniel Macon, on the other hand, felt some addition should be made to the navy in view of the threat of war, but he thought that fewer gunboats should be built as long as no one was sure how useful they were. Despite this assault the bill passed the House with only a handful of Federalists and Quids in opposition.[22]

There was some rationality in the opposition of the Quids to the bill, for Jefferson's gunboats never justified the President's faith in them. The gunboat scheme, however, had long been advocated by the Republican party, and the Quids seemed to be opposing all efforts to build up the nation's defenses. Indeed, the gunboats themselves were a conservative proposition; what the nation really needed was more frigates. Their opposition seemed even more irresponsible when Randolph disclosed his plan for handling the British by attacking Canada and descending on Jamaica. John Taylor of Caroline, thoroughly disillusioned with Randolph's leadership, expressed the reaction of most of the Republican conservatives:

Poor Randolph is lost, and his party has vanished. A conviction of his honour and integrity, and a very warm approbation of his conduct in the Yazoo business had procured him a considerable position of respect; but some of his speeches lately delivered, exhibit him as so blinded by something, supposed to be passion or prejudice, as to have led him into censures of Mr. Jefferson's conduct, in some cases where it is universally approved, and in others upon contradictory grounds, in the opinion of those I have conversed with. What can be more astonishing than to be opposed to war with England at the time of the non-intercourse bill—to be for it now—to talk of suffering a ship captain to involve two nations in war, of invading Canada & descending on Jamaica—to complain that Congress was not called sooner, and now to do nothing, because they have met too soon for their materials—and to censure buying a little timber and salt peter, whilst the projects advocated required it.[23]

The inconsistencies lay more in Randolph's language than in his actions, for his actions for the most part during this session were in accordance with long-cherished conservative principles. Such, for instance, was his resolution of December 18 that "an embargo be laid on all shipping, the property of citizens of the United States, now in port or which shall hereafter arrive." Randolph no doubt had in mind a temporary embargo designed to keep American shipping out of British hands should England decide to declare war. The Senate on that same day passed a more general embargo and hurried it over to the House. Opposed in the Senate only by the Federalists and Crawford, the Senate bill instantly aroused the opposition of the Quids in the House because it imposed no limitations on the embargo in time or scope. The House debated the bill behind closed doors for two days while the administration forces fought various attempts to restrict its provisions. On December 19 the House passed the bill virtually intact by a vote of 82–44. Jefferson's estimate that the opposition consisted of "one-half Federalists, ¼ of the little band [Quids], the other fourth of republicans happening to take up mistaken views of the subject" was generally accurate, though Macon, Clay, and Williams, who like Randolph favored the principle of an embargo, abstained from voting.[24]

Randolph was hard put to defend his sudden reversal, even to his friend Nicholson. He suggested that Nicholson visit him, "I will then show you how impossible it was for me to have voted for the embargo. The circumstances under which it presented itself were peculiar and compelled me to oppose it; although otherwise a favorite measure with me, as you well know."

The "peculiar circumstances" were no doubt the general terms in which the Senate's bill was written. Randolph was not alone in his opposition. A sizable minority of the Republican party agreed with him, and even Gallatin had no relish for the sort of embargo the Senate's bill contemplated. "In every point

of view," the Treasury Secretary wrote to Jefferson, "priva-
tions, sufferings, revenue, effect on enemy, politics at home, etc.,
I prefer war to a permanent embargo." [25] Randolph must have
agreed; he had conceived of the embargo as a temporary prelude
to war, not as a long-term measure designed to coerce the
European powers. Throughout the rest of the session he called
for strong measures of defense and criticized the administration's
proposals as weak, halfhearted, and expensive.

On December 1 Randolph introduced a resolution to provide
funds to arm the whole militia of the United States. Like Jefferson's gunboats, the militia was an old stand-by of the Republican
party, which considered it less expensive, less dangerous, and no
more inefficient than a regular army. John Taylor, temporarily
forgetting his disappointment with Randolph, considered the
resolution "the most effectual, principled, and grand measure,
which has been introduced since the government has been in
operation. He ought to nurse his popularity in Congress, if for
no other end, but to carry the one point." No Republican could
afford to vote against it. The House quickly passed it, forgot it,
and in February the administration Republicans introduced their
own measure—a bill to increase the regular army from four thousand to ten thousand men. The Quids immediately objected to
this departure from party principles, and by clever delaying
tactics they managed to keep the bill before the House until
the first week in April. It was clear, however, that some sort of
defensive preparations had to be approved before the end of the
session, and several of the conservatives supported the army
bill. Nathaniel Macon, who thought the government ought to
raise troops "for some very defenseless places," wrote to Nicholson: "We must either repeal the law which authorized the
President to issue the proclamation or take some measures to
enforce it." [26]

The debate on the bill occupied the whole first week in April.
Randolph, Williams, Stanford, and Garnett fought the measure
all the way, resurrecting the old fear of standing armies, point-

ing out that there was no immediate danger of invasion and that
ten thousand troops were inadequate even if there were a danger,
and reminding the House Republicans of their opposition to a
regular army in 1798. Even Macon was unimpressed with their
arguments, however. He informed Nicholson on April 6: "Stanford yesterday gave historical account of all the votes given in
'98, and Randolph a very able speech both against, though
neither of them convinced me that the state of our affairs were
the same now as in '98." [27]

After the longest discussion since the debate on the Nonimportation Act, the House passed the bill on April 7 by a vote of
95–16. In the minority were Randolph, Garnett, Edwin Gray,
Stanford, and Williams, plus a few Republicans who occasionally voted with the Quids, like Matthew Clay of Virginia and
William Hoge of Pennsylvania. The rest of the minority were
Federalists, except for Sloan of New Jersey, who found himself
in an antiadministration minority for the first time. Macon,
Trigg, Bibb, and Troup supported the bill, although Bibb later
changed his mind and asked for a revote.[28]

Macon later told Nicholson, "I never regretted differing with
him [Randolph] so much in my life as I did on the bill raising
troops. He followed his judgment, I mine." The administration
Republicans were quick to exploit the temporary division in
the conservatives, for Macon reported to Nicholson the next
day that he had been approached by "one of the great or leading men in the House," who wanted him to take a more active
part in the debates and told him that a great majority of the
House respected his opinions on foreign relations.[29] Except
for Randolph, there was no impassable gulf between the conservatives and the administration Republicans, and overtures of this
sort are not surprising. Nor is it surprising to find Macon in the
next session of Congress introducing the administration measures.

Randolph's opposition to the army bill during a threat of war
cost him heavily in popularity. An increase in the regular army
seemed justified to the majority of people, if only, as the admin-

istration forces argued, to provide a nucleus for the militia system. On his return to North Carolina Macon "found almost everyone of every political description condemning the conduct of our honest friend J.R." Even Randolph had some difficulty in explaining his tactics to his constituents.[30] The complete reliance on militia in the face of war, though a long-cherished concept, was one of the weakest of the Republican doctrines. The militia proved all but worthless in the Revolution (and, except at New Orleans, they were of little value in the War of 1812). Randolph's faith in the militia in time of danger was utterly unjustified. One cannot help but respect his stand, however, insofar as it was based on a fear of standing armies. That ancient ghost, inherited from English Whiggism, was one of the more wholesome facets of the conservative tradition and an aspect that justified to some extent what otherwise might seem an irresponsible opposition.

By the spring of 1808 John Randolph and his tiny band of Quids in Congress were in virtual isolation, estranged from the majority of Republican conservatives as well as from the administration. Their isolation was temporarily obscured, however, by the approaching presidential election, as the conservatives closed ranks in support of their candidate, James Monroe.

For several years it had been evident that Madison was the probable successor to Jefferson, and the conservatives had accordingly turned to Monroe, one of the founders of the party and a man whose political ideas seemed to be more in conformity with old Republican principles. The process of grooming Monroe for the presidency had not gone very far when John Randolph and the Quids rebelled against the administration in the winter of 1805–6. Despite Randolph's pledges of support, Monroe in 1806 had no intention of running against Madison for the presidency. One visitor to London quoted him as saying he would "rather be constable" than oppose Madison.[31]

In a letter of June 16, 1806, Monroe made it clear to Randolph that he intended to abide by the present order of presidential succession and that any other course would wreck old friendships and perhaps ruin the party. Randolph replied that such arguments would be valid if there were no differences between Monroe and Madison, but he had a "decided preference" for Monroe and felt that the principles of the Republican party were being subverted by the "cold and insidious moderation" of Madison. By the end of 1806 Monroe was resisting less strongly. He felt keenly the implied rebuke of the Pinkney mission, as well as the frustrating strictness of Madison's instructions in regard to the treaty with England. Confiding his feelings to Randolph he wrote: "circumstances have occurred during my services abroad which were calculated to hurt my feelings and actually did hurt them, which may produce a change in the future relation between some of them and myself, unless satisfactorily explained." [32]

In December, 1806, Monroe and Pinkney ended six months of negotiations and signed a treaty with Great Britain. In their efforts to reach some point of agreement with England the commissioners exceeded their instructions from the Secretary of State, and the treaty contained no settlement of the outstanding American grievances and few concessions to American commerce. The subject of impressment of American seamen, which Madison considered a *sine qua non*, was omitted entirely. The treaty arrived in Washington on the last day of the congressional session, March 3, 1807. Jefferson and Madison had serious doubts as to whether the treaty would be approved by the Senate, and at a hastily called cabinet meeting it was decided not to submit it to the Senate at all.[33]

The rejection of his treaty, news of which reached Monroe in June, seemed to confirm all the insinuations of Randolph. Pinkney had been sent to deprive him of credit, and the treaty had been rejected to injure him politically. Although disappointed with the reception of his treaty, Monroe nevertheless avoided any commitment on his presidential ambitions before he left London. His arrival in Norfolk on December 13, 1807, occasioned a flurry of activity among Virginia conservatives. The Governor's Council, a majority of which supported Monroe, presented a highly complimentary address, which Governor Cabell refused to sign, evidently out of fear of advancing Monroe's political fortunes. After visiting several old friends in Richmond, Monroe journeyed to Washington to report to the President on the state of affairs abroad. In Washington he was ignored by the President and saw Madison only briefly. Neither sought his advice on the state of affairs with England or on domestic politics. Utterly distressed with his cold reception, Monroe returned to Virginia a willing candidate for the presidency.[34]

The campaign for Monroe was centered largely in Virginia, both because he had more popular appeal in that state and because he could not hope to make a showing in the national election without the backing of his home state. Though the campaign was handled primarily by conservative leaders in Virginia, such as Littleton Waller Tazewell, Benjamin Watkins Leigh, and Creed Taylor, Randolph and the congressional Quids made some effort to organize a campaign on a national scale. Randolph's support probably did more harm than good—he had so completely alienated Virginians by his irresponsible actions. Alexander McRae, one of those managing Monroe's candidacy in Virginia, informed Monroe that he would lose most of his support in the General Assembly if he endorsed Randolph and the open critics of the administration.[35]

Outside Virginia the strongest support for Monroe came from Georgia where Crawford, Bibb, Cobb, and Troup were all working for Monroe. In North Carolina there was little support for Monroe outside of the prosperous and conservative Roanoke Valley. Nathaniel Macon, with more insight into the political ideas of Madison and Monroe than most conservatives possessed, felt there was little choice between the two. He actually preferred Gallatin as better qualified than either. He also felt that when two candidates for President were in the same political party, it seemed "too much like a contest for the loaves and fishes." In regard to the campaign he wrote to Judge Nicholson: "I shall not trouble myself, and Stanford, I imagine will be afraid to make a stir before his own election is over."[36] From Pennsylvania Joseph Clay reported that the people were opposed to Madison, a report that was more hopeful than true. Alexander James Dallas, the Republican leader of Pennsylvania, was a moderate who supported the administration and favored the succession of Madison. William Duane and Michael Leib made sporadic efforts to stir up opposition to Madison but they were more interested in the Pennsylvania gubernatorial contest. The Duane-Leib faction, which called itself the "Democratic Society of the Friends of the People," seems to have been divided between Madison and George Clinton. There was no evident support for Monroe in any case.[37]

In New York the newspapers of the Clinton machine were booming the candidacy of Vice-President George Clinton on the battle-cry of "too much Virginia," and they continued attacking Madison while Madison's supporters were nominating Clinton as the party candidate for the vice-presidency. Neither Clinton nor Monroe had a chance for election unless one retired from the race and threw his support to the other. The Federalists would have been willing to support either in preference to Madison. No serious attempt was made at alliance, however. In 1806 the Clintonians, according to one Virginian visiting in Albany, considered courting Randolph and the Virginia Quids, but abandoned the idea for fear that Randolph's anticommercial speeches might damage their cause in New York. The Virginians were even less anxious for an alliance. John Taylor told Monroe that he thought Monroe's friends in Virginia would prefer even Madison to Clinton.[38]

For the Monroe campaign all depended on a caucus of the members of the Virginia legislature to be held toward the end of the session. Realizing the importance of this meeting, Madison's managers in Washington—William Branch Giles and Wilson Cary Nicholas—arranged for the expected congressional caucus to meet earlier than usual (it had met in February in 1804) with a view to influencing the Virginia meeting. As a result the caucuses were held almost simultaneously, and neither influenced the other.

On January 21 the Madison forces invited all members of the Virginia General Assembly who supported Madison to meet that evening in the Bell Tavern. One hundred and twenty-three delegates attended the meeting, and all voted for Madison. That same day a spokesman for Monroe invited the whole Assembly to meet that night in the capitol. The meeting was attended by many leading conservatives, personal friends of Monroe, and a number of political opportunists. General John P. Hungerford, a Federalist, was elected chairman. Tazewell of Norfolk and Taylor of Caroline were placed on the Monroe electoral ticket, along with John Coalter, Randolph's brother-in-law, and Creed Taylor, who had managed Randolph's first steps in politics. The central corresponding committee included George Hay, Monroe's son-in-law, and Dr. John Brockenbrough, a Randolph intimate. James M. Garnett headed the Essex County committee, while Benjamin Watkins Leigh served as chairman of a similar body in Petersburg. Also prominent among the delegates was Henry St. George Tucker, Randolph's step-brother, who had been denouncing the embargo in the Assembly.[39] The leadership of this meeting testifies to the close-knit family ties of the Virginia squirearchy—a nascent form of the "Richmond Junto," which eventually became the clearinghouse for Old Republican doctrine in Virginia.

In this meeting at the capitol 57 votes were cast for Monroe and 10 for Madison. Counting 3 votes cast on the following day, Madison had the support of 136 members of the Assembly to Monroe's 57. And one observer friendly to Monroe admitted that at least 20 of his votes were cast by Federalists. This was a stunning defeat for the conservatives, who as late as December had been claiming a majority of the legislature. Two days later, January 23, the Republicans in Congress held their caucus to determine the party nominee. With 94 senators and representatives present, Madison received 83 votes for President, Monroe 3, and George Clinton 3, 5 not voting. The votes for Monroe were cast by the 3 Georgians—Crawford, Bibb, and Cobb.[40]

Expecting defeat, most of the Monroe supporters in Congress had refused to attend the caucus in Washington. They published instead an address, "To the People of the United States," protesting the principle of nomination of the President by congressional caucus and objecting to the choice of Madison as "unfit for the office of President." It was signed by seventeen Congressmen, six of whom were Quids—Randolph, Clay, Trigg, Garnett, Gray, and Williams. The rest represented the Duane-Leib faction in Pennsylvania or the Clinton faction in New York.[41]

Despite the counterattack engineered by Randolph, the caucuses in Washington and Richmond squelched the movement for Monroe before it barely started. The lukewarm among his followers hastened to join Madison, and even many of his close friends advised him to drop out of the contest. Walter Jones and Matthew Clay, Virginia congressmen who occasionally voted with the Quids, told Monroe that his persistence would only divide the party and isolate him politically.[42]

Even Taylor of Caroline, one of the most influential and certainly the most disinterested of Monroe's supporters, began to express some doubts to Monroe. Taylor had never been very sanguine about Monroe's chances for election, and in February he told Monroe that he ought to accept the President's offer of a governorship in Louisiana. He pointed out to Monroe that he could not win without an alliance with the Federalists and dissident factions among the Republicans, alliances that were not only contrary to his principles but which would ruin him politically. As governor of Louisiana, Taylor noted, Monroe would be removed from the taint of political factions, and he would be available when the West began demanding a Western

man for President. This latter suggestion was not altogether un-
reasonable, and the prophecy was borne out by the career of
William Henry Harrison, the Virginia planter who was then
governor of the Indiana Territory. Despite the crushing defeats
in the caucuses, Randolph, almost alone among Monroe's supporters, refused to abandon hope. On March 9 he sent Benjamin
Watkins Leigh to Monroe with news of the campaign in Washington and wrote, "The Prospect before us is daily brighten-
ing. . . ." [43]

Monroe, of course, never had any illusions about his ability
to defeat Madison. He sought only a vindication of his actions
abroad by demonstrating that he had the support of a substantial
number of citizens.[44] At the same time he felt the necessity of
remaining aloof from the campaign so he could retreat grace-
fully should it prove hopeless. On February 27 he wrote to the
President: "In regard to the approaching election, I have been
and shall continue to be an inactive spectator of the movement.
Should the nation be disposed to call any citizen to that station,
it would be his duty to accept it. On that ground I rest." He
used the same phrasing in letters to Randolph and Tazewell, declining to discuss politics since he was a "distant and inactive
spectator of the movement." On March 26 Randolph wrote to
Monroe that he was breaking off their correspondence lest Monroe's reputation be damaged by clandestine contact with one
who had been "proscribed" by the administration. He did not
resume the correspondence until after the election in January,
1809.[45]

The campaign started slowly, as both sides glossed over the
basic issues that had brought on the conservative revolt. Monroe's supporters confined themselves to criticism of the manner
in which the caucuses had been held. The first note of excitement was injected by the publication in March, 1808, of the
Monroe-Pinkney Treaty and its related correspondence. The
publication of this correspondence was a blow to Monroe's
candidacy, for it revealed the real force of Madison's diplomacy.
The Secretary of State, many discovered, was a skilled negotia-

tor capable of defending American rights against both England and France. Madison emerged as the champion of American nationalism; Monroe and Pinkney had violated his instructions and bowed needlessly to the demands of the British. Whatever its effect on public opinion, the publication of the treaty only confirmed the faith of Monroe's supporters. The conservatives were convinced that a *rapprochement* with England was necessary, even at the price of abandoning the American stand on impressment and blockades. Indeed, so convinced were they of the correctness of Monroe's diplomacy that they looked on its publication as a vindication.[46]

The campaign for Monroe, never very fervid, slowed to a crawl during the summer, largely due to the diffidence of Monroe's supporters in refusing to attack the administration directly. By August the lethargic campaign discouraged even John Randolph, who at last came around to John Taylor's view that a halfhearted campaign would only divide the party and damage Monroe politically. Randolph asked Garnett to "Tell Col. T[aylor] that I agree with him so far, in this matter, that such a languid support of M[onroe] is calculated *only* to injure him, & that it would have been better not to have brought him forward if this is the kind of support that he is to receive." [47]

In the meantime, ironically, Monroe was beginning to sound more like a candidate. In July he wrote to John Taylor to discuss the strategy for the campaign. A direct attack on the administration was unthinkable, Monroe wrote.

My idea is that the committee should form a general view of my services, opportunities, and character, address the publick in my favor, & recommend the appointment, as furnishing the best hope of adjusting honorably our differences with foreign powers without war, or of supporting the war if necessary with suitable energy and decision.[48]

Later he wrote to Nicholson that he had definitely decided to run and would make his issue the embargo, which had aroused discontent throughout the country as Southern agricultural products piled up on the wharves and New England ships rotted at their moorings. "We are now approaching a great crisis. Such is the state of our affairs, and such is the compromitment of the Administration at home and abroad by its measures, that it seems likely that it will experience great difficulty in extricating itself. . . . " To Littleton Tazewell he enlarged further on this line of reasoning. He was fairly certain of losing, he told Tazewell, but by refusing to withdraw he could maintain his neutrality and withhold or lend support to the new President depending upon his "conduct." Then if Madison proved unable to extricate himself from the embargo without assuming dictatorial powers at home or losing prestige abroad, at least the whole Republican party would not fail with him, for "there remain within the republican pale the means of preserving the cause, while there are so many independent republicans who have had no agency in the present system of measures. . . . " [49]

To further the Monroe campaign a conservative newspaper, *The Spirit of '76*, was founded in Richmond in September, 1808, by Edward C. Stannard. The politics of the paper was indicated by its motto: "A frequent recurrence to fundamental principles is essential to the liberties of a republic." As expounded in *The Spirit of '76* the essence of the Monroe platform was opposition to the embargo and a demand for a return to the "principles of 1798" in the operation of the government. In the embargo the conservatives had a good issue, not only because it was generally unpopular but because it tended to subvert every principle the Republicans had fought for in 1798. It gave the federal government too much control over the economic affairs of the country, and it gave the President himself too much discretionary power. Moreover, it forced the government to make up the deficiency in revenue by increased taxes or by contracting loans. Finally, the embargo aided manufacturers who needed protection at the expense of farmers who were dependent on foreign markets. All these objections were brought up by John Taylor of Caroline in a series of letters published in *The Spirit of '76*. Taylor thought that acceptance of the Monroe treaty would have rendered an embargo unnecessary and might have paved the way for better relations with England. If war to up-hold the nation's honor was necessary, Taylor preferred fighting France rather than England; but a better policy, he thought, would be to sweep away all the restrictions on American commerce and retaliate against both England and France by seizing the property held by their citizens in the United States.[50]

The embargo proved to be the only strong point on the conservative side, and it was not enough. The conservatives, without effective organization and without popular support for their pleas for principle, were no match for the force of party discipline and the personal popularity of Madison. Though *The Spirit of '76* had confidently expected Monroe to receive the votes of Federalist New England, as well as Virginia and Georgia, Monroe received not a single electoral vote. Madison won with 122; the Federalist Charles C. Pinckney obtained 47; and George Clinton received six. Monroe's only strength was in the Tidewater counties of Virginia, where the vote was largely a protest against the embargo. The protest vote in the valley of Virginia went to the Federalist candidate Pinckney. Madison carried Virginia 12,451 to Monroe's 2,770.[51] The vote was mute testimony to the weakness of conservative opinion and the strength of party orthodoxy.

The overwhelming defeat ended the incipient rebellion. In Virginia the movement disintegrated, and the Quids made no appearance as an organized group in the next session of the General Assembly. In Congress John Randolph found himself completely isolated with a dwindling group of followers. The repeal of the embargo, March 3, 1809, was more a general admission that the system had failed than a victory for the Quids or their Federalist allies. Yet the conservative wing was by no means dead. An important segment of the Republican party retained a healthy respect for the principles of old. The conservative undercurrent in the party, having crested once in the campaign for Monroe, would come forth in a new ground swell under President Madison.

Conservatives and

War Hawks

The disastrous defeat of the conservatives in the election of 1808 precluded the formation of a Southern-oriented third party.[1] Not only did there seem to be no public support for their program, but their numbers diminished rapidly after the election. In Virginia the Quids disappeared as a group in the legislature, and in Congress under Madison the number of Quids could be counted on one hand. Joseph Clay resigned his seat in the House at the end of the session in 1808, and Garnett did not even bother to run for re-election. David R. Williams failed to be re-elected in 1808. Gauging correctly the new political trend, he returned to South Carolina, and reappeared in 1811 as a War Hawk. Even the larger body of conservatives remained a relatively small group of men without organization or political connection other than a similarity of ideas. It is true, however, that as late as 1810 there was some sentiment among them for the formation of a third party. Both Tazewell and Taylor wrote to Monroe in 1810 to sound him out on the possibility of a third party on the assumption that, as Taylor expressed it, "a manly avowal and defense of their principles will be more likely to raise their little party in the public esteem. . . ." Monroe, already trying to mend his political fences, scotched the idea.[2]

Except for the occasional mention of the "minority" in the letters of Taylor and Tazewell and the continuing opposition of Randolph, Gray, and Stanford in Congress, the party schism was healed by 1810. Yet, while no third party or even identifiable faction existed by 1810, it should not be assumed that the party schism of 1806–8 was of no long-range significance. The Randolph schism was a rebellion on the part of a small group of conservatives against the gradual compromising of party doctrines. As a rebellion it is of interest largely because of the genius of the men involved and the spectacular oratory and political maneuvering it occasioned. But it is much more significant as an indication of a strong element of conservatism that helps to explain much of the later history of the Republican party. The Randolph schism was the momentary eddy on the surface that evidenced the stronger current beneath.

The rebellion failed because Jefferson the idol had not completely lost his power to inspire awe, and Randolph was too extremist and erratic to inspire confidence. But the undercurrent of conservatism remained, though in the troubled years preceding the War of 1812 it underwent a subtle change. This change was wrought by the threat to American security presented by the European belligerents, England and France, and by the incursions on American neutral rights which led ultimately to the declaration of war.

Historians have differed widely concerning the causes of the War of 1812. A generation ago a number of scholars, in search of the economic motives for the war, concluded, with some variation among themselves, that the war was the product of Western land hunger and a desire to remove the Indian threat from the frontier. Although satisfactory in explaining the nearly uniform support for the war among Westerners, this thesis did not explain the war sentiment in the mid-Atlantic states and the South, which provided most of the votes for war in Congress. A more sophisticated interpretation, combining economic interest with patriotism, emphasizes the extent to which British restrictions on American commerce created a price depression in the West and South. War sentiment grew in the fertile soil of economic depression; the planter who demanded a militant response to British restrictions not only furthered his interest in free trade but soothed his wounded national pride.[3]

Two recent and comprehensive studies of the war, by Reginald Horsman and Bradford Perkins, emphasize the threat to the nation's honor and integrity by the commercial depredations of both England and France. Horsman, though recognizing that the War of 1812 stemmed primarily from the conflict between England and France, stresses the importance of the Indian conspiracy on the frontier. The threat to American honor on the high seas was paralleled in the interior of the continent by the threat to American sovereignty posed by British intrigues among the Indians. Perkins focuses his attention on the problem of maintaining neutral rights on the high seas; he finds that after a protracted series of efforts to defend their rights Americans concluded by 1812 that they had no honorable alternative to war. National honor, in short, has become the comprehensive explanation that embraces not only the economic factors operative in certain localities but the deeper psychological attitudes that produced the climate for war.[4]

Most recently, Roger H. Brown has taken this interpretation one step further. He concludes that the humiliation Americans suffered at the hands of the European belligerents was such that it imperiled the very existence of the republic. Further submission to the edicts of Britain and France might have caused a popular disillusionment with the republican experiment itself. In defense of their own political supremacy, possibly in defense of republican institutions, the leadership of the Republican party was driven to war. The war, concludes Brown, was primarily political rather than sectional in origin. It was supported generally by Republicans and opposed unanimously by Federalists.[5]

Although agreeing generally that the war was a nationalistic reaction to humiliation at the hands of the European belligerents, recent scholars do differ to some extent in regard to the timing of this reaction. Mr. Horsman feels that the evolution of public opinion began in 1809 with a misunderstanding concerning the repeal of the orders in council that heaped new humiliation upon the United States. In the awakening realization that economic coercion had failed "America gradually plucked up courage to declare war on England." Perkins finds no well-defined war sentiment until 1811 when a band of War Hawks began to push an unwilling, apathetic nation into war. The process was gradual and continuous, for as late as the spring of 1812 the public remained generally indifferent, and Congress was distracted by an important "scarecrow" faction.[6]

Roger Brown, on the other hand, maintains that there was no visible sentiment in favor of war until the summer of 1811, when the vast majority of Americans suddenly decided that they had no choice but war or humiliating submission. By November, 1811, when the House Foreign Relations Committee published a highly belligerent report, there was "a general consensus" among Republican leaders in favor of war. The subsequent debates were concerned only with exploring the various alternatives—confining the war to the sea, for instance, or to privateers—a debate carried out in the full realization that total war might mean absolute military defeat.[7]

American nationalism would indeed seem to be the primary factor responsible for the war. The emergence of nationalism in the Western world was one of the most important developments of the age. The era that had begun in 1789 was one of revolution and intermittent warfare. The attendant feelings of anxiety and insecurity forced men to turn for relief to the nation-state. Britain and the nations of central Europe experienced the first pangs of nationalism under the pressure of oppression from Napoleonic France.[8] Similarly, under the pressure of British aggression on the high seas, Americans turned to the central government and demanded a more militant policy that would uphold the nation's honor and integrity. In this age commercial equality was often identified with national security.[9]

The emergence of this phenomenon in the United States was necessarily gradual. The threshold of belligerency, at which a man decides to fight rather than endure further humiliation, varies with each individual. A few were ready for war at the time of the embargo, and the succeeding years saw the gradual conversion of the Republican leadership from pacifism to militance. To be sure, war sentiment increased dramatically during 1811 in the region south and west of the Hudson, but there remained an important "scarecrow" faction within the Republican party that sought an honorable alternative to war down to the very eve of the declaration. It was this development that created a new division in the Republican party after the election of Madison, and it changed subtly the character of Republican conservatism.

By 1810 three distinct groups are discernible in the Republican party: the Quids, negligible except that Randolph could not be ignored; middle-of-the-road administration Republicans including conservatives who had returned to the fold; and a growing band of men who believed that war with England would ultimately be the nation's only recourse and felt that military preparations ought to be undertaken immediately. This last group, reinforced in 1811 by the election of a host of young War Hawks, was attempting to respond positively to a rapidly changing situation; in a sense, it was the progressive element in the party.

The middle group, however, included the vast majority of Republicans in 1809–10. It embraced the former supporters of Monroe, as well as a large number of Republicans who had remained consistently faithful to the Jefferson Administration and its compromises. But, unable to adjust their philosophy to the rapidly changing times—the classic definition, after all, of conservatism—they continued to approach the great problems, foreign and domestic, that faced the nation within the doctrinal framework of strict construction and pacifism created by the Republican party in the 1790s. Opposition to the administration is thus after 1809 no longer a satisfactory criterion for conservatism, for the Madison Administration itself was slow to accept the necessity for more energetic foreign and domestic policies. With numerically minor exceptions—Randolph on one extreme and the Senate "invisibles" on the other—War Hawks and conservatives alike gave loyal support to the President.

Henry Adams has accused the first Congress under Madison of "incapacity" and "inanition," and it is true that the predominant conservative sentiment prevented it from taking any significant steps toward solving the important national problems of the day.[10] A lack of leadership, moreover, allowed it to submit to the disruptive tactics of John Randolph, who led the House from one pointless debate to another in his crusade to re-establish the old "principles of 1798."

The confused condition of Anglo-American relations prevented Congress from accomplishing anything positive in 1809. Within a month after his inauguration Madison announced the conclusion of an agreement with the British ambassador, David Erskine, that promised redress for the *Chesapeake* and a repeal of the orders in council in return for a renewal of commercial intercourse. Unfortunately, when word of this agreement reached London, British Foreign Minister George Canning repudiated it, recalled Erskine, and sent to the United States the notorious "Copenhagen" Jackson. Jackson arrived in August, refused to discuss either reparations for the *Chesapeake* or revision of the orders in council, and in November Madison suspended all further communication with him.

Despite the apparent British duplicity and Jackson's provocative diplomacy, the war party in Congress remained a small minority. In the House only eleven Republicans (four of them Southerners) voted consistently for military preparations in

1809–10.[11] In the Senate the demand for a more militant foreign policy was confined to the erratic "invisibles," who made it the basis for their opposition to the administration. As a result, Congress, even under extreme provocation from abroad, continued to manifest a strict Republican pacifism. The prevailing sentiment was well expressed by Richard Stanford in a letter to George Logan:

I cannot say I can find any apology for the apparent folly & infatuation of Mr. Jackson and Mr. Jackon's government, but I cannot bear that our councils & government should commit themselves by a like degree of madness and folly. That government may deserve war at our hands, but our *blessed & happy* Country does not deserve that worst of all human calamities . . . to be inflicted on . . . [it] by . . . [its] own government.[12]

One Tennessee senator felt that nothing short of a direct act of hostility on the part of Great Britain could induce Congress to prepare for war.[13] Any attempt to vindicate the honor and integrity of the nation was to be undertaken within the old framework of commercial retaliation. Neither Congress nor the administration was ready yet to free itself from the fetters of Jeffersonian dogma.

The subject of foreign affairs was introduced in the spring of 1810 when the Nonintercourse Act, which had replaced the embargo, expired. In view of the British actions, complete submission was unthinkable, and in December, 1809, the House had referred the whole matter to a special committee headed by Nathaniel Macon. Macon probably went to the treasury for instructions, for the bill he submitted to the House on December 19 was designed to continue the principle of commercial retaliation without seriously damaging the customs revenues. Drawn up by Gallatin the new plan would close American ports to all British and French vessels, but it would admit all British and French merchandise imported in American vessels. More a navigation act than a nonintercourse law, the measure would, in effect, give American shipping a monopoly of the American trade. Its chief merit was that it struck at Britain's merchant marine, which was chiefly responsible for Britain's commercial policy.[14]

The Federalists immediately objected that it would invite retaliation, and American vessels would be excluded from British and French ports. Macon replied that in that case Britain and France would actually be helping us to enforce the present Nonintercourse law, which had proved impossible to enforce without their aid. Moreover, because it would effectively hurt England without damaging the United States, it would give the President a strong instrument with which to bargain. Macon did not really consider the bill a strong measure, but he felt that without damaging the American economy it was "a fair protest against the acts of both Great Britain and France. And can you do more at this time and preserve peace?" [15]

William A. Burwell of Virginia, a former private secretary to Jefferson who had won the seat of Christopher Clark of Lynchburg, was willing to go even further than Macon in defending the measure. He approved the bill not only because it was a pacific protest against British and French depredations but, more important, because it repealed the old Nonintercourse Act. Burwell had supported the policy of commercial retaliation in the time of Jefferson, but he had since become disillusioned with it because it hindered the sale of Southern agricultural products. This bill, thought Burwell, would encourage the nation's trade and at the same time uphold its honor. This speech was quite reminiscent of Randolph's fulminations against the embargo in behalf of Southern agriculture, and the Quid newspaper *The Spirit of '76* did not hesitate to make the comparison. Had one not seen and heard Burwell himself, the newspaper noted, one "would have supposed that Mr. Randolph had resumed his seat in Congress. . . ." "It is obvious to us and will soon be to the world that the Congress is becoming (if we may be permitted to use the expression) a little more Randolphian, than what it has been for a long time past." [16]

Understandably enough, Macon's bill did not satisfy the advocates of a stronger foreign policy. Duane of the *Aurora* denounced it as weak and harmful, while Ritchie of the *Enquirer* pointed out that it was more of a commercial measure than any serious attempt to force a recognition of American rights. Ritchie demanded that Congress undertake immediate military preparations and issue letters of marque and reprisal. On January 25 George M. Troup of Georgia, a new convert to the war party in the House, offered an amendment to Macon's bill authorizing the government to issue letters of marque and reprisal to shipowners whose vessels had been captured by Britain or France. The idea found little sympathy in the House, however, and Troup shortly withdrew his motion.[17]

On January 29 Macon's bill passed to the third reading 73–52. "I have rarely seen such a discordancy of opinions upon almost any subject," wrote a Massachusetts Federalist. "Some voted for it because they thought it would keep us out of war, at least keep off the adoption of more violent measures, others I believe because they could not carry anything more hostile but in hopes that Great Britain may retaliate in such a way as to make a war popular." In general the Republican moderates voted for the bill, while the Federalists opposed it because it was too strong and the war party because it was too weak.[18]

When Macon's bill reached the Senate, Samuel Smith moved to strike out all but the enacting clause and the provision excluding belligerent warships from American harbors. Smith charged that the bill was too weak to be effective in securing redress while at the same time it would invite retaliation. Smith preferred instead to arm American merchant vessels and provide convoys for them—a proposal that reflected his own mercantile interests. Federalists were overjoyed at Smith's action, but administration Republicans protested. Henry Clay, the new Senator from Kentucky, considered the bill sent up from the House to be weak and in need of revision, but he thought Smith's amendment to remove all the vital parts mere submission to England and France. Clay was willing to go along with peaceful resistance as embodied in the system of commercial retaliation, but when that system was abandoned Clay preferred war. Submission was out of the question. Nevertheless a combination of Federalists and Republican "invisibles" adopted the Smith amendment 16–11, and Macon's bill, thus emasculated, was returned to the House.[19]

The House refused to accept the Senate amendment and sent the bill back to the Senate in its original form. A long wrangle ensued, and a committee of conference failed to reach agreement. In the meantime Randolph took his seat in the House and marshaled his small band—Stanford, Gray, and Bibb—in support of the Senate amendment. Randolph, as he wrote Nicholson the previous December, wished "to repeal all the laws restricting trade; and as we will not, or cannot, protect it, let it shift for itself." Matthew Lyon of Kentucky also favored the Senate's amendment and wished to abolish the whole retaliatory system because it hindered the only legitimate trade—the export of agricultural products. The great majority of Republicans, however, preferred to retain some vestige of the Jeffersonian system, and on March 31 the House voted to adhere to its disagreement with the Senate.[20] The issue thus ended in stalemate.

Taking advantage of the confusion Randolph that same day, March 31, introduced a resolution to repeal the Nonintercourse Act of 1809. The move seemed to crystallize the growing dissatisfaction with the system of commercial retaliation, and even John Taylor of South Carolina, administration spokesman on the Foreign Relations committee, seemed sympathetic to repeal. The House voted to consider the resolution, but no further action was taken.[21]

Though the House was vaguely dissatisfied with the restrictive system, it was clearly unwilling to adopt any stronger measures. On March 5 John Wayles Eppes, a temporary convert to the demand for stronger measures, introduced a bill providing for the arming and convoying of American merchant vessels.

The bill slept in committee until April 12 when Eppes moved to call it up for an immediate vote, arguing that there was not enough time left in the session for debate on it. The House summarily rejected Eppes's motion, and the convoy bill was dead.[22]

Having rejected the thought of any stronger measures the House returned to the subject of replacing the Nonintercourse law. In April, 1810, Macon reported out of his committee a new bill, which naturally became known as Macon's Bill Number Two. It apparently had the support of the Cabinet though Macon himself neither framed nor favored it. Drawn up by John Taylor, a member of Macon's committee, the new bill embodied an attempt to force the two great European powers to bid for American support. It repealed the Nonintercourse Act of March 3, 1809, thereby removing all restrictions on American commerce, but it authorized the President, "in case either Great Britain or France shall, before the 3rd day of March next, so revoke or modify her edicts as that they shall cease to violate the lawful commerce of the United States," to prohibit intercourse with the nation that had not revoked its edicts.[23]

Macon's Bill Number Two was a very weak bill that actually satisfied no one completely. It abandoned the restrictive system and thus even that feeble protest against the British and French edicts, while at the same time it laid American rights on the bargaining table. "This plan is said to be a cabinet project," Macon wrote to Judge Nicholson; "if so it satisfies me, that the cabinet is hard pushed for a plan, but it may have been taken to prevent a worse [one], or to prevent the continuance of the present non intercourse system." The bill satisfied neither the advocates of strong measures, like Duane and Ritchie, nor the Federalists and Randolphites who demanded a complete abandonment of the restrictive system.[24] Yet a stronger measure could not have passed the House, and despite the discretionary power delegated to the President the plan fitted into the framework of the Jefferson-Madison foreign policy. Madison's most recent biographer maintains that from the beginning of his administration the main object of Madison's foreign policy was to choose an enemy so the United States would not have to fight both Britain and France to maintain its rights. This policy fitted the prevailing mood of Congress, which intended the bill to be "a weapon in the hands of the President to enable him to treat with the belligerents" by playing one off against the other.[25]

When the House debate opened on April 11, the bill came under immediate attack. Thomas Gholson of Virginia, who a week later voted to reduce the army and navy, offered an amendment to re-enact the Nonintercourse law and to authorize the President to use the army and navy to enforce it. Gholson objected to Taylor's bill because it "held up the honor and character of this nation to the highest bidder. . . ." This amendment immediately brought Taylor to his feet in defense of his bill, and he carefully adapted his arguments to the conservative temper of the House. Not only was this a peaceful measure, he informed the House, designed to prevent all the horrors of war, but it was sound economically because a restoration of trade was essential to the treasury. His bill would abandon the old nonintercourse system, which had "operated unequally on different parts of the Union" and had, in effect, been a tax on "the people generally of the Southern States . . . under the pretense of resistance," yet it would provide the President with a lever with which to force a recognition of American rights. As to Gholson's amendment to employ the army and navy in enforcing the nonintercourse system, Taylor scornfully dismissed it as a design to "pour into the mud, into the rotten hulks of the navy, the whole revenue of the country. . . ."[26]

Taylor had gauged correctly the mood of the House, and the next day Gholson withdrew his amendment because of the "decided opposition to it." As a mild protest against the actions of England and France, Macon's Bill Number Two reflected the dominant conservatism of the House, and it passed on April 19 by a vote of 61–40. Mild as it was, it was still too provocative for some of the extreme conservatives—Macon, Bibb, Stanford, Clay, and McBryde—who voted against it along with the Federalists and a few war Republicans.[27]

In the Senate the bill was referred to a select committee headed by Samuel Smith. Smith struck out a House proposal to place a tariff duty of 50 percent on goods imported from England and France and replaced it with an amendment authorizing the President to employ the public armed vessels in protecting American commerce. This amendment, in effect readopting the convoy principle, was adopted by a combination of Federalists and "invisibles," and on April 27 the Senate passed the bill 21–7. The only Republicans voting against it were Crawford of Georgia and Turner of North Carolina, probably because they objected to the convoy amendment. The House refused to agree to the Smith amendments, but in conference each house receded. Convoys were abandoned in exchange for omission of the tariff duties, and on May 1, the last day of the session, the bill was passed.[28]

The debates on the system of commercial retaliation illustrate the prevailing conservatism in the Republican party, but a more striking example of adherence to ancient formulas can be seen in a debate on the reduction of the armed forces in the spring of 1810. Significantly enough, the original impetus for the move came from Treasury Secretary Gallatin, who suggested in his annual financial report that a reduction in military and naval expenditures of $3 million might compensate for an expected deficit due to the restrictions on commerce. Randolph, who had been delayed in Virginia by illness, had no sooner taken his seat than he introduced on March 22 a resolution that the military and naval establishments ought to be reduced. An expensive standing army, argued Randolph, was an unnecessary drain on the treasury. There was, moreover, no enemy in sight; France had no navy and England was too preoccupied with the war in Europe.[29]

The House found it hard to dispute Randolph's argument.

The military establishment was always unpopular with old Republicans, and it was doubly so when a budget deficit threatened. Armies and navies, in the words of Taylor of Caroline, "only serve to excite wars, squander money, and extend corruption." There was, moreover, the gnawing suspicion that an army under Wilkinson was not worth maintaining, a view Macon expressed privately to Judge Nicholson:

I am decidedly for reducing the army and navy or rather for putting them altogether down, and if we have any military force take a new start. The present army is destroyed by the hatred of those who are opposed to W[ilkinson] . . . [for] those who support him, or more properly, they hate each other too much, to be in the same service.

In line with his idea of "putting them altogether down" Macon moved an amendment that the whole army ought to be disbanded on the ground that internal dissension and intrigue had rendered it useless anyway.[30]

Macon's proposal to abolish the army altogether was a little too extreme, but the House was generally sympathetic to the idea of some reduction. John Taylor of South Carolina suggested disbanding the extra troops raised in 1807 and returning to the normal peacetime establishment. The navy he felt could be completely laid up except for the dispatch vessels. Samuel McKee of Kentucky expressed the opinion that "even if war itself was certain, it would be perfectly unnecessary to keep on foot this establishment." In any emergency McKee preferred the militia to "men who have loitered out their days in camps and in the most luxurious ease and vice." The demand for economy even received some support from frustrated War Hawks. Richard M. Johnson of Kentucky wanted to defend American rights even if it meant going to war with both England and France, but since the government had made no effort to defend its rights he felt there was no need to maintain an expensive military establishment. "Unless you use them, the Army and Navy, in time of peace, are engines of oppression. . . ." The resolution was passed, 60–31, by a combination of Federalists and Republican conservatives; in the minority were mostly Northern and Western Republicans.[31]

After passing this remarkable resolution the House seemed to have second thoughts. In the face of the threat from abroad the attempt to reduce the armed forces seemed on reflection absurd to many a moderate Republican. When Randolph a few days later brought in a bill to effect a reduction in the navy, the House temporarily shook itself free from his leadership; majorities were found to sustain the navy and eliminate the key features of Randolph's program. A more moderate bill to reduce the army was introduced by John Smilie of Pennsylvania, but the session ended before the debate ceased.[32]

The prevailing conservatism extended also to internal issues, most important of which was the Bank of the United States, whose charter was due to expire in 1811. A bill to recharter the bank was introduced in January, 1811, but the subject involved a number of ramifications which clouded the basic issue. The bank had proved a valuable adjunct to the treasury, and Secretary Gallatin was known to favor recharter. On the other hand, President Madison, who had delivered the classic statement against the bank twenty years before, chose to remain noncommittal. To most Republicans, however, the bank was a continuing reminder of Federalist mercantilism and a symbol of the doctrine of implied powers. State banks, multiplying in numbers throughout 1810 in anticipation of the demise of the federal bank, also had their adherents in Congress who did not hesitate to play on Republican prejudice and the fear of foreign control. Perhaps most important were the anti-Gallatin "invisibles," predominant in the Senate, but with sympathizers in the House, who could not resist the opportunity to embarrass the treasury by killing the bank.

The motives that governed the votes of the members of Congress were no doubt as varied as the membership itself, yet it is not surprising that in the debate opponents of the bank settled on two general themes—its unconstitutionality and the fear of foreign influence, that is, that British stockholders by controlling the bank could control the economy of the country. Both arguments were vague enough to be conducive to impressive oratory, both were general enough so the orator could not be accused of special interests, and both were at least secondary considerations in the mind of every member. Historians have pointed out that the Republican party had its speculative-entrepreneurial wing that was deeply involved in the state banking systems, which stood to gain by the removal of the conservative influence of the federal bank. Thomas Ritchie, for instance, who attacked the bank on constitutional grounds in the *Enquirer*, was a stockholder in the Bank of Virginia. In the House debate Robert Wright, former governor of Maryland and member of the Smith faction which not only was anti-Gallatin but had banking interests in Baltimore, had the temerity to rely on constitutional arguments in opposing the bank bill. And from William Crawford of Pennsylvania, member of the war party and advocate of a protective tariff, the constitutional argument must have sounded a little hollow.[33]

On the other hand, it would be a mistake to assume that the constitutional argument was necessarily insincere. This Congress habitually treated new issues in the context of Jeffersonian dogma, and the Republican party still contained many men whose political philosophies were shaped by the great debates of the 1790s. The agrarian wing in particular tended to look upon all bankers as mere speculators in paper growing rich at the expense of all honest producers of wealth, a prejudice that merely reinforced a political philosophy of strict construction. Joseph Desha of Kentucky deplored the fact that the state banks were petitioning Congress against renewal of the charter of the federal bank, but he felt that, despite the fact that special interests would be benefited, the charter should not be renewed for constitutional reasons. John Clopton of Virginia, who did not enter the debate on the bill, expressed in a letter to his son his fear that rechartering the bank would further the principle of broad construction of the Constitution, "under which in future times powers would be assumed one after another so as to alter the very character of the government. If it should be renewed, a severe blow will, I apprehend, be given to the republican cause." Nor is there any reason to doubt the sincerity of William A. Burwell of Virginia, whose whole record in Congress was conservative. Burwell argued that since the government deposits could be placed in the state banks, the Bank of the United States was not absolutely necessary as required by a literal rendering of the Constitution. Finally, it is difficult to explain, other than by a lingering attachment to old Republican doctrine, the vote against the bank of a number of future War Hawks, such as Peter B. Porter, Richard M. Johnson, Ezekiel Bacon, and Langdon Cheves, who must have realized that a bank would be indispensable in any future war.[34]

A number of conservatives were torn between constitutional scruples and the desire to protect Gallatin from the intrigues of the "invisibles." Nathaniel Macon "was as clearly of the opinion that it was expedient to renew the charter, as he was that it was unconstitutional." Macon finally resolved the dilemma in favor of the Constitution and against the bank, but Randolph, who was more deeply committed to strict construction than any other member of the House, proved himself, for once, more the statesman than the doctrinaire. More solicitous than Macon for Gallatin and for the government should it get into the hands of the Smith faction, Randolph kept his opinion to himself and refused to enter the floor debate. But he did cast his vote for the bank, and in so doing he was joined by his North Carolina friends, Richard Stanford, John Stanly, and Archibald Mc-Bryde.[35]

After two weeks of debate the House on the motion of Thomas Newton of Virginia voted 65–61 to postpone the bill indefinitely. The voting pattern was of course confused, but the geographical distribution of the votes and the political backgrounds of the members indicate that the bank was defeated by a combination of Southern conservatives and state banking interests. "It is a matter of astonishment," wrote a Massachusetts Federalist, "that every representative of the great commercial towns, with the exception of Mr. Quincy and Mr. Pickman of Mass., voted for the indefinite postponement." Voting in support of the bank were pro-Gallatin Randolphites, Northern Republicans who invariably supported the administration, members of the war party friendly to energetic government, and Federalists.[36]

By voting to postpone the bank bill the House in effect threw the problem into the lap of the Senate, where a bill to recharter the bank had already been introduced. The only able defender of Gallatin and the treasury in the Senate was William Harris Crawford, whose later reputation and political career were based largely on his defense of the bank in 1811. Crawford's defense of the bank marked a shift toward a more nationalistic political philosophy, which he maintained until the 1820s when he again became the idol of the Old Republicans. On February 11 Crawford delivered a brilliant speech in support of the bank, which even Macon called "a better argument in favor of it on constitutional ground than ever has been made. . . ."[37]

Three days later Giles of Virginia opened the case against the bank. As a member of the anti-Gallatin faction he was only too willing to see the bank die in order to embarrass the treasury, yet for over a year Giles had been advocating a stronger foreign policy and demanding greater energy in government. Hence he was obliged to admit that the government possessed all sorts of broad power, but it did not possess the power to establish a bank. Randolph called it "the most unintelligible speech on the subject of the Bank of the U.S. I ever heard," and Clay, who succeeded Giles on the floor the next day, twitted Giles for proving "that it was constitutional and unconstitutional, highly proper and improper to prolong the charter of the bank."[38]

Clay's speech against the bank was probably the ablest exposition of Republican doctrine on the subject since Madison's war on the bank in 1791. After taunting Giles for making no real contribution to the antibank argument, Clay turned his scorn on Crawford, who had deplored the fact that the bank had been made a party issue. "And if, on this occasion," retorted Clay, "my worthy friend from Georgia has gone over into the camp of the enemy, is it kind in him to look back upon his former friends, and rebuke them for the fidelity with which they adhere to their old principles?" The most fundamental of these "old principles" was that there was no clause in the Constitution that specifically granted Congress the power to create a bank. Even the advocates of a bank had not agreed among themselves whether the bank was justified under the money power or the taxing power, either of which required a liberal interpretation of the "necessary and proper" clause. Where, demanded Clay, was the specific provision that conferred "this vagrant power to erect a bank . . . [which has] wandered throughout the whole Constitution in quest of some congenial spot whereupon to fasten."

Clay then turned to the argument used by a number of Republicans to justify their change in attitude—that the constitutionality of the bank had been established by precedent. This Clay answered with the irrefutable argument that mere passage of an act does not make it constitutional, "and to legislate on the ground merely that our predecessors thought themselves authorized, under similar circumstances, to legislate, is to sanctify error and perpetuate usurpation." Clay had more difficulty explaining why the Republicans had failed to repeal the bank charter as soon as they came to power, but he finally settled on the idea that the Federalist-dominated judiciary would have annulled such a law as the impairment of a contract between the government and the bank. Since nothing in the Constitution prevented the federal government from impairing the obligation of a contract, this argument was probably intended more as a criticism of Marshall's recent decision in the Yazoo case of *Fletcher v. Peck* than as a serious point of debate.[39]

In view of his later career it is rather surprising to find Henry Clay opposing a federally chartered bank on strict constructionist grounds. In his biography of Clay, Bernard Mayo points out that Clay had been on the board of directors of the Bank of Kentucky and was thus connected with local interests desiring a removal of the restraints on the banking system provided by the federal bank.[40] Yet, as Mayo also points out, the importance of local banking interests can be overemphasized, particularly in the case of Clay, for he championed the cause of the Bank of the United States from 1816 until his death in 1852. A lingering attachment to Jeffersonian principles must be accepted as at least a partial explanation for his stand in 1811.

Senator Anderson of Tennessee had moved to strike out the enacting clause, and on February 20 the Senate finally came to a vote. A tie vote of 17–17 was broken by Vice-President Clinton, who after a short speech condemning the bank as unconstitutional, voted to kill the bill. Voting for the bank were nine Federalists and eight administration Republicans; against the bank were one Federalist and sixteen Republicans, representing a combination of anti-Gallatin "invisibles," representatives of state banking interests, and Republican conservatives like Jesse Franklin of North Carolina, John Gaillard of South Carolina, and Thomas Worthington of Ohio.[41]

Gallatin thought that the defeat was the result of "the *personal* opposition to Mr. Madison or myself of the Clintons, the Maryland Smiths, Leib, and Giles," while a New York Republican, Erastus Root, writing some years after the event, attributed the defeat of the bank bill to the fear of foreign influence and British control of the bank.[42] Both views were no doubt partially correct, but the importance of Old Republican doctrine, particularly among Southern agrarians, also played a part. How else could one explain the votes of men who were normally conservative in thought, who supported Gallatin and detested the "invisibles," and who gave no indication of fearing British influence in the bank—men like Macon, Burwell, Desha, Bibb, Clopton, and Eppes in the House, and Gaillard, Franklin, and Worthington in the Senate? [48] Had these men supported the bank the bill would have passed.

The refusal of both the administration and Congress to depart significantly from Old Republican doctrine after the election of Madison, despite the fears of John Randolph, made it apparent that there was no important difference between the administration and the rebels who had supported Monroe in 1808. Any lingering distrust was ended in the spring of 1811 when Monroe joined the government and brought his followers back into the fold. Significantly, the reconciliation resulted from a showdown between Madison and his critics in the Senate. The conflict between the President and the Smith faction had been impending since the beginning of the administration when Madison made Robert Smith, brother of Senator Samuel Smith, Secretary of State so as to secure the Senate confirmation of Gallatin as Secretary of the Treasury. This anti-Gallatin faction, whom Macon dubbed "the invisibles," was led in the Senate by Smith of Maryland, Giles of Virginia, and Leib of Pennsylvania, with frequent support from Obadiah German of New York and Joseph Anderson of Tennessee. It had its allies in the House in Robert Wright of Maryland and Samuel L. Mitchill of New York, and it had the general sympathy of William Duane and the Philadelphia *Aurora*. Insofar as the group had any political principle it was the demand for a stronger foreign policy and a more energetic attempt to cope with the major problems facing the country. Their dislike of the Secretary of Treasury was both personal and political. Gallatin was a foreigner, a Genevan who spoke with a decided French accent. He was, moreover, the most important conservative influence in the administration, the last great representative of the Republican party of the 1790s that demanded unobtrusive, frugal government. Could Gallatin but be replaced the way would be cleared for the strengthening of the central government under the predominant influence of the Smiths and Giles.[44]

Most Republicans, including Jefferson, deprecated both the methods and the objectives of the "invisibles," but those most alarmed were the Old Republicans like Randolph and Macon. Macon saw "no great difference between invisibility and federalism," while Randolph considered them "the worst men in our country." *The Spirit of '76* saw in the vendetta against Gallatin nothing more than an attempt "to make way for one of their own faction."As early as May, 1809, Macon had recognized the danger of the "invisibles" and wished that some of his old friends, such as Joseph Clay, David R. Williams, Peter Early of Georgia, and Thomas Worthington of Ohio were still in Congress to help fight them.[45]

The appointment of Robert Smith to the Cabinet kept the "invisibles" loyal to the administration for almost a year, but in the spring of 1810 the *Aurora* began a series of personal attacks on Gallatin, while Smith and Giles began sniping at the Secretary from the Senate floor. The fight over the bank in early 1811 brought matters to a head. Judge Nicholson, who from Baltimore kept Macon and Randolph informed of Maryland politics, wrote Macon urging him to warn the President that the Smiths were organizing a combination against his whole legislative program. Finding his position utterly intolerable, Gallatin offered to resign as Secretary of the Treasury.[46] Faced at last with the absolute necessity of choosing between the two, Madison instead dismissed Robert Smith and appointed Monroe Secretary of State.

The replacement of Smith by Monroe reunited the party in a way it had not been since Jefferson's first administration. Not only was the divisive Smith faction removed from administration councils and virtually stripped of its influence in Congress, but the selection of Monroe healed at last the party split in Virginia. Monroe had begun his efforts to heal the breach in the party immediately after the election of 1808. In an amiable letter to William Wirt a few weeks after the election he had intimated that his candidacy had been promoted largely by his friends and that he himself had not intended to divide the party. Jefferson had talked to him the following spring and found him anxious to disclaim any connection with the Randolph group, and a few months later Jefferson was surprised to learn that Monroe would have accepted a seat in the Cabinet.[47]

After Monroe's election as governor of Virginia in 1810 with the aid of administration Republicans, it was clear that for practical purposes the party schism in Virginia was ended. Even Monroe's friend, John Taylor, who still considered himself one of the "minority," advised Monroe to accept a post in the administration if one "not derogatory to your character and station" were offered. In the winter of 1810–11 rumors were circulating in Washington that Monroe was to be offered a cabinet post. Randolph, who never could become reconciled to the Madison Administration, warned Monroe that he ought to scotch the rumors lest his political character be damaged by the suspicion that he had compromised his principles.[48]

After Madison's open break with Robert Smith in March, Monroe was approached by Senator Brent of Virginia on the possibility of his entering the Cabinet. Though not himself averse to joining the administration, Monroe was anxious to avoid compromising his previous stand or alienating his friends in Virginia. The main difficulty was that since 1806 Monroe had been publicly advocating closer ties with England, while the foreign policy of the Madison Administration, particularly since Macon's Bill Number Two and Napoleon's offer to revoke his decrees, had been decidedly pro-French. Aware of the difficulty Monroe told Tazewell that he feared acceptance of a post in the administration would damage his reputation by associating him with a policy he was known to disapprove. He also sought an interview with Randolph, but received neither advice nor sympathy. "We had a great deal of talk," Randolph reported to Garnett, "but I declined giving any opinion." On the other hand, both Tazewell and Taylor, Monroe's closest friends and the leading "minority" men in Virginia, advised him to accept the post.[49]

On March 23 Monroe wrote to Madison a partial acceptance of the overture made through Senator Brent. The main obstacle, he informed the President, was that he had felt since 1806 that some sort of accommodation with England was preferable to war. Madison removed the obstacle Monroe had raised by pointing out that he was not averse to a settlement with England and that his differences of opinion with Monroe in 1806 need not hinder agreement now since the outstanding disputes with Britain—the *Chesapeake*, the orders in council, and paper blockades —had arisen since 1806. This was only partially true and in essence Madison was yielding nothing of his stand in 1806. It satisfied Monroe, however, and he accepted the State Department, though in doing so he accepted and, as events proved, carried out loyally the Madison foreign policy.[50]

Most of the Republican "minority" in Virginia followed Monroe back into the good graces of the administration, and many felt that Monroe would have a salutary effect on the administration's foreign policy.[51] Randolph's stepbrother, Henry St. George Tucker, informed Garnett that he expected negotiations with England to be conducted henceforth with "more sincerity and more mildness," and he expected "more firmness and fewer criminal suppressions of facts than heretofore on the subject of foreign affairs." John Taylor of Caroline expressed similar hopes to Garnett, suggesting that Monroe's appointment was a concession to the "minority." Garnett was unimpressed with these arguments and felt that Monroe had betrayed the "minority." Shortly Jefferson was reporting to Madison that John Randolph too was "open-mouthed" against Monroe. But by the spring of 1811 Garnett and Randolph were all that remained of the schism of 1806.[52]

Although conservative sentiment prevailed in the Republican party at least through 1811, it was not universal. By 1811 a number of important figures had concluded that the old doctrines no longer furnished an adequate response to the foreign crisis. The failure of the embargo and continued British intransigence eventually convinced many a conservative Republican that war might ultimately be necessary—a conversion that paralleled and to some extent shaped the evolution of public opinion.

This subtle shift in opinion began even while the embargo was in effect. In the spring of 1808 William A. Burwell reported to Jefferson on the current of opinion in Virginia: "All look forward to a change by fall. I am convinced by that period it will be indispensably necessary to remove the embargo & give new direction to the energy of the nation." Jefferson himself felt: "Should neither peace nor a revocation of the decrees and orders take place in Europe, the day cannot be distant when . . . [commercial restrictions] will cease to be preferable to open hostility." By the time the embargo was repealed Jefferson's close friend Wilson Cary Nicholas had become completely disillusioned with the policy of commercial retaliation. "We have tried negotiation until it is disgraceful to think of renewing it," he wrote to Jefferson. "Commercial restrictions have been so managed as to operate only to our own injury. War then or submission only remain. In deciding between them I cannot hesitate a moment." George Campbell came to a similar conclusion as early as the spring of 1808 and was one of the abler members of the small war party in Madison's Congress.[53]

The gradual realization of the need for a stronger foreign policy was also reflected in the prominent Republican newspapers. Thomas Ritchie considered the embargo the only honorable alternative to war, and when the embargo was repealed Ritchie became an outspoken advocate of war. William Duane had supported the system of commercial retaliation, but the repudiation of the Erskine agreement disillusioned him. After the failure of the Jackson mission he began advocating military preparations, arming of American merchant ships, and if that failed to intimidate Britain, "defensive war." [54]

The repudiation of the Erskine agreement and the high-handed diplomacy of "Copenhagen" Jackson greatly accelerated this conversion of public opinion, and the result was the appearance in 1810 of a small but identifiable war party in Congress. "There is a sincere desire for peace," wrote a Pennsylvania representative, "but really Congress is embarrassed. It wishes to avoid war and to preserve its rights—but how can it carry on any trade while the Orders in Council exist. . . . The people are sick of embargoes and nonintercourse laws—the war spirit is increasing." [55] To all appearances, this growing war spirit in the country crystallized in the congressional elections of 1810–11.

Historians have long felt that this election provided the initial impetus for the War of 1812. Earlier historians noted the large number of new faces in the Twelfth Congress, but Henry Adams was the first to emphasize the importance of the "revolution" of 1810 in providing new leadership for the Republican party that had scant respect for the old doctrines of '98. Men like Henry Clay and William Lowndes, John C. Calhoun and Felix Grundy, Langdon Cheves and Peter B. Porter, "whatever else they might at times say, cared little for Jeffersonian or Madisonian dogmas." Moreover, the election, by providing 63 new faces in a House of 142 members, represented a popular judgment of the Eleventh Congress. "Seldom if ever," observed Adams, "was Congress overwhelmed by contempt so deep and general as that which withered the Eleventh in the midst of its career." The election of 1810, concluded Adams, was at least as important a revolution in favor of energy in government as the "revolution of 1800," which had been a reaction against the energetic Federalist administration.[56]

Until recently, historians tended to follow the lead of Adams, pointing out, for instance, that New Hampshire had a complete turnover, electing 5 new congressmen, that 10 of New York's

18 were new, that Massachusetts elected 9 new members and Pennsylvania 7.[57] In sending to the House men like Clay, Calhoun, and Lowndes the election of 1810 certainly ensured strong and effective leadership in the Twelfth Congress, but as evidence of a revolution in popular sentiment throughout the nation it can be overestimated. The complete turnover in the New Hampshire delegation furnishes a striking example of the effect of the election, but it should be noted that 2 of the 5 voted against the declaration of war in June, 1812, and that the popular vote in the election was so close that early reports indicated a Federalist sweep and a runoff election had to be held.[58] Though New York elected 10 new men in 1810, the state's delegation divided 11 to 3 against war in 1812, and of the 3 votes for war 1 was cast by a holdover from the Eleventh Congress. Of Pennsylvania's 7 new men in the Twelfth Congress 2 cast the state's only votes against war. Speaking strictly in numbers the actual War Hawks elected in 1810 were out-voted by Federalists and antiwar Republicans in the Twelfth Congress.

To be sure, the election of 1810 was more than a turnover in numbers, and to some extent Henry Adams was right in stressing the revolution in leadership. Though supported wholeheartedly by no more than a third of the House, the War Hawk leaders by force of will and intellect alone dragged Congress toward war almost in spite of itself. Yet they could not have done so if a majority of the Republican party had not come to the realization that war was the only alternative, a process of conversion that had begun with the embargo and continued down to the very eve of the war declaration. The core of Republican strength was in the states of the South Atlantic seaboard from Maryland to Georgia, which cast 39 or nearly half of the 79 votes for war in 1812. Any satisfactory explanation of the war must place primary emphasis on these congressmen and their reaction to events.

Most of these Southern congressmen were Old Republicans,

conservatives whose political Bible was the Jeffersonian platform of 1800 and who had been in Congress for years. In the
election of 1810 in the South there is no evidence of a sudden
popular demand for more energetic government and a more
aggressive foreign policy. Maryland, which voted 6 to 3 for
war in June, 1812, had 4 new members in the Twelfth Congress, 1 a Federalist. The 3 new Republicans were either elected
without opposition or replaced men who had supported military
preparations and a stronger foreign policy in the Eleventh
Congress.[59]

Virginia, which held her elections for the Twelfth Congress
in the spring of 1811, returned a virtually identical delegation
of 17 Republicans and 5 Federalists. The Quids Randolph and
Edwin Gray were re-elected, as were most of the conservatives
of the Eleventh Congress. The Valley remained as solidly Federalist as it had been in 1800, and the tramontane region elected
Thomas Wilson, its first Federalist representative since 1793. The
election produced 5 new Republican members, none apparently
elected on the issue of peace or war. John Wayles Eppes, the
only strong leader Virginia furnished in the Eleventh Congress,
moved to John Randolph's district in the Southside and was
defeated by Randolph in the election. The contest was close
even though Eppes never formally declared himself a candidate, but the objections to Randolph centered on his vigorous
opposition to the Madison Administration. No one maintained
that the election of Eppes would ensure stronger measures toward Great Britain.[60]

Eppes's seat in his former district was taken by James Pleasants, a war Republican who later reverted to the old strict constructionist doctrines. In Jefferson's own district David S. Garland was replaced by Hugh Nelson, a close friend of Monroe
and one-time member of the "minority," who entered the
Twelfth Congress with a decided preference for peace. In the
Fredericksburg area the administration regular Walter Jones
declined to run again, and in the canvass Major John P. Hun-

gerford defeated John Taliaferro by six votes. Hungerford
was a former Federalist who sat on the Monroe electoral committee in 1808, and when Taliaferro contested the election he
was seated with the aid of the War Hawks in the House. In
the Fauquier-Culpeper district John Love, who had generally
supported preparedness measures in the Eleventh Congress, declined re-election and was replaced by another war Republican,
Dr. Aylet Hawes.[61]

Nearly half the Virginia delegation was elected without opposition; even where there was a contest the election seldom
turned on the issue of foreign policy. Typical of Virginia conservatives re-elected in 1811 was John Clopton, who had represented the Richmond district since 1801. If a letter to his constituents published in the *Virginia Argus* was a fair summary
of his campaign platform, Clopton was running in support of
the Nonintercourse law and against the Bank of the United
States, giving no indication of any departure from the Jeffersonian system. Clopton had two opponents, one of whom withdrew before the election while the other made statements agreeing with him on every issue.[62]

The election of 1810 in North Carolina similarly produced
no great turnover in her representation. Of her 12 congressmen
8 were re-elected, 2 of them Federalists and Richard Stanford,
a Randolph Quid. Two of the 4 newcomers had served in Congress during the Jefferson Administration (William Blackledge
from 1803 to 1808 and Thomas Blount from 1804 to 1808).
The only new faces in the North Carolina delegation, Israel
Pickens and William R. King, were War Hawks, but neither
defeated an incumbent.[63]

The political revolution in South Carolina in the election of
1810, which produced a unanimous vote for war in June, 1812,
was more apparent than real. The election of the great War
Hawk leaders—John C. Calhoun, William Lowndes, and Langdon
Cheves—was more an addition of talent than numbers to the war
party in Congress. Calhoun openly advocated war in the cam-

paign, but he was elected without opposition since the incumbent—his cousin Joseph Calhoun, a War Hawk in the Eleventh Congress—declined re-election and supported him. William Lowndes succeeded to the seat of John Taylor, one of the administration leaders in the Eleventh Congress, who had been elected to the Senate. Langdon Cheves, a former Federalist, was elected in 1810 to fill a vacant seat in the Eleventh Congress and was re-elected to the Twelfth. The other prominent War Hawk, David Rogerson Williams, succeeded his brother-in-law Robert Witherspoon, who declined re-election and threw his support to Williams. A follower of John Randolph in his first term in Congress, Williams fits more into the pattern of the converted conservative. Indeed, as late as May, 1812, a Federalist member of the House observed that Williams was still trying to make up his mind between peace and war. The only real contest in South Carolina was the defeat of Lemuel J. Alston by Elias Earle, but no current issue was involved for the two men had taken turns defeating each other for years.[64]

Under Georgia's general ticket law the 4 candidates receiving the highest number of votes were elected. In October, 1810, 7 candidates ran for election but 3 incumbents—William Bibb, Howell Cobb, and George M. Troup—were re-elected. The fourth, Dennis Smelt, did not enter the race and was replaced by the war Republican Bolling Hall. Bibb and Cobb had entered Congress in 1807 in vague alliance with the Randolph group and had consistently opposed strong measures ever since. Bibb was converted to the war party in the Twelfth Congress, and Cobb never took his seat. Troup had joined the war party in the House by 1810.[65]

If it is highly doubtful that the election of 1810–11 represented any fundamental changes in public opinion, it can scarcely be doubted that it infused new energy into the government. Though the War Hawks elected in 1810 may not have been numerous, they were certainly able, and largely by force of character alone they led an unwilling and apathetic country to war. Yet was leadership alone enough? Several of the leading War Hawks—Clay, Johnson, Bacon, Cheves, and Porter—were members of the Eleventh Congress, but despite their ability they had been unable to lead that body in any consistent direction. At least as significant as the sudden appearance of a few talented War Hawks in the Twelfth Congress was the gradual conversion of the average Republican from Jeffersonian pacifism to a vigorous defense of America's neutral rights. It was these men, most of them Southerners who had been in Congress for years, that provided the necessary votes for war, just as they had provided the main support for the embargo and Nonintercourse laws. And their conversion seems to have stemmed primarily from a disillusionment with the old system of commercial retaliation and a growing realization that the only alternative to war was submission and national disgrace.

Jesse Franklin, senator from North Carolina, wrote later that he had supported the War Hawks, "but not until I believed that every effort had been made to preserve the peace of the nation, that every point of the political compass had been tried, and every Honorable offer made to the present enemy. . . ." [66] Every expedient to avoid war while retaining honor had been tried without success. Submission to the orders in council presaged a return to the colonial status; war seemed the only alternative. The war, at least as far as the South was concerned, was a nationalistic response to British provocations. It was brought on by men who had already retreated too far and who wished to reassert the independence and sovereignty of the nation. [67]

Very few Southern Republicans were elected in 1810–11 on a war platform; many were not converted to war until the spring of 1812. The votes and speeches of Nathaniel Macon were typical of the Old Republican struggling with a Jeffersonian conscience. In the Eleventh Congress Macon had uniformly supported the Madison Administration though he went along with Randolph's efforts to reduce the size of the army and navy. By the opening of the Twelfth Congress in November, 1811, he had concluded that a war to defend American rights was inevitable. He cooperated generally with the War Hawks, but could not bring himself to support all their measures. He voted against all efforts to arm and prepare the navy, he opposed the attempt to expand the War Department by adding assistant secretaries, and he voted against all increases in taxes. Yet he voted for war.

A number of conservatives remained undecided on war up till the last moment. As late as May, 1812, the Massachusetts Federalist Samuel Taggart felt, perhaps somewhat wishfully, that a majority of the Virginia delegation was against war. Besides the Virginia Federalists and Quids, he listed Taliaferro, Burwell, Smith, Nelson, and Clay as probably opposed to war.[68] John Smilie of Pennsylvania as late as April, 1812, favored commercial retaliation to war, but he still ended by voting for war in June.

Surely the War Hawks, both Southern and Western, provided with their skill and energy the necessary impetus to war. But they could not have done so unless the majority of the Republican party, particularly in the South, had not become gradually converted to the idea that war was the only alternative to national humiliation and disgrace. In this sense the War Hawks acted as the catalyst for a reaction the basic elements of which were already present.

Relations with England degenerated even further in the interval between sessions of Congress. Monroe took over the reins of American diplomacy in April, 1811, but despite his avowed determination to reach some sort of understanding he was unable to make any progress. At London in February the American minister William Pinkney had presented a virtual ultimatum demanding the repeal of the orders in council, and when rebuffed by the Tory Perceval ministry he departed for home leaving only a chargé d'affaires to handle the routine business in London.

Tension increased during the spring of 1811 as British warships stepped up their activity in American waters. The situation came to a head one night in May when the *President* was fired on by a British warship thought to be the frigate *Guerrière*, notorious for her recent captures and impressments. Unwilling to repeat the disgrace of the *Chesapeake*, Commodore John Rodgers returned the fire and in fifteen minutes silenced his foe. The next morning revealed her to be the British sloop-of-war *Little Belt* with a loss of thirty-two killed and wounded. Great was the popular excitement, for Rodgers had at last avenged the *Chesapeake* and reaffirmed American dignity.

In the midst of this clamor the new British minister, Augustus J. Foster, arrived in Washington. His instructions, however, which permitted only a tardy reparation for the *Chesapeake*, made further negotiation all but impossible. Foster was instructed to insist that the French decrees had not actually been repealed, and he was permitted to offer a revocation of the British orders only after France had repealed the decrees that affected Britain. Britain, in short, would remove her restrictions on American commerce only when France freely admitted British goods into Europe. An honorable settlement on such grounds was impossible.

It was thus with the general feeling that war was inevitable that the Twelfth Congress assembled on November 4, 1811, a month earlier than usual. This feeling permitted the war party to seize the initiative and capture the vital committee machinery. The advance planning of the war party was evident in the selection of Henry Clay as Speaker on his first day in the House. His ability was widely recognized; even John Randolph, who voted for Macon and objected to the selection of Clay by an invisible caucus, admitted that Clay was "as good a

Speaker as we could have elected." Clay immediately organized the House to suit the War Hawks. To head the Ways and Means committee he appointed Ezekiel Bacon of Massachusetts, supported by Langdon Cheves and four conservatives, with only one Federalist. To the all-important Foreign Relations committee Clay appointed Porter, Calhoun, Grundy, and Desha, along with two old administration Republicans, Smilie of Pennsylvania and Ebenezer Seaver of Massachusetts. Having assured a prowar majority, he tossed in Randolph and two Federalists. The army committee headed by David R. Williams and the naval committee under Langdon Cheves were both loaded with War Hawks from the previous Congress.[69]

The House then marked time with a debate on the admission of Louisiana while the Foreign Relations committee deliberated the problem of peace or war. On November 29 Porter submitted the report of the committee, which found that the French decrees, insofar as they affected American commerce, had been repealed, enumerated the transgressions of Britain, and concluded that "the period has arrived when . . . it is the sacred duty of Congress to call forth the patriotism and resources of the country." To effect this the committee offered a series of six resolutions authorizing the President to fill up the present military establishment, to increase the size of the army to 10,000 regular troops, to accept the service of 50,000 additional volunteers, to order out the militia when needed, to fit out and commission all the vessels in the navy, and to arm American merchant vessels. Lest there be any doubt, Porter explained that the committee had "unanimously" agreed that American rights were to be defended by force and that the resolutions were offered "with a view to make preparations for such a war." [70]

Hoping to gain time Randolph moved that the committee report lie on the table, but his motion was shortly negatived. Then the first resolution, a harmless recommendation that the

President fill up the ranks of the presently authorized military establishment, was passed 117–11, only Randolph and Stanford among Republicans voting against it. The second resolution, which clearly contemplated war by authorizing an increase in the regular army to 10,000 men, sparked a debate that occupied the House through the second week in December. This was the first general debate on the issue of war or peace and Randolph made the most of it. On December 10 he spoke for several hours iterating all the Old Republican arguments against saddling the people with corrupt and expensive armies and navies, debts and taxes. None of these disadvantages could be overweighed by the need to defend abstract rules or remote economic interests. War Hawks like Porter and Grundy had mentioned the acquisition of Canada, but Randolph answered that even if Canada could be conquered, which he doubted, the attempt would leave the seaboard undefended and at the mercy of the British navy. "Virginia planters," he warned, "would not be taxed to support such a war—a war which must aggravate their present distresses; [a war] in which they had not the remotest interest."

Randolph then turned to a comparison of England and France, maintaining that England was the last bulwark of free men while Napoleon was the scourge of mankind, an argument that he had used in 1806 and a point that had considerable appeal among Virginians.[71] America's whole cultural heritage came from England,

whose form of government is the freest on earth, our own only excepted; from whom every valuable principle of our own institutions has been borrowed—representation, jury trial, voting the supplies, writ of habeas corpus—our whole civil and criminal jurisprudence . . . our fellow Protestants identified in blood, in language, in religion with ourselves.

Napoleon, on the other hand, could be compared with Attila, Tamerlane, and Kubla Khan, "malefactors of the human race, who ground man down to a mere machine of their impious and bloody ambition." By declaring war on England the United States would "become a party to his views, a partner in his wars." [72]

The speech of Nathaniel Macon two days later depicted the conservative struggling to reconcile current necessity with Jeffersonian dogma. Macon announced he would vote for the committee resolution because an increase in the regular army to 10,000 men seemed reasonable preparation for a war he had concluded was inevitable. Recent British interference with the direct trade, the sale of American agricultural products in Europe, had converted Macon. Though opposed to war in general he was willing to fight to protect this trade, but he would not go to war to protect the carrying trade or to conquer Canada or to encourage manufactures, as some of the War Hawks seemed to wish.[73]

The following day, December 13, Hugh Nelson of Virginia, who had been elected in 1811 and was expected to give wholehearted support to war measures, delivered a speech on the committee resolutions that, according to a Federalist observer, "carried terror and dismay into the ranks of the war party." Nelson was an old friend of Monroe, and in the schism of 1806 he had supported the Jefferson Administration as a member of the Virginia House of Delegates while sympathizing with the "motives" of the "minority." Upon arriving in Washington in November, 1811, he took up residence with a group of Federalists and Republican "minority" men, including Randolph. A few days before his speech he had written to a friend in Charlottesville: "I am a messmate of J[ohn] R[andolph]. The more I see him the more I like him. He is as honest as the sun, with all his foibles, and as much traduced as any man has ever been. . . . Do not be surprised if before the session closes I am classified with him as a minority man." [74]

Nelson began his speech in true Old Republican style by

pointing out the effects of war on "our political institutions, our habits, our manners, and republican simplicity." The disadvantages were such, he contended, that

> few circumstances besides invasion would justify war. It would strengthen the Executive arm at the expense of the Legislature. The Chief Magistrate would have to carry on the war. . . . The Constitution would be sapped. . . . [I] care not for the prices of cotton and tobacco as compared with the Constitution.

Moreover, it was quite unlikely that the United States could ever gain recognition of her neutral rights, particularly since the only program the War Hawks suggested was a territorial war begun by an invasion of Canada. Canada could not be conquered, but even if it could would this enforce our maritime rights? "Certainly not. The way to enforce these rights was by a great maritime force, which the nation were incompetent to raise and support."

Nelson agreed with Randolph that even if the war were successful and brought England to her knees it would leave Napoleon master of the world. Reluctant as he was to go to war, Nelson nevertheless thought that the country should prepare for any eventuality: "I shall vote for the increase of the regular force; to go hand in hand with my friends, even in a war, if necessary and just. I have not made this speech to prove that I am against war." [75] Nelson bespoke the confusion of the old Jeffersonians, who only reluctantly abandoned their old principles and submitted to the leadership of the War Hawks.

On December 16 the second resolution of the Foreign Relations committee raising the regular army to 10,000 men passed the House 110–22, a handful of Federalists and three Republican Quids—Randolph, Stanford, and Gray—in the minority. Even those conservatives who had not yet made up their minds on war felt that an increase in the army as a gesture of preparation was desirable. The House then passed the third resolution 113–16, which authorized the President to enlist 50,000 volunteers—Randolph, Gray, and Stanford again the only Republicans in the minority. The fourth resolution, which permitted the President to order out detachments of militia "as in his opinion the public service might require," was then passed without debate, only a handful of Federalists in opposition. The fifth resolution, which authorized the fitting out and commissioning of all the vessels in the navy, was also passed without debate, 111–15, but received the tacit opposition of eleven or twelve Republicans, including those who opposed war and a few half-converted conservatives, like Macon and D. R. Williams, who habitually voted against the navy.[76]

The most striking aspect of the debate and votes on the resolutions of the Foreign Relations committee was the near unanimity of the House. But for the Quids Randolph, Gray, and Stanford, Republican dissension was stilled, and even many of the Federalists cooperated on these initial preparedness measures. The primary purpose of the Federalists was apparently to embarrass the administration, and a few even felt a short war worthwhile if it served to turn the Republicans out of office. It is also evident that many of the Federalists had as yet no real conception of the determination of the War Hawks.[77]

After passing its series of warlike resolutions the House settled down to routine business, and the initiative passed to the Senate where the portion of the President's annual message dealing with foreign affairs had been referred to a select committee headed by William Branch Giles. Giles and the "invisibles" had long advocated a more energetic foreign policy and a sterner attitude toward Great Britain, and they quickly assumed the leadership of the war party in the Senate. On December 6 Giles reported out of committee a series of bills designed to gird the nation for any possible conflict, the key measure of which was a bill to increase the regular army to 25,000 men and increase the term of enlistment to five years. Since the President had asked for only 10,000 as a start and there was some doubt that the government with a nearly empty treasury could afford to maintain an army of that size, the measure aroused the suspicion that Giles was more interested in embarrassing the treasury than in preparing for war. Monroe at least felt that Giles's move so endangered the treasury that "the means for making war were put at a distance." Giles's series of bills nevertheless breezed through the Senate in four days with no opposition in principle from either party.[78]

The House began debate on the Senate army bill on January 5. Several Republicans including Macon objected to the bill because it provided a separate organization for the new force that would keep it distinct from the present army, a feature which Macon felt would "introduce disorder and confusion." Only Randolph and Stanford in the debate opposed the bill in principle, and both fought a rear-guard action based on the "principles of '98." Reminding Republicans that they had opposed armies and navies in 1798, Stanford accused them of deserting their principles. It was even probable, and he submitted documents to prove it, that the foreign crisis of 1798 had been more serious than the present one. If true, the Federalists had been more justified in raising an army in 1798 than Republicans were in 1812.[79] The argument was directed at the Old Republicans who could remember the experience of '98 and whose support was vital to the War Hawks.

Randolph adopted the same theme, reminding conservatives that the War Hawks with their demand for strong and energetic government meant a return to the Hamiltonian system. There was no middle ground:

Gentlemen must either stop on the good old Virginia ground, or they must scout it, and go into Federalism, and adopt Federal doctrine to its full extent. They must take one or the other; and if they are prepared for this system of internal taxation, this system of patronage, this vast Army and Navy, and the point of honor . . . it is hardly worth while to keep up the old distinction.

Ignoring this warning that the real battle front was the Liberal state, the House passed the army bill 94–34, with the Federalists and only a few conservatives, Randolph, Stanford, McBryde, Macon, and Smilie in opposition.[80]

An effort to increase the navy, on the other hand, ran into considerable opposition. Republicans had traditionally disliked the navy as designed to serve only the New England shipping interest, and the navy had suffered under Republican administration. On January 17 Langdon Cheves, chairman of the naval committee, began a two-day speech in support of a bill to appropriate $7.5 million for the construction of twelve 74s and twenty frigates. In answer to the usual argument that the United States could not afford to compete with Britain on the seas, Cheves pointed out that England had world-wide commitments and could not afford to keep more than a few ships on the American station even in time of war. The United States, Cheves concluded, could hardly expect to fight a war with England without a navy. The argument was distinctly un-Republican, and Federalists gleefully noted the change. Cheves, wrote Samuel Taggart of Massachusetts, "has done himself honor and deserved well of his country, but whatever he may be nominally he is in reality as high a toned Federalist as ever was Alexander Hamilton." [81]

Cheves was answered by both Republican conservatives who could not stomach the thought of a navy under any conditions and some Western War Hawks who contemplated only a relatively inexpensive land war against Canada. Regardless of their motives, however, all couched their arguments on Old Republican grounds. Jonathan Roberts of Pennsylvania, a War Hawk elected in 1810, had the temerity to remind Republicans of their opposition to a navy in 1798, while Adam Seybert of Philadelphia, who had taken the seat of Joseph Clay in 1809, predicted that Cheves's bill would lead to a permanent naval establishment with the horrendous result that "the public debt will become permanent; direct taxes will be perpetual; the paupers of the country will be increased; the nation will be bankrupt; and, I fear, the tragedy will end in revolution." Successive amendments removed the provisions for additional ships and dockyards, and thoroughly emasculated, representing little more than a small annual appropriation for repairs of existing ships, the bill passed on January 29. On the key votes Western War Hawks teamed up with Southern conservatives to ensure that any war the country began would not be fought on the sea.[82]

Next came the ticklish subject of taxes to finance the war that was now generally considered to be inevitable. In January Gallatin submitted to the House Ways and Means committee his estimates for the coming fiscal year. He estimated the cost of running the government at $9.6 million and the additional charge for conducting a war at $10 million for the first year. The fixed cost of the government Gallatin thought could be met by increasing the customs duties and the internal taxes; the conservative estimate of $10 million as the cost for a year of war he proposed to meet by a loan.[83]

Despite Gallatin's optimistic estimates, which were carefully tailored to prevent dampening the war fever in Congress, the House was reluctant to face the cost of war. Not until February 17 did Ways and Means Chairman Ezekiel Bacon submit to the House a report containing fourteen resolutions to provide an increase in revenue, and not until February 25 did the House take up the subject for debate. Bacon's resolutions included a 100 percent increase in customs duties, additional tonnage duties on American and foreign vessels, increased excises on salt, spirits, and carriages, and finally a direct tax of $3 million to be apportioned among the states. The duties were not to go into effect until war had been declared, and they were to continue until one year after the conclusion of peace.[84] They were explicitly war taxes but even so, similar excises had sparked bitter Republican opposition and even open rebellion in the 1790s.

The crucial measure was the salt tax, which Republicans had

long opposed as a burden on the poor. On February 28 the House rejected the tax on salt, 60–57. The War Hawks begged the House to reconsider on the grounds that rejection threatened the whole tax structure and in effect the war effort. They managed to convince a few conservatives, and on March 2 the House reconsidered and adopted the tax. The rest of the resolutions were then quickly passed, and the committee report was finally approved 56–34. In the minority on the final vote besides Federalists were the North Carolina conservatives Macon, Stanford, McBryde, and Cochran, Randolph, and a few anti-Gallatin Republicans, like Robert Wright of Maryland. Despite this victory for the War Hawks, a bill embodying the increases was not introduced into the House until June 26, and then final action was postponed until the next session.[85]

Despite considerable progress in passing warlike resolutions, it was still apparent by early spring that Congress was badly divided on the ultimate measures to be taken. The unity achieved thus far was largely superficial and resulted from the general feeling that some sort of military preparations were in order, even apart from the question of peace or war. In the Senate the "invisibles" supplied much of the leadership in behalf of stronger measures, but it was still unclear whether the nation's honor or the embarrassment of the treasury was their primary aim, particularly since they and their allies in the House had opposed all efforts to finance the war by taxation. In the House the Federalists abandoned their cooperation with the War Hawks and were now solidly opposing all efforts at mobilization. The War Hawks gained important adherents, but there remained a third group, what the Federalist Samuel Taggart described as the "scarecrow party"—"those who vote for war measures without any sincere intention to go to war, but in hopes that Great Britain may be intimidated by the din of our preparations to relax her system so that they will eventually come off with flying colours."[86] Aware that something had to be done but afraid to take the ultimate step, the conservatives were being reluctantly dragged forward until it was too late to back down without utter disgrace.

It was partly to crystallize the war sentiment in Congress and partly to embarrass the Federalists in the spring elections in New England that the administration released the Henry correspondence early in March. On March 9 Madison laid before Congress the instructions and dispatches to Captain John Henry, a British secret agent whom Governor Craig of Canada had sent to New England at the time of the embargo to stimulate disunionist sentiment. The uproar in Congress and in the country was deafening; the war press, such as the *Aurora* and the Baltimore *Whig*, raised their cries for action to a new pitch. The Federalists were at first alarmed, for they did not know what Henry might have reported, but a closer examination showed that his correspondence contained nothing more compromising than the editorials, sermons, and addresses that had been printed in every Federalist paper in New England. The Federalists called for an investigation and a House committee discovered that the administration had paid Henry $50,000 out of the State Department contingent fund and then allowed him to leave the country before releasing the correspondence. The motive was patently political; Randolph called it "a poor, shabby, shallow, dirty electioneering trick—played off to affect the Massachusetts elections." [87]

Though it stimulated the demand for war, the Henry affair in all other respects backfired on the administration. Its influence on the Northern elections was disappointing, and it seemed to have no effect, despite Madison's hopes, on the alliance in New York between DeWitt Clinton and the Federalists. In Congress the unauthorized expenditure of $50,000 for frivolous purposes alienated a number of conservatives. John Clopton wrote home to his wife:

I know not how I can vote for Mr. ——'s [Madison scratched out] re-election, for I have not the least idea that the purse-strings of the nation should be placed in the hands of any man whatsoever to be drawn at his pleasure. I am decidedly in favor of Principle in exclusion of every other consideration. I am afraid that there is too much cabal and intrigue in the composition of the atmosphere that surrounds the executive department.[88]

Despite some misgivings many conservatives concluded that it was too late to turn back when on April 1 the President sent a confidential message to Congress requesting a sixty-day embargo on American shipping. Probably in an effort to sound the sentiment of the House, Secretary Monroe appeared before the Foreign Relations committee a few days before. He informed the committee that the sole purpose of the administration in recommending an embargo was to defer war for two months to furnish additional time for preparation. The committee met again, probably on March 30 or 31, to discuss the possibility of an embargo. Apparently a majority of the committee favored it, and the only issues were secrecy and speed, which were essential to prevent wholesale ship departures. Unfortunately Randolph denied the power of the committee to impose secrecy and refused to be bound by it. Moreover, he declared, the secret was an open one. He had just returned from Baltimore where he had found merchants already aware of an intended embargo. Randolph's intransigence precluded further efforts at secrecy, and Calhoun himself authorized Josiah Quincy to inform his Boston constituents of an impending embargo.[89]

The only effect of Randolph's stand was to increase the sense of urgency in the House. When the President's message was received on April 1 the Foreign Relations committee was ready with a bill, which was read twice and committed to debate. The bill was generally viewed as the final preparation for war. Clay whipped the conservatives into line by reminding them that they had gone too far to back out. If Congress stopped now after all the war measures it had passed, it would cover itself "with shame and indelible disgrace." That this argument was effective was proved when old John Smilie followed Clay on the floor. Smilie, whose Western Pennsylvania Republicanism dated back to the fight over the Constitution in 1788, admitted that from the beginning of the session he had preferred commercial retaliation to a war and an army of 25,000 men. But since the House and the administration clearly favored war he would "go to war." "If we now recede we shall be a reproach among all nations," he told the House.[90] The human impulse to "join the bandwagon" was an effective political weapon for the War Hawks.

However, no such weakness affected Randolph, who had accused the War Hawks of "bludgeoning" the House into war. Pleading for time, Randolph repeated to the House Monroe's admission before the Foreign Relations committee that the country was unprepared for war. "If you mean war," he taunted the War Hawks, "if the spirit of the country is up to it, why have you been spending five months in idle debate?" This was too much for Clay, who realized that a good part of the five months had been wasted by Randolph himself. He called Randolph to order for accusing the House of spending time in idle debate, but the temporary chairman, Burwell Bassett of Virginia, ruled that Randolph was not out of order, and his decision was upheld by the House.[91]

When Randolph sat down several Federalists arose to state their objections, but the debate was cut off by a motion for the previous question, which was carried. Passage of the bill in one day was contrary to a standing rule of the House, and Macon proposed that the final reading be postponed to the next day. Though the idea received the support of D. R. Williams, the War Hawks overrode the suggestion; the bill was read a third time and passed 70–41. Randolph, Stanford, and McBryde were the only conservatives in the minority.[92]

The Senate extended the embargo to ninety days and passed it 20–13 without recorded debate. Voting against it were six Federalists and seven Republicans. The "invisibles" opposed it ostensibly because they feared it might be regarded as a return to the policy of commercial retaliation and, in the words of

Samuel Smith, give Madison "a fair occasion to sneak out of war." [93] This seems more like a pretext than an explanation; it seems more likely that the "invisibles" were beginning to get cold feet. In any case the bill as amended was repassed by the House, and the President signed it on April 6.

That same day the injunction of secrecy, imposed at the time of the confidential message, was removed; and the editor of the Alexandria *Herald* was brought before the bar of the House for publishing confidential information on the embargo. The editor was dismissed when it became evident that the embargo had been a matter of general knowledge. There was some inclination to blame Randolph for insisting that the deliberations of the Foreign Relations committee be made public until Macon reminded the House that the subject had not been considered confidential until the message was received from the President and that prior to that time a mere committee had no power to impose secrecy.[94] The incident illustrates the determination of Randolph to keep the public informed of the trend of events in the hope that it might come to the aid of the minority. In the meantime he no doubt felt that any incidental embarrassment to the War Hawks was all to the good.

Shortly after the embargo was passed it became evident that the facilities of the War Department were inadequate to administer the proposed increase in the size of the army. At the suggestion of the President a bill was introduced on April 30 to provide two assistant secretaries of war, but it ran headlong into conservative opposition. Suspicious of all government bureaus, Old Republicans were doubly suspicious of the War Department, which they regarded as a monstrous collection of parasites sucking the blood of the body politic. Even some of the War Hawks joined the fray. D. R. Williams thought additional secretaries unnecessary and felt that "there were thousands of individuals perfectly adequate to the correct arrangement and prompt execution of all the duties of the Department." If the War Department was disorganized and unprepared it was primarily the fault of the Secretary, and adding more clerks would only increase the confusion. To Williams, "a monster with three heads" was no better than a monster with one.[95]

Randolph, whose political ideas seldom advanced beyond the whiggery of Edmund Burke, gave the *coup de grâce* to the idea.

This system will effectually create all our great departments of government into sinecures. So that, after having gotten pretty good subordinate men, you will only have to fill the highest place with some man of straw, who will cut a pretty good figure in the drawing room or at the head of a table at an official dinner. This is a state of things which I do not wish to see produced.

Randolph opposed all measures of military preparation because they strengthened the federal government and the Executive, and at least he was being consistent if not wise. But War Hawks like Williams, who permitted themselves the luxury of an occasional lapse into Old Republicanism, were inviting disaster. Despite the conservative opposition, the bill passed 58–43, partly through Federalist support.[96]

On May 29 rumors that Congress would shortly go into closed session to vote a declaration of war induced Randolph to make one last public effort to commit the House to peace. He prefaced his motion with a few remarks designed to show that the French decrees had not been repealed, that the administration had not negotiated fairly with Britain, and that war was not justified. If despite this war were declared, Randolph continued, "this government will stand branded, to the latest posterity . . . as the panderers of French despotism—as the tools, the minions, sycophants, parasites of France." [97]

This accusation was too much for Calhoun, who called Randolph to order for debating a subject when there was as yet no motion before the House. The chair, occupied temporarily by the former conservative William Bibb of Georgia, ruled that Randolph had declared his intention to offer a motion and a few prefatory remarks were permissible. Randolph, who had already been speaking for over an hour, continued his harangue. A few

moments later when Clay returned to the chair Calhoun again
called him to order. This time Clay decided that Randolph must
submit his motion without further ado. Randolph appealed to
the House and lost; he thereupon submitted his resolution:
"That, under existing circumstances, it is inexpedient to resort
to war against Great Britain." His purpose was to force the hand
of the War Hawks prematurely and obtain, if possible, a public
debate on the issue of peace or war.

Clay forestalled this by ruling that the House could not debate
the merits of the proposition until it had voted to consider it.
Randolph again appealed to the House declaring that this decision along with the rule of the previous question drastically
abridged freedom of debate. But when Macon pointed out that
the House could not possibly debate the resolution until it had
voted to entertain it, Randolph withdrew his appeal. The House
then voted 72–37 not to consider the resolution. Voting in the
minority besides the Federalists were the Republicans who opposed war and a few conservatives, such as Macon and Willis
Alston of North Carolina, Burwell Bassett and Hugh Nelson of
Virginia, who still considered the question of war an open one.[98]

Madison sent his war message to Congress on June 1. Two
days later Calhoun in closed session introduced a bill declaring
war on England. Randolph and Quincy moved to make the debate public so the country would at least know what was going
on, but the move was defeated 77–45. The bill passed its second
reading by the same vote, and the next day it passed, 79–49.
Voting in the minority were thirty-one Federalists and eighteen
Republicans. All the Republicans but the Quids Randolph, Stanford, and McBryde were Northerners.[99]

In the Senate the declaration of war was referred to a select
committee of Anderson, Smith, Leib, Campbell, Howell, Lloyd,
and Taylor. While the committee deliberated the Senate called
for information from the War Department on the condition of
the army. The answer was not very encouraging, for apparently
the enlistments had not even filled up the old authorization of

10,000 men. This seems to have reinforced the tremors of the "invisibles," who favored, at most, a limited maritime conflict. Smith and Leib eventually joined with the Federalists on the committee to convert the declaration of war into a bill to authorize the President to issue letters of marque and reprisal and commission privateers to operate against British commerce. In the end it was Smith, not Madison, who tried to "sneak out of war." Thus emasculated the bill was reported out of committee on June 12, but the amendments failed when the Senate tied 16–16 on the question of accepting the committee's bill.[100]

After the move to substitute commercial retaliation failed, Obadiah German, a Clintonian who had opposed military preparation since his entrance into the Senate in 1809, moved to postpone the declaration to the following November on the grounds that the country was not prepared for war. He was not opposed to war, he said; he merely wished to wait until the ranks of the army were filled and the seaports fortified. The problem of the country's poor defense system, stressed by Randolph without success in the House, had considerable weight in the Senate. It was on this ground primarily that the two senators from Ohio, Worthington and Campbell, preferred commercial retaliation to war. German's motion was negatived, and on June 17 the declaration of war was passed, 19–13. Voting against war were eight Federalists and five Republicans (German of New York, Gilman of New Hampshire, Lambert of New Jersey, Reed of Maryland, and Worthington of Ohio).[101]

"The bold talk of the War Hawks in 1812 concealed an extraordinary incapacity for warlike endeavor. The country was sorely unprepared whether from the point of view of finance, of military readiness, of competent leadership, of national unity, or of administrative capacity to sustain a large-scale military operation."[102] This opinion by a modern student of administrative history confirms the arguments of the conservatives in 1812, but what was more galling to them than the possibility that the war might be unsuccessful was the certainty that it would mean the end of the Jeffersonian system. A huge army, an expensive navy, high taxes, vast quantities of paper money afloat, added government offices and bureaus—in short, all the trappings of Hamiltonian Federalism. And for what? Nothing, conservatives thought, but a point of honor. The honor of the nation, to be sure, but nevertheless, as Falstaff said, "A word." Air. "What hath it? He that died on Wednesday."

"This metaphysical war," John Taylor of Caroline called it— "a war, not for conquest, not for defense, not for sport— . . . this war for honour, like that of the Greeks against Troy, may terminate in the destruction of the last experiment in . . . free government. . . ." [103]

"This Metaphysical War"

The Old Republicans entered the War of 1812 with many misgivings for the future of the Liberal Republic. An apprehension that a belligerent foreign policy led inevitably to domestic centralization, born in the Federalist era, had been confirmed by the exercise of executive influence during the West Florida dispute and by the vast increase in federal power during the embargo. Nor were their fears groundless. The war engendered a wave of popular nationalism that eventually swept aside the Jeffersonian system. Even the Southern conservatives were not immune to this surge of nationalism. Though a few retired from politics, most surrendered temporarily to the tide. Except for an occasional issue that involved too radical a departure from conservative principle, the Old Republicans gave loyal support to the Madison Administration during the conflict.

On the extreme right the Randolph Quids continued to oppose the war and the Madison Administration, but by 1812 their numbers were insignificant. Randolph and Edwin Gray were defeated for re-election in 1813, leaving Richard Stanford the sole Quid in the Thirteenth Congress. James M. Garnett continued to express his opposition to the war in the columns of *The Spirit of Seventy-six* under the pseudonym "Timothy Turfcutter," but even that lone voice was silenced when *The Spirit of Seventy-six* died in the spring of 1814 for lack of subscribers.

One of the more interesting aspects of this small Republican opposition was its alliance with the Federalists. This unnatural association was largely the result of the impotence of the two minority groups. Wrote Randolph to the Maryland Federalist Francis Scott Key: "Be assured that nothing can be done with effect without union among the parts, however heterogeneous, that compose the opposition. They have time enough to differ among themselves after they shall have put down the common foe; and, if they must quarrel, I would advise them to adjourn to that distant day." [1] Randolph clearly considered the new nationalism of Clay and Calhoun more dangerous than the earlier Federalism. He also could respect ability, even in an opponent, and many of the Federalists, such as Josiah Quincy, were indisputably able men.[2] The Quids, moreover, for years associated socially with Virginia Federalists, a fact that often raised eyebrows among Republican leaders in Richmond.[3] It was only natural to extend their circle of acquaintances in Washington.

In the Twelfth Congress the advocates of peace, Republican and Federalist, drew closer together. Randolph befriended a number of Federalists, and with at least three—Josiah Quincy, Francis Scott Key, and Harmannus Bleecker of Albany—he corresponded for a number of years after the war. Randolph was not alone in this association with Federalists. The Old Republican George Logan of Philadelphia, whose Quaker pacifism had led him to oppose war in 1812 just as he had opposed it in 1798, became reconciled with the Massachusetts Federalist Timothy Pickering through their mutual desire for peace. Pickering frequently visited Logan's home at Stenton, and the two kept up a correspondence through the war and for some time after. In the Thirteenth Congress Richard Stanford became quite close to Francis Scott Key, who was a brother-in-law of Joseph H. Nicholson and of Governor Edward Lloyd.[4]

At least on the part of Republicans there was no real compromise of principle in this cooperation with the Federalists. It was the Federalists, after all, who during the war adopted the old opposition philosophy of weak government and states' rights.

When, for instance, Congress in January, 1813, was proposing to finance the war by issuing treasury notes, the Federalist Elisha Potter of Rhode Island predicted that the issue of public paper would create "a new system of patronage and favoritism in the Treasury Department" in a speech that would have done justice to John Taylor of Caroline. The Republican conservatives can hardly be blamed for welcoming with open arms these new adherents to the "principles of '98." When in 1814 Harrison Gray Otis began making speeches in the Massachusetts legislature repeating the doctrines of the Virginia and Kentucky resolutions, Randolph wrote Josiah Quincy asking him to congratulate Otis on his conversion to "the side of liberty of the subject and the rights of the states." [5]

When nullification sentiments among the Federalists became more extreme toward the end of the war, Randolph became quite alarmed, for he, like Jefferson and Madison, regarded the philosophy of the Virginia and Kentucky resolutions as no more than a last resort in the defense of individual freedom, not as a prelude to disunion. Any resistance to the arbitrary acts of the federal government, he wrote to his cousin in Rhode Island, Richard Kidder Randolph, "must be made by the *State authorities* and restricted to those acts, or parts of acts, which are manifestly *unconstitutional* as well as *oppressive,* or the most dreadful consequences will ensue." At the same time he was warning his friend Josiah Quincy with as much tact as possible: "Rash counsels are not always, if ever, wise. I trust we [i.e., the nation] shall hold together. . . ." [6]

An incidental result of this Federalist-Quid alliance was to raise Federalist hopes that Republican conservatives might be induced to join them in supporting the candidacy of DeWitt Clinton against Madison in the election of 1812. Clinton himself was an antiwar Republican whom the Federalists were supporting in an effort to unite the various peace factions into a single anti-Madison party. The North Carolina Federalist, John Steele, was even willing to offer the vice-presidential nomination to a

Republican conservative in an effort to woo them away from the war party. "We have taken measures," he wrote to a North Carolina Federalist in Congress, "to sound Mr. Macon and Governor H[awkins] of this state as to the manner in which such an overture w[oul]d be relished by them."[7] Hawkins was a member of the "Warren Junto," a group of North Carolina conservatives whose political mentor was Nathaniel Macon. The overture to Macon was foredoomed to failure, for whatever reservations he might have about the direction of events he was loyally supporting the war effort and the Madison Administration. Nor were any of his friends disposed to support Clinton; he even wrote Judge Nicholson that he knew of only one pro-Clinton man in his part of North Carolina.[8] Indeed the whole thought of supporting the likes of DeWitt Clinton was obnoxious to most conservatives, who considered him on the same level of political morality as the "invisibles" in the Senate.[9] *The Spirit of Seventy-six*, though it predicted the defeat of Madison, gave no open support to Clinton, and it reported the election results as votes for "peace" or "war," rather than by political party.[10]

Apart from John Randolph and his tiny band but equally opposed to the war was John Taylor of Caroline. No longer active in politics, Taylor was forced to resort to his pen to express his discouragement with the trend of events. In 1814 Taylor published his longest and most important work, *An Inquiry into the Principles and Policy of the Government of the United States*. Although it might seem twenty-five years too late, Taylor's essay was intended as an answer to John Adams' *Defense of the Constitutions of the United States*, in which Taylor professed to see a defense of government by aristocracy. Actually Adams' work was no more than a springboard which Taylor used to launch into an attack on the wartime extension of federal powers and expenses.

Readopting a theme he had made familiar in the 1790s, Taylor demonstrated how the pure simplicity of the early republic had been undermined by corruption and patronage. Although the

American Revolution had been a struggle against the ancient forms of privilege—monarchy, nobility, military, and clergy—its ideals had unfortunately been prostituted by the substitution of a new order of privilege created by "paper and patronage." Originating in the Federalist system, this new aristocracy flourished on the war with England, and the nation was now burdened with a wholly new order of privilege with none of the benefits of the old system. The people were "submitting to be taxed and enslaved by patronage and paper, without being deluded or terrified by the promises of heaven, the denunciation of hell, the penalties of law, the brilliancy and generosity of nobility, or the pageantry and charity of superstition." [11] This theme is elaborated through the rest of the book. Taylor felt that this new aristocracy spawned on the wartime finance, the vast increase in public paper and the national debt. He also lamented the impetus which the war gave to the demand for a new bank and a protective tariff, symbols of the unnatural alliance between government and commerce against the landed interest.

Although Charles A. Beard regarded Taylor's *Inquiry* as one of the few important systematic studies of American politics, its contemporary influence was slight. Written in a prosaic, discursive style, Taylor's incisive ideas were so obscured by dull and unnecessary verbiage as to be all but unreadable. As a disappointed Randolph wrote to Taylor's friend Garnett, "For heaven sake, get some worthy person to do the second edition into *English*." [12] It is unlikely that it was read by anyone except a few interested Virginians.

The overwhelming majority of conservatives loyally supported the war effort and the Madison Administration. The only Randolphite left in the Virginia legislature, Benjamin Watkins Leigh, gave unstinted support to the war until 1813 when he resigned to accept a commission in the militia. In Maryland, Nicholson's brother-in-law, Edward Lloyd, governor until 1811 and a member of the state senate through the war, loyally echoed administration policies. In Congress the Republican opposition to the war was confined to Randolph, Gray, and Stanford, though they received occasional support from such conservatives as Matthew Clay of Virginia and Archibald McBryde of North Carolina. And even this tiny band of dissent was decimated by the elections of 1812–13. Randolph, defeated for the first and only time in his life, lost his seat to an ancient foe, John Wayles Eppes. Edwin Gray, Archibald McBryde, and Matthew Clay all fell victim to the wave of nationalism stimulated by the war. In the Senate David Stone was censured by the North Carolina legislature for his opposition to the war and resigned his seat at the end of 1813. Only Richard Stanford survived—a lone and misplaced voice of doom.

The harmony in Republican ranks, however, was fairly superficial, induced by the emergency, and it was confined largely to measures directed toward the immediate prosecution of the war. On the more remote features of the program of the War Hawks, such as a federally chartered bank to help finance the war, the party redivided into its "old" and "new" wings. Many a conservative had feared the effects of the war in strengthening the federal government, and another Bank of the United States was a frightening prospect. Congress was forced to consider the possibility of another federal bank by the condition of the treasury, which by early 1814 was on the verge of bankruptcy. It was evident that a bank would relieve the treasury and straighten out the tangled strands of wartime finance, but the question remained whether the emergency was acute enough to overcome traditional Republican scruples. The Federalists were divided on the issue—favoring in general the idea of a bank but disliking the idea of a bank run by Republicans. The War Hawks were similarly divided between those who demanded a bank to finance the war and those who, influenced by state and local banking interests, opposed a federal bank. The balance in the House seems to have been held by the agrarians who had defeated the bank bill in 1811 and who considered a federal bank unconstitutional and potentially dangerous.

The subject was brought to the attention of the House by a petition of several inhabitants of New York City demanding the establishment of a bank to aid the fiscal operations of the government. This petition was referred to the House Ways and Means committee headed by John W. Eppes. On January 10, 1814, Eppes reported that it was the opinion of his committee that Congress had no power to create a corporation within the states without their consent, that the power to create a bank was not delegated by the Constitution nor could it be inferred from the "necessary and proper" clause.[13]

On February 4 John C. Calhoun offered a resolution to inquire into the expediency of establishing a national bank in the District of Columbia. This proposal at least had the merit of sidestepping the Constitutional issue, and it was adopted without opposition. This move stirred the Ways and Means committee into action, and two weeks later John W. Taylor of New York reported a bill to incorporate a federal bank in the District of Columbia. In the ensuing debate Eppes explained that the Ways and Means committee, though divided, still considered a bank unconstitutional, but it had reported a bill because it thought the subject ought to be brought before the House. A majority of the committee, moreover, considered a bank chartered in the District of Columbia constitutional though Eppes himself did not.[14]

The committee's bill languished, however, primarily because a bank in the District of Columbia would be of little use to the treasury and the creation of branch banks would resurrect the constitutional issue. Finally on April 2 Felix Grundy proposed to start all over again and appoint a special committee to investigate the whole subject of a national bank. This resolution was immediately countered by a motion of Thomas Newton of Virginia to postpone the subject indefinitely. Newton argued that Congress had no power to create such an institution, and in any case there was not enough time left in the session to give it adequate consideration. Newton's resolution was voted down

71–80 by a combination of Federalists and nationalist Republicans, and Speaker Cheves appointed a committee of War Hawks and probank Federalists to investigate the subject. It was strictly a moral victory, however, for it was too late in the session for further action. On April 8 the committee was discharged from further consideration of the subject, and a week later it was postponed indefinitely by common consent.[15]

In the meantime something had to be done to rescue the treasury, which anticipated a deficit of $29 million for the fiscal year 1814. Eppes proposed to meet this with a loan of $25 million and the issuance of $5 million in treasury notes. The size of the loan was wholly unprecedented, even in Federalist times, but it aroused little opposition except from the Federalists. Most conservatives no doubt rationalized the necessity for it in the same way as Nathaniel Macon, who reminded the House that

No man dislikes . . . [a national debt] more than I do. It never was my opinion that a national debt was a national blessing. And I dislike taxes as much as I do a national debt; but I do not dislike them quite as much as I hate impressment; and before I would acknowledge the right of Great Britain to impress American citizens, I would bear as much of both as I could without complaining.

In the division only Stanford, Adam Boyd of New Jersey, and Thomas Bayly of Virginia among Republicans voted against it.[16]

The summer of 1814 was the low point of the war for the United States. The American armies had been generally unsuccessful in Canada and now faced an invasion down the Lake Champlain route. The army was disheartened and under-strength; the treasury was empty. As a final humiliation the British in August captured and burned Washington. The cries for more men and more money echoed in the ears of congressmen as they reassembled in Washington in September, 1814. It was clear that the difficulties of the treasury could be solved only by the creation of a national bank and the ranks of the army could be filled only by conscription. Both proposals were anathema to Old Republican doctrine, but even a conservative like Hugh Nelson of Virginia realized that the only alternative was defeat and a humiliating peace settlement. Indeed, so willing were conservatives, as well as War Hawks, to adopt any measure that might further the war effort that Nathaniel Macon, the watchdog of the liberties of the citizen and the rights of the states, began to fear they might go too far. "The majority," he wrote Judge Nicholson, "are well disposed to raise money and men, and I really fear, that the proper balance in both cases will be surpassed." [17]

The question of money presented itself before the House first when on September 27 John G. Jackson of Virginia offered an amendment to the Constitution authorizing the establishment of a federal bank. Jackson's purpose was to overcome by constitutional amendment the objections of those who felt a bank useful but unconstitutional. The amendment should have pleased everyone, but it was voted down 86–44, defeated by representatives of state banking interests, who wanted no federal bank at all, and nationalists, Federalist and Republican, who feared an amendment would merely raise a question of constitutionality which they considered already settled in favor of the bank.[18]

On October 10 the chairman of the Ways and Means committee, John Wayles Eppes, offered a plan to finance the war by issuing treasury notes which would be receivable in all payments owed the government, but which would not be legal tender. The notes would be redeemed by a predetermined percentage of the annual receipts from the internal taxes.[19] By providing a useful paper currency with the stability of bank notes this plan recommended itself to conservatives who disliked the idea of a national bank in any form. This scheme, however, was misliked by the Secretary of the Treasury, Alexander James Dallas, who preferred a more permanent system of handling the nation's finances. On October 18 Dallas sent to Congress his plan for a national bank to be incorporated for twenty years with a capital stock of $50 million, two-fifths of which was to be subscribed by the government. In accordance with the ratio then popular among economists, one-fifth of its capital was to be in specie. Eppes dutifully submitted a resolution declaring the expediency of establishing a national bank, though he himself later admitted that he considered a bank unconstitutional. Clopton and Burwell of Virginia also objected to the bank on constitutional grounds, but the resolution was adopted 93–54.[20] The nineteen Republicans who had voted earlier in favor of the constitutional amendment but now opposed the bank resolution can be presumed to have opposed the bank on constitutional grounds alone.[21] This, however, is not an exact indication of the number of Old Republicans in the House, for the list does not include such agrarians as Richard Stanford, John Clopton, and Hugh Nelson, who voted against the bank on both divisions.

In the meantime the Senate had been working on a bill to charter a bank similar to that envisaged by Dallas. The Senate fought off a series of amendments by Federalists and Western Republicans to reduce the size and capital of the bank and passed it on December 9 by 17–14. In opposition, besides Federalists and antiadministration Northern Republicans, were John Gaillard of South Carolina and the senators from Louisiana, James Brown and Eligius Fromentin.[22]

When the Senate bill came before the House on December 23, John Clopton immediately moved to strike out the first section in order to test the principle. He supported his motion with a lengthy speech that iterated all the old Republican arguments against a bank—even if expedient it was not absolutely necessary as required by the Constitution, and would prove to be "a very dangerous political machine to this country." Clopton's motion was lost 50–71, and the House proceeded to debate the bill.[23] The debate was conducted with a good deal of bitterness. Conservatives charged their colleagues with violating the principles of the party, and within the probank party the followers of Calhoun were at swords' points with the friends of Dallas. "All is confusion at O," wrote John Randolph from Bizarre.

Letters this morning express doubts whether the bank bill will or will not pass. Dallas reviled by the Jacobins (the democratic ones I mean) who are at daggers drawn with each other. [Thomas] Newton . . . talking of 'revolt.' [Thomas] Gholson . . . complaining that if you mention the Bank Bill to a brother Demo[crat] you are in danger of being insulted.[24]

On January 7, 1815, the House passed the bank bill 120–38. It is difficult to distinguish motives, for the constitutional argument was a handy tool in debate even for those more interested in protecting state banking interests. The Massachusetts Federalist Samuel Taggart thought perhaps twenty members of the House opposed the bank on constitutional grounds.[25] Of these about fifteen were Old Republicans, such as Macon, Stanford, Burwell, and Clopton, whose votes were normally determined by Jeffersonian doctrine. There was also a few new members elected in 1812–13, like Philip Pendleton Barbour and James Johnson of Virginia, who can be classified as conservatives only on the basis of their performance in later years. In the case of Barbour, at least, a letter to his brother, Senator James Barbour, indicates he thought the bank unconstitutional.[26] Also in the minority on the bank vote were a number of Western agrarians, such as Joseph Desha and Richard M. Johnson of Kentucky, whose votes were not normally conservative. Finally, there were a handful of Federalists and representatives of state banking interests voting against the bank.

On January 30 President Madison vetoed the bank bill on the practical grounds that the proposed institution would not be linked closely enough with the government, would not help the public credit, nor provide a circulating medium for the collection of taxes. On February 6 James Barbour, the new Senator from Virginia, introduced a revised bank bill more in line with the desires of the President. The Senate debated it for five days and passed it 18–16. The bill was sent to the House, and that body was engaged in sharp debate on it when news of peace arrived. The peace seemed to remove the immediate need for a bank, and on February 17 the House voted 74–73 to lay the subject aside.[27]

Congress was no more successful in finding ways to raise the needed men than it was in providing money. The farce conducted along the Niagara River in December, 1813, when the militia refused to enter Canada, and the defeat at Bladensburg had produced a general disgust with the militia system. The strength of the regular army, on the other hand, was largely on paper, and there was little prospect that its ranks could be filled by voluntary enlistments. The military situation deteriorated further in the fall of 1814. A large British force at Kingston menaced Sackets Harbor while another was preparing to march down Lake Champlain; a third was known to be on its way to New Orleans. Something had to be done, but just how far was Congress willing to go toward creating a large standing army of conscripts? The following letter of Jefferson represents the reaction of most Republican conservatives to the emergency:

we must prepare for interminable war. To this end we should put our house in order, by providing men and money to indefinite extent. The former may be done by classing our militia, and assigning each class to the description of duties for which it is fit. It is nonsense to talk of regulars. They are not to be had among a people so easy and happy at home as ours. We might as well rely on calling down an army of angels from heaven.[28]

Even in the face of invasion and defeat Jefferson was unwilling to abandon the old reliance on a voluntary army of citizen-soldiers.

Those responsible for conducting the war, however, were somewhat more flexible. Secretary of War Monroe had lost all confidence in the militia and preferred to rely on the regular army for the nation's defense. To fill the ranks of the army he asked Congress to pass a draft law. Aware that many Republicans considered conscription unconstitutional, he pointed out in a letter to Senator Giles that the Constitution had given Congress an unqualified power to raise and support armies. "It would be absurd to suppose that Congress could not carry this power into effect otherwise than by accepting the voluntary services of individuals," concluded Monroe.[29] Plausible as it seemed, this argument did not answer the objections of the conservatives. What effect, for instance, might such a law have on the liberties of the individual? If the Virginia doctrine of states' rights and weak government had any lasting value, it was as a bulwark for the freedom of the individual. "Can a man," asked Nathaniel Macon, ". . . be put under military law without his consent, and what has become of the habeas corpus act if he can be put in the regular army, where military law governs." Something like military conscription was exactly what the conservatives had in mind in the spring of 1812 when they were predicting that the war would have dire effects on the old system. "Who could have believed," wrote Macon, "when Mr. Adams was President, that the party which opposed his administration on constitutional principles, would be the advocates for conscription. I am sick at the thought of the change which has taken place." [30]

The bill that was finally agreed upon between Monroe and Giles was a compromise between the needs of the army and the demands of Virginia doctrine. It proposed to draft an army of 80,000 militia, each man to serve for two years within the limits of his own or an adjoining state. Giles reported it to the Senate on November 5, and the Senate passed it two weeks later without serious objection. In the House Giles's bill was taken up in committee of the whole on December 2. The military committee, headed by Troup of Georgia, would have nothing to do with it. Troup objected to the bill because, instead of providing a regular army, it provided only more untrained, expensive, ineffective militia. On the other side the conservatives viewed it as too strong, and they centered their attack on the two-years term of service. On December 8 John Wayles Eppes, who had assumed the leadership of the Southern conservatives during the currency debate, offered an amendment to reduce the term of service from two years to one. This was adopted in committee by a majority of about twenty votes, and on December 14 the House passed the bill 84–72. Voting in the minority were Federalists, New England Republicans, and about a dozen conservatives who opposed the bill in principle.[31]

In conference the Senate committee objected to the House amendment reducing the term of service to one year, and Troup finally compromised on eighteen months. On December 27 the House decided 73–64 to reject the compromise, and the next day the Senate voted to postpone the bill indefinitely. Again the deciding votes were cast by Southern conservatives. At the end of the session in February Troup reported that his committee

found that no efficacious measure, calculated certainly and promptly to fill the regular army, could be effectually resorted to. Measures were matured and proposed by the committee, but were not pressed on the House from the solemn conviction that there was no disposition in the Legislature to act finally on the subject.[32]

This was putting it mildly, for by this time news of peace had arrived and the House was busily hacking away at the military establishment.

Throughout 1813 and 1814 Republican conservatives had to cooperate in the war effort, but they were anxious to return to the old Jeffersonian system when the war was over. On February 20 President Madison transmitted the peace treaty to Congress with a message recommending that some of the regular army and navy be preserved for future defense. This suggestion was made more specific by a letter of Monroe urging that an army of 20,000 men be retained as a peace establishment. Recognizing the mood of the House, Troup's committee watered down Monroe's proposal, and on February 22 it submitted a bill fixing the peacetime army at 10,000 men.[33]

Joseph Desha of Kentucky immediately moved to reduce the army further to 6,000 men, arguing that the battle of New Orleans proved the value of militia and precluded the need for a large standing army. A drastic reduction, moreover, would permit the House to remove the wartime taxes.[34] With Desha's amendment the issue was joined between the War Hawks and the revitalized conservatives. The War Hawks pointed out that an army of 6,000 was smaller than the country had had for several years before the war, and they predicted that even 10,000 would not interfere with a reduction in taxes. Nathaniel Macon answered that the country had been on the verge of war since the *Chesapeake* affair and that the normal peace establishment before that time had been limited to one brigade. Macon thought this the best time to reduce the army. "His experience had shown him that, if there was a difficulty in raising men and laying taxes, there was a greater difficulty in getting rid of both." Desha's amendment was adopted 75–65, the Federalists voting with about fifteen conservatives.[35]

The House then passed the army bill without further debate and sent it to the Senate. On March 2 the Senate struck out 6,000 and inserted 15,000 as the authorized limit of the peacetime establishment. A conference between the Houses compromised on the original provision for 10,000 men, and on the last day of the session the House, rather than leave intact the wartime establishment, voted to accept the compromise.[36]

The emergence of a discernible group of Old Republicans at the end of the war showed that the Jeffersonian system was not quite dead. Most of them shared in the efforts of Congress to avoid open conflict before 1812, though only two, Macon and Stanford, had been in Congress since the 1790s. Their conservatism was a combination of age and a temperamental inability to adjust to rapidly changing times. And their reaction to the various proposals of the nationalists in 1814 foretold their reaction to the new nationalism of the postwar period.

Students of nationalism have often observed that the phenomenon, particularly in its early stages, was most viable in time of war. As a result, the economic features of nationalism were concerned primarily with promoting national self-sufficiency vis-à-vis potential enemies. This program was quite reminiscent of the ancient theory of mercantilism, and, in fact, a sort of neo-mercantilism emerged in Europe and America in the wake of the Napoleonic wars. A perfected form of the older variety, including tariffs, quota arrangements, and state-connected monopolies, neomercantilism paralleled the development of political and cultural nationalism.[37] The United States entered the War of 1812 in a burst of patriotic fervor and a determination to defend the honor and integrity of the nation. The war in turn provoked a demand for an end to America's colonialistic economic dependence on England. Determined upon national self-sufficiency, the Republican party after 1815 adopted with embellishments of its own the old Hamiltonian system that included a national bank, a protective tariff, and a federally sponsored system of internal improvements. This meant the final abandonment of "the principles of 1798."

The weakness in the Virginia doctrine itself was that, though treated as a theology by its more ardent preachers, it was to a large extent a rationale for economic and sectional interests. In the 1790s the strength of the Republican party had been in the South and in rural regions of Pennsylvania and New York. A tradition of individualism and distrust of strong government led this area to embrace the Virginia theory of states' rights. Primarily agrarian in interest, this region distrusted banks and factories and demanded hard money and free trade. It is hardly surprising, therefore, that when economic interests changed the Virginia doctrine was abandoned by those whom it no longer benefited.

During the period since Jefferson's Administration the mid-Atlantic states matured economically. The embargo and the war fostered the growth of manufactures, and a more sophisticated financial system developed. Likewise in the West a new entrepreneurial class arose with interests that were frequently counter to the Virginia school, and infant industries were appearing and demanding protection from foreign competition. By 1815 this area, that extended from New York to Kentucky, replaced Virginia as the focal point of the Republican party, and its economic demands—for a bank, a tariff, and internal improvements —replaced the old Virginia system. True, a number of the strongest spokesmen for this new nationalism, like John C. Calhoun, came from the South, but most of Calhoun's support came from the North and within a few years his ideas would be counter to the dominant feeling within his own state.

The Old Republican minority that opposed this new nationalism was a reflection in reverse of the majority. Sectionally they represented the planter-dominated South with its eighteenth-century colonial economy. The Southern planter had no need for an elaborate financial system; at best he tolerated the local bank whose policies he could control. Dependent upon Europe for markets for his cotton and tobacco as well as for his supplies, he preferred free trade and considered the protective tariff a special tax levied on him for the benefit of Northern industry. Since he could use the Tidewater rivers of the South to transport his produce to the coast, he had little use for a system of internal improvements, and he felt little desire to tax himself to open new competing lands in the West. Though a minority in Congress, the Southern planter still dominated his state government, and in reaction to the nationalism of Congress he became increasingly dependent upon the defensive mechanism of states' rights. In answer to Calhoun's defense of his bank bill in January, 1816, John Randolph defined the main difference between the two Republican factions:

As the gentleman from South Carolina has presented the question to the House . . . the question is whether or not we are willing to become one great consolidated nation, under one form of law; whether the state governments are to be swept away; or whether we have still respect enough for those old, respectable institutions to regard their integrity and preservation as part of our policy.[38]

The various measures of the new nationalism were passed through Congress by close votes with a large minority in dissent on each issue. But the vote of most members was determined by local economic interest and was not an opposition in principle to the system. Kentucky, for example, would support a tariff and internal improvements and oppose a bank; Maryland might support a bank, but vote against a tariff or internal improvements; New York might be divided on all three issues with the vote of each congressman dependent upon the interest of his district. The actual number of Old Republicans who opposed all three issues, for economic as well as doctrinal reasons, was very small—only ten in all—and, significantly enough, most of them represented the tobacco-growing areas in Virginia and North Carolina which had been the first to criticize Jeffersonian nationalism.

The war bolstered the strength of the nationalists in Congress, and their talented leadership was expanded by the election of John Forsyth of Georgia and Henry St. George Tucker of Virginia. Tucker was a former Quid who was swept up in the fervor of nationalism that accompanied the war. In Congress he represented a district in the lower Shenandoah Valley that had formerly voted Federalist and differed in economic interest from the conservative Tidewater. The revitalized Federalists were able to muster such notables as Daniel Webster, Timothy Pickering, and Thomas Grosvenor of New York; and they received new blood with the election of William Pinkney of Maryland, the latest product of the brilliant Maryland bar.

On the other hand, the war had thinned considerably the ranks of the Old Republicans, and age continued to take its toll. Richard Stanford died in 1816—"the best political friend that I had left on the floor of Congress," wrote Randolph in eulogy.[39]

John Clopton retired the same year, while Macon was elevated to the Senate. These losses were partially offset by the election of Philip Pendleton Barbour and James Johnson of Virginia in 1813. Barbour represented the tobacco-growing area of the central Piedmont, while Johnson replaced Edwin Gray in the Portsmouth district south of the James. Though both men were elected on prowar platforms, they reacted unfavorably to the postwar nationalism. Equally important was the return of John Randolph, who had spent two years mending political fences and defeated Eppes in 1815. But it was still a small and scattered group of conservatives that fought the nationalistic measures of the Republican majority through 1816 and 1817.

The first feature of the new program was a tariff bill, brought on by the demands of American manufacturers for protection against the postwar influx of British goods. In the debate on this measure in the spring of 1816 Randolph assumed the leadership of the conservatives and made the issue the focal point for his opposition to the new nationalism. This was a shrewd choice, for the tariff seemed to be a tax on the nation at large for the benefit of the manufacturing interest. "On whom do your impost duties bear?" he asked the House. "Upon whom bears the duty on coarse woolens and linens and blankets, upon salt, and all the necessaries of life? On poor men, and on slaveholders." [40]

In the debate on the bill Randolph nevertheless received remarkably little support. Many Southerners were still breathing the roseate air of nationalism and the conservatives seemed too overawed by the overwhelming protectionist sentiment in the House to rise in debate. In desperation Randolph made an effort to gain the support of the "*bona fide* American merchants" against the "mushroom" manufacturing interest "which had sprung into favor" and moved to strike out the duty on cotton goods. This maneuver was an attempt to unite the merchants engaged in importing cotton goods with the Southern planters who had to purchase them. The Federalists substituted an amendment merely to reduce the duty on cottons, and when the House voted this down, Randolph withdrew his proposal altogether. After speeches against the bill by Randolph, Telfair of Georgia, and Wright of Maryland, the House on April 8 passed the tariff by a vote of 88–54. In the minority were 34 Southerners, 28 of them Republicans, while 23 Southerners voted for the bill.[41]

The geographical distribution of the vote is significant. Kentucky generally supported the tariff in response to the needs of her infant manufactures and the demands of her hemp industry. The representatives from Tennessee, South Carolina, and Georgia were evenly divided. In those areas the support for the tariff stemmed partly from the desire to stimulate their own manufactures and partly from the need to unify the nation by offering a sop to New England discontent. Significantly, the parts of the South that supported the tariff had been the first to respond to the wartime nationalism. North Carolina cast only one vote in favor of the tariff, and in Virginia the opposition was centered in the South and the West.[42]

The tariff bill breezed through the Senate in four days; no objections to the bill in principle were recorded in the debate. The only consistent opponent of the new nationalism in the Senate was Nathaniel Macon. For years he had opposed the idea of a protective tariff, and he blamed its sudden popularity on the war and the need for revenue. "A war undertaken for sailors rights and free trade," he wrote Judge Nicholson, "will I fear produce a system to tax all classes for the benefit of the manufactories; so that the glorious war will produce an effect not calculated on, by some who voted for the declaration." [43]

The bank bill of 1816 caused even less division among Republicans. A bill to create a second Bank of the United States was drawn up by Calhoun in consultation with Dallas and submitted to the House on January 8. The new bank would be incorporated for twenty years with a capital of $35 million, one-fifth of which would be subscribed by the government. Of the bank's twenty-five directors five would be appointed by the government to represent its share of stock. The main opposition to the bill was conducted by the Federalists, who disliked several features of Calhoun's scheme though they approved the general idea of a bank. The Republican opposition, as in 1811, was composed of those who feared that a federal bank would threaten state banking interests and of the agrarians who were suspicious of all banks. Randolph, who had voted for rechartering the first bank in 1811, actually disliked the state banks more than the projected federal bank. He supported the general principle of a bank on the grounds that it might curb the activities of the state banks, but he objected strenuously to the "monstrous alliance between the bank and the government." He wished to delete the section authorizing the government to purchase stock in the bank and sever all connection between the bank and the government.[44]

In the House debate John Clopton of Virginia was the only member to raise the constitutional question. In his message vetoing the bank bill in 1815 President Madison waived the question of constitutionality, "as being precluded . . . by repeated recognitions, under varied circumstances, of the validity of such an institution, in acts of legislative, executive, and judicial branches of the government, accompanied in different modes by a concurrence of the general will of the nation. . . ."[45] Though this opinion might seem to have settled the issue, Clopton objected to the idea that time and usage made an act of Congress constitutional. Henry Clay used the same argument in 1811: if Congress could legally create a bank merely because it had done so twenty-five years before, then it could constitutionally pass another sedition law. The Constitution, after all, was not common law; it could not be changed by mere precedent. Clopton, however, was alone in opposing the bank on constitutional grounds, and his argument was virtually ignored. "I am at a loss to account for the fact," Nathaniel Macon complained, "that I seem to be the only person of those who were formerly in Con-

gress, that still cannot find the authority for a bank in the constitution of the U.S." [46]

On March 14 the House passed the bank bill 80–71; of the
minority 38 were Federalists and 33 Republicans, only 15 of
them from the South or Southwest. The opposition of the Federalists led by Webster had been factional, rather than on principle, and in the end about 15 of them voted for the bank. Their
wavering and factional conduct, however, at last led Randolph,
who cooperated with them for years, to conclude that they
possessed "neither the courage, the talent, nor the integrity to
conduct an opposition." [47] The Southern opposition was confined largely to Virginia, though Kentucky and Tennessee, evi-
dencing some frontier distrust of banks, were evenly divided.
In Virginia the opposition centered in the tobacco-producing
counties of the middle Tidewater, central Piedmont, and the
Southside, all districts where a relatively unsophisticated, eighteenth-century economy predominated.

In the Senate the Federalists also led the attack on the bank
bill. Their tactics involved several amendments designed to retain
congressional control and to limit the operations of the bank.
Most failed, but one important amendment preventing the bank
from suspending specie payments passed with the aid of the conservatives, Macon, Armistead Thompson Mason of Virginia, and
Gaillard and Taylor of South Carolina. On April 3 the bill
passed the Senate 22–12, eight Federalists and four Republicans
in the minority.[48]

When the bill returned to the House on April 5 for concurrence in the Senate amendments, Randolph, whose opposition in
the early debate had been mild, denounced the bank as unconstitutional in origin, inexpedient in operation, and dangerous in its
connection with the government. He was supported by Benjamin Hardin of Kentucky on the same grounds. Randolph's views
seem to have been hardened by the concurrent debate on the
tariff, for he linked the two together when he predicted in the
debate that if both the bank and the tariff passed "the present

session would be looked back to as the most disastrous since the commencement of the Republic." [49] The conservative is of necessity a prophet, but the young nation was too busy to heed the dire predictions of a Jeremiah. Both the tariff and the bank bill were passed and signed by a President who a few years before had opposed them.

The third important feature of the postwar nationalism was the subject of federally financed internal improvements. The war had furnished dramatic evidence to bolster the long-felt need for better communications between the Atlantic Coast and the Mississippi Valley. Some even felt that the nation would not long hold together unless the federal government provided better transportation facilities. Thus the demand resulted both from economic necessity and the new spirit of national unity. President Madison, in his annual message to Congress in December, 1816, recommended the construction of interstate roads and canals, but conservatively suggested that an amendment to the Constitution authorizing such projects would be necessary. In the House John C. Calhoun responded on December 16 with a motion for the appointment of a select committee on the subject. A week later Calhoun for the committee reported a bill to set aside the bonus of $1.5 million paid by the bank for its charter and all future dividends from bank stock held by the government "as a fund for constructing roads and canals." [50]

The bill was debated off and on through January, 1817, with few objections to it in principle, though several opponents pointed out that if the government was too insolvent to reduce the wartime level of taxation it could not afford a system of internal improvements. A number of conservatives, moreover, objected to control of the proposed system by the federal government. On February 4 Thomas B. Robertson of Louisiana offered an amendment to distribute the proposed fund among the states on the basis of population and let the states determine on what projects the money would be spent. Robertson feared that if the federal government undertook various projects within the states the bill might be unconstitutional. Thomas Telfair supported Robertson's amendment because it "deprived the General Government of a mass of patronage in the appointment of a great many persons to superintend the various works." Telfair, however, thought that Congress ought to designate the projects to be undertaken by the states, particularly those of an interstate nature, while leaving the actual construction to the states. Both proposals were accepted without a division.[51]

Two days later, February 6, Philip Barbour for the first time in the debate voiced objections to the bill on constitutional grounds. After pointing out that the defenders of the bill themselves could not agree as to which section of the Constitution authorized Congress to appropriate money for roads and canals, Barbour proceeded to give a lucid exposition of the appropriate clauses of the Constitution as they were then understood. Calhoun's defense of his bill turned on the clause giving Congress power "to lay and collect taxes . . . to provide for the Common Defense and General Welfare. . . ." In answer Barbour explained that the phrase "general welfare" was intended as a qualification of the taxing power and did not confer additional power on Congress to appropriate money that was not justified by one of the other enumerated powers.[52] Nor were internal improvements authorized under the power "to establish post offices and post roads." The word *establish* in this clause meant to Barbour that Congress could designate as post roads certain already existing roads. If the Constitution intended to confer a power to construct new roads, Barbour argued, it would have said so.

Finally, Barbour took up the clause which today authorizes the construction of national highways, but which at that time was seldom invoked by the federal government—the power to regulate interstate commerce. "To regulate" meant to Barbour, as it did to most people before John Marshall's broad interpretation of it, the power "to prescribe the manner, terms, and conditions, on which that commerce should be carried on"; it did not confer a right to subsidize or aid commerce by the construction of roads and canals. Unable to find any authority for the bill, Barbour was forced to conclude that it was unconstitutional.[53]

The following day Robert Wright of Maryland also expressed objections to the bill on constitutional grounds, but he also admitted an economic motive—he disliked the idea that the older Eastern states, who had already built roads at their own expense, were being taxed for roads to be built in the West. On February 8 Randolph delivered a three-hour speech against the bill, none of which was reported, and then the House passed the bill by the narrow margin of 86–84.[54] As in the previous divisions on the bank and the tariff, most of the votes were determined by economic and sectional interest. The Northeast, except for New York and Pennsylvania, was generally opposed; the South was evenly divided; the West was generally in favor.

Even in Virginia, which divided fourteen to eight against the bill, the vote was partly sectional. Four of the eight votes in favor were cast by Federalists from the Valley and the West. Yet Virginia's opposition was not based exclusively on economic grounds; she stood to gain as much as New York or Pennsylvania by a link with the Ohio Valley financed with federal funds, and she was far less able to finance a program of her own.[55] It seems probable that doubt of the bill's constitutionality was at least a secondary consideration in the minds of most of the Virginia delegation.

North Carolina divided evenly, the East against and the West in favor of the bill. South Carolina and Georgia, continuing their nationalistic trend, generally supported the bill. More difficult to explain is the behavior of Kentucky and Tennessee, which together supplied only three votes for the bill. It may be significant that the six votes against the bill in Kentucky all came from districts bordering the Ohio River, and the three districts in Tennessee that opposed the bill flanked the Tennessee River.[56] But, as in Virginia, lingering constitutional scruples cannot be ignored. Both Kentucky and Tennessee shared to some extent in the conservative reaction that swept Virginia in 1817.

When the bonus bill reached the Senate floor on February 26, David Daggett, a Connecticut Federalist, moved that it be postponed until March 4, which would have killed it for that session. Nathaniel Macon supported the motion. Macon disliked this "new plan of legislating" by general authorization. Heretofore, he reminded the Senate, appropriations for internal improvements had been made for specific projects, like the Cumberland Road. No estimate was made of the ultimate cost of this program; Congress had no idea even where the new roads and canals would be placed. Too much, it seemed to Macon, was being left to Executive discretion in this plan to set aside the bonus received from the bank. Macon also had some doubts as to the constitutionality of the bill. He recognized that for years Congress had been making appropriations for the Cumberland Road, but that specific project, he felt, did not justify the undertaking of a broad program of internal improvements. The argument of constitutionality based on precedent was a dangerous one, for by it any unconstitutional act could become a precedent for others.[57]

Despite support for the move by conservatives and Federalists, the motion for postponement was defeated, and two days later, February 28, the Senate passed the bill 20–15. Voting for it were 15 Republicans and 5 Federalists; voting against were 6 Federalists and 9 Republicans, including George W. Campbell and John Williams of Tennessee, John Gaillard and William Smith of South Carolina, Troup of Georgia, and Macon.[58] Of this group only Macon and Gaillard can be considered Old Republicans. The opposition of Campbell and Williams of Tennessee is puzzling. Campbell was a former War Hawk and Secretary of the Treasury. Williams had just entered the Senate, and in the 1820s he was to become a nationalist and the leading political opponent of Andrew Jackson in Tennessee. The fact that their stand paralleled the opposition of the Tennessee delegation in the House suggests that Tennessee still looked to its river system for the transportation of its cotton and saw little benefit to be derived from expensive roads. William Smith, on the other hand, was a new conservative whose election to the Senate in 1816 indicates the beginning of a shift in political opinion in that state. In the early 1820s he was to become one of the leaders of the states' rights movement in South Carolina.

On March 2 Calhoun and a group of Republicans called at the Executive mansion to present their official farewells to the retiring President. As the group was leaving, Madison called Calhoun aside and broke the news: he was vetoing the bonus bill. Madison's views expressed in the veto message followed closely the arguments of Philip Barbour. No section of the Constitution specifically authorized the construction of roads and canals by the federal government. To justify it by the "general welfare" clause, Madison argued "would have the effect of giving to Congress a general power of legislation. . . ." That clause did not give Congress an unrestricted power to appropriate money; it was merely a qualification of the taxing power. The power to appropriate was nothing more than "the ordinary and necessary means" for carrying out a specifically delegated power, and the construction of roads and canals was not one of these. Nor was the difficulty circumvented by obtaining the consent of the states involved; the consent of a state could not endow Congress with powers that were not listed in the Constitution. "Not unaware of the great importance of roads and canals, and the improved navigation of the water-courses . . . ," Madison believed, however,

that such a power is not expressly given by the Constitution; and believing that it cannot be deduced from any part of it without an inadmissable latitude of construction, and a reliance on insufficient precedents; believing also that the permanent success of the Constitution depends on a definite partition of powers between the General and State governments, and that no adequate landmarks would be left by the constructive extension of the powers of Congress as proposed in the bill, I have no option but to withhold my signature from it, and to cherish the hope that its beneficial objects may be attained by a resort for the necessary powers to the same wisdom and virtue in the nation which established the Constitution in its actual form, and providently marked out in the instrument itself a safe and practicable mode of improving it as experience might suggest.

The veto was hailed by Old Republicans like Thomas Ritchie, who thought Madison deserved "the thanks of every Republican, who will calmly set down to review the incontrovertible doctrines of '98 and '99." [59] But the veto took Washington completely by surprise. For two years Madison had been urging Congress to exercise its "existing powers" over internal improvements, and now it turned out that Congress had none after all. "No circumstance," said the exasperated Henry Clay later,

not even an earthquake that should have swallowed up half this city, could have excited more surprise than when it was first communicated to the House that Mr. Madison had rejected his own bill—I say his own bill—for his message at the opening of the session meant nothing if it did not mean such an exercise of power as was contemplated in that bill.[60]

The surprise was the more complete since the President and his cabinet officers had cooperated actively with the nationalists in Congress on the other features of their program. "After swallowing the national Bank and the Cumberland Road &c," wrote DeWitt Clinton who had hoped for federal aid on the Erie Canal, "it was not to be supposed that Mr. Madison would strain at canals. . . ." [61]

Yet in Madison's mind a line had to be drawn somewhere, lest the concept of implied powers completely subvert the spirit and intent of the Constitution. As a member of the Federal Convention and author of the Virginia Plan, Madison had played a central role in the establishment of the Constitution; no one was more qualified to interpret its provisions. Far from being doctrinaire, he had demonstrated considerable elasticity in the course of his long political career. The Cumberland Road, begun by the

Federalists in 1796, he had supported as a single appropriation for an isolated project. Even the bank he could justify by 1816 on the grounds of precedent and public acquiescence. But, instead of regarding these actions as an excuse for a further extension of congressional powers, he felt it was time to call a halt. The Constitution, he had warned the nation in authoring the Virginia Resolution of 1798, was the limit of his nationalism. It had precisely enumerated the powers given the central government; so far would he go, and no further.

It is generally assumed that the group of Old Republicans evident in Congress after the war appeared as a reaction to the measures of the young Republican nationalists—the bank, the tariff, and internal improvements.[62] This is only partially true, however. Though each of the three was passed by a narrow margin, the vote in each case was determined almost completely by local interests. There was almost no objection to any of the three in principle. Only ten Republicans voted against all three, and of these only six had been in Congress before the war.[63]

It is true, however, that this represents only the hard core of Old Republican sentiment. It does not include, for instance, Philip Barbour, who voted for the tariff, or Hugh Nelson, who supported the bank and abstained on the vote on it. Perhaps absolute consistency is too rigid a criterion, particularly since the administration had backed the bank and the tariff and had hinted at the advisability of internal improvements. Of the Republicans who voted against two of the three major issues and supported the idea of tax reduction there were twenty-five—perhaps a better indication of conservative opinion in the House. Even this, though, is a small minority. The major Southern reaction to the postwar nationalism appeared, not in Congress, but at home. It began in Virginia and North Carolina in 1817 and over the next decade spread gradually through the rest of the South.

····❧❀❧ VII ❧❀❧····

"This Era of Good Feelings and Bad Principles"[1]

The first years of President Monroe's Administration, frequently described as the "Era of Good Feelings," are a landmark in the history of the Old Republican movement. Heretofore the conservative Republicans in Congress were a small and uninfluential minority whose only brush strokes on the landscape of American History had been the prewar jeremiads of John Randolph and an ineffectual opposition to the postwar nationalism. But the neomercantilism of the postwar nationalism and the implications of the Missouri controversy forced upon Southerners a deepening realization of the broad threat to their institutions. It became increasingly evident that a society dominated by gentlemen and a colonial economy could not long survive in a majoritarian democracy that had the power of the national government at its disposal. A growing consciousness of its minority status led the South to embrace once again the doctrines of states' rights and strict construction as the most convenient tools for the defense of its institutions. Led by the Old Republicans the upper South experienced a conservative reaction during the first administration of James Monroe, and in the 1820s it passed on the banner of states' rights to a new generation of Southern sectionalists.

The conjunction of the economic depression and the Missouri

debate in 1819–20 marked the climax of the Old Republican movement. As an aftermath of the Panic of 1819 the criticism of the Second Bank of the United States and the demands for retrenchment and tax reduction reached a crescendo, and in the Missouri controversy the Old Republicans spearheaded the defense of slavery and states' rights. Ironically, these events also sounded the death knell for the Old Republicans, for after 1820 the South began to develop a self-conscious sectionalism.

The distinction between Old Republicans and Southern sectionalists may seem arbitrary, but it has to be made. Prior to 1820 the South was not a unified, self-conscious minority. It was quite diversified, geographically, economically, and socially; since 1800 at least it had been the dominant region and the heart of the union. After 1820 the Missouri controversy, the agricultural depression, and the success of the nationalists in obtaining a protective tariff and internal improvements provoked the first realization of its minority status and provided the emotional impulse needed to unite Southerners into a self-conscious sectionalism. The Old Republicans, as a dissenting faction within a ruling party, were concerned with issues of national scope, whereas Southerners of the later period were concerned with the minority rights of the South and a defense of her institutions in an age of majoritarian democracy.

The Old Republican movement did not die out in the 1820s. Instead it was swallowed up. Its doctrines and slogans were adopted by the new Southern sectionalists for local purposes—to attack the tariff in South Carolina, the Indians in Georgia, and the bank in Kentucky. Its membership was absorbed into the broad-based political movement in behalf of the presidential candidacy of William Harris Crawford. Not surprisingly, the allies of the Old Republicans in the Crawford campaign of 1824 were Northern Liberals led by Martin Van Buren. *Laissez faire* was the new slogan of the 1820s, and it appealed to Southern agrarians and Northern businessmen alike. After the election of 1824 this coalition moved into the presidential camp of Andrew

Jackson, whose pronouncements and political affiliations were vague enough to appeal to all. The ultimate irony is that the election of Jackson in 1828 did not bring the final triumph of Southern conservatism. Rather it marked the birth of a new age, an age of democracy and commercial liberalism.

At the core of this conservative reaction that began in 1817 was a change in the political sentiment of Virginia, which since the 1790s had been the oracle of Republican doctrine. There had been little opposition among Virginia politicians and editors to the acts of 1816 that set up a second Bank of the United States and a protective tariff; the reaction began to appear only with the internal improvements debate of early 1817. The matter is easily explained: To some extent Virginia shared in the postwar feeling of nationalism and with one of her own sons in the Executive chair she felt secure in the apparent supremacy of Virginia principles. Equally important, the Republican minority in Congress made little effort to carry the issues of the bank and the tariff to the people, and the leader of the minority, John Randolph, was still under a cloud in Virginia for his opposition to the war.

The internal improvements issue of 1817, on the other hand, bore the threat of taxing Easterners to pay for roads and canals that would open the new fertile lands of the West. So clearly contrary to the economic interests of Virginia planters was it that it awakened Virginians to the potential danger of the postwar nationalism. Editors such as Ritchie of the *Enquirer*, William F. Gray of the Fredericksburg *Virginia Herald*, and James O'Connor of the *Norfolk and Portsmouth Herald* attacked the concept of a federal scheme of roads and canals and claimed that they had always been opposed to the other elements of the new nationalism, the bank and the tariff.[2]

Economic factors were at the heart of the conservative reaction in Virginia. After a brief flurry of wartime prosperity, Virginia agriculture succumbed to a chronic state of depression.

Tobacco culture moved into the Piedmont as the Tidewater area shifted largely to wheat. But even wheat proved no panacea, as John Taylor had hoped; in 1817 one-third of the wheat crop in Virginia was destroyed by the Hessian fly. Moreover, the price of both wheat and tobacco skidded under the pressure of competition from the West after the war. Virginia planters began to reap the harvest of centuries of poor soil practices as the familiar story of overproduction, low prices, declining yields, and heavy debts reappeared by 1817.[3]

One result was a mass migration from Virginia to the new lands of the Southwest. Those who remained tended to blame their ills on the actions of the federal government and developed a narrow agrarian particularism, a phenomenon that would reappear a decade later in South Carolina and Georgia. The whole issue was brought into bold relief by the Western demand for internal improvements, which threatened to reduce further the marginal utility of lands in eastern Virginia.

Though economics was usually at the root of Virginia political philosophy, superficial political developments frequently had a more immediate impact. Contributing to the reaction of 1817, for instance, was a conflict with the Supreme Court which brought home to Virginians the many implications of the new nationalism.[4] In the *Fairfax* land grant case, which involved the seizure of Tory lands by the state during the Revolution, the Virginia Supreme Court of Appeals led by Spencer Roane in 1814 denied the power of the Supreme Court of the United States to accept jurisdiction of a case on appeal from a state court.[5] In 1816, in *Martin v. Hunter's Lessee* involving this issue alone, Justice Joseph Story handed down an opinion that affirmed on broad grounds the appellate jurisdiction of the federal Supreme Court over all cases that arose under the Constitution, treaties, or laws of the United States, whether the court in which they originated was state or federal. Reaffirming the supremacy of the national government, this decision in effect reduced the state courts to inferior tribunals, a reminder to Virginians of the broad threat to their cherished state sovereignty.

By 1817, moreover, the moderate influence of Jefferson and Madison was gone, and President Monroe had never been on close terms with the political leaders of Virginia, who distrusted him for his association with the Quids in 1808 and for his moderate nationalism after 1811. At first both the Virginia assembly and the editor of the *Enquirer* were indifferent to the candidacy of Monroe in 1816. A caucus of the Virginia assembly nominated electors without expressing a choice for the presidency. Not until the congressional caucus nominated Monroe in February, 1816, did Ritchie have much to say in his favor.[6]

With less influence coming from Washington after 1817 the Virginia Republican party fell into the hands of agrarian particularists, who pushed the doctrine of states' rights into a prominence it had not known since 1798. At the heart of this leadership was the Richmond Junto, a small group—at most twenty—of political leaders drawn mainly from the eastern half of the state. The Junto had guided the Virginia party since 1800, but until 1817 it had submitted to national direction. During Monroe's Administration it reverted to a rigid strict constructionism and pursued a course quite independent of the national leadership. It became, in fact, the focal point of the conservative reaction in Virginia and the guiding hand of the Old Republicans in Congress.[7]

The most important member of the Junto was Spencer Roane, who served on the Virginia Supreme Court of Appeals from 1794 until his death in 1822. A son-in-law and protégé of Patrick Henry, Roane devoted his life to a jealous guardianship of the sovereignty of the Commonwealth. His revival of this doctrine after his conflict with Marshall and Story in the *Fairfax* case made him the outstanding figure in Virginia politics from 1817 to 1822. Another important member of the Junto was Thomas Ritchie, cousin of Spencer Roane and editor of the influential party organ, the Richmond *Enquirer*. Though never a strong nationalist Ritchie gave wholehearted support to the war and demanded a strong army and navy after the peace settlement. He raised only a feeble protest against the bank and tariff in 1816, but by 1817 his editorials were reflecting the ideas of Roane and John Taylor of Caroline.[8]

Other prominent members of the Junto were Dr. John Brockenbrough, president of the Bank of Virginia, cousin to both Ritchie and Roane, and a long-time friend and correspondent of John Randolph; Andrew Stevenson, brother-in-law of Dr. Brockenbrough and leader of the House of Delegates since 1812; the brothers Wilson Cary and Philip Norborne Nicholas; William Wirt, Monroe's Attorney General, and George Hay, Monroe's son-in-law; and James and Philip Pendleton Barbour.[9] The close family as well as political ties between the leaders in Richmond and the Old Republicans in Congress are at once evident.

The elections of 1816–17 could almost be described as a political revolution, for they unseated nearly two-thirds of the House of Representatives, providing 126 new faces in a House of 185. The occasion for the dissatisfaction of the people with their elected representatives was the compensation law of 1816 whereby Congress had undertaken to raise its own salary. Though the Republican conservatives had been divided in their reaction to the law and even that symbol of purity in politics John Randolph had supported it, the conservatives gained most by the turnover. It was natural that a man who based his election campaign on opposition to the compensation law, with its implications of influence and corruption, would frequently vote with those who were suspicious of all government.[10] Among the Virginia delegation, however, the change was due more to a growing conservatism that paralleled the evolution of popular sentiment in the state, rather than to a change in membership.

The Virginians in the House suffered least in the election of 1817. Most of the members were re-elected, and conservatives, such as Philip Barbour, James Johnson, Peterson Goodwyn,

William A. Burwell, and Hugh Nelson, were re-elected without opposition. The most important change was in the Botetourt-Abingdon district of the Southwest where the conservative John Floyd replaced the Federalist James Breckinridge, who declined to run for re-election. As a member of the General Assembly Floyd was an outspoken supporter of the war, but he reacted against the postwar nationalism and entered Congress in 1817 a sound conservative.[11] In the Fredericksburg district the conservative Robert Seldon Garnett, son of the Quid James M. Garnett, was elected without opposition to replace William Roane, the son of Spencer Roane.

In the central Piedmont George F. Strother, a probank and anti-internal improvements Republican, replaced the nationalist Aylett Hawes. John Randolph declined to run for re-election for reasons of health, but his constituents in the Roanoke Valley elected the equally conservative, if less talented, Archibald Austin. In the upper Shenandoah Valley the "Anythingarian" Daniel Sheffey declined to run for re-election and was replaced by the ultraconservative General Alexander Smyth, the commander of the regular troops at Fort Niagara, during the war, who had refused to aid in a militia attack on Queenstown in October, 1812, because a militia action was no concern of his.[12]

Among others re-elected in 1817 were two important conservatives who had been sent to Congress in special elections the year before—William Lee Ball, who had replaced Major John P. Hungerford of the Northern Neck, and John Tyler, who had been elected in December, 1816, to the seat of John Clopton of Richmond. Tyler's conservatism was evident from his first appearance in the Virginia House of Delegates where in 1812 he led a move to censure Senators Giles and Brent for voting in favor of rechartering the Bank of the United States. Though not, so far as is known, a member of the Richmond Junto, he remained popular with his conservative Richmond constituency, which had returned John Clopton to the House for sixteen years.

The Virginia delegation of twenty-three in the House of

Representatives contained nine new faces, but the main change was in conservative leadership: John Tyler, John Floyd, and Alexander Smyth were important additions to the Old Republican faction in the House and joined Philip Barbour in assuming leadership of the group, which until then had been borne almost singlehandedly by John Randolph.

Even with these changes, however, the Old Republicans would not have had a majority of the Virginia delegation but for the growing conservatism among other Virginians in the House—partly a result of the revolution in political sentiment in the state and partly, perhaps, a matter of age. The most striking change was in James Pleasants, who had been elected in 1811 as a nationalist and who had supported large appropriations for the army and navy, internal taxes, the Second Bank, and the tariff of 1816. His conversion began with an opposition to the bonus bill in 1817, and until he resigned in 1822 to become governor of Virginia he voted consistently with the Old Republicans, opposing even the bank and the tariff. William McCoy, another War Hawk elected in 1811, also supported the bank and the tariff in 1816, but thereafter he followed the Old Republican leadership on every issue except the bank. The new spirit among Virginians was best expressed by Hugh Nelson, who wrote to a friend in Charlottesville at the beginning of the Fifteenth Congress: "I shall be much more on the alert this session, if I have my health, than I have ever been. . . . I will do all I can to support the old republican doctrine in the construction of the Constitution." [13]

North Carolina also experienced a political reaction in 1817, and, as in Virginia, it had roots in her economic geography. Virtually isolated from the rest of the nation by a dangerous seacoast and poor roads, North Carolina was cursed by a poor soil which through most of the state yielded a bare subsistence. A people who lived largely from one harvest to the next felt they could ill afford the taxes necessary for governmental services such as roads and schools, and they had little interest in affairs outside the state. These conditions fostered an endemic provincialism that was interrupted briefly by a wave of nationalism generated by the war and the wartime prosperity. But by 1817 soil exhaustion, worn-out lands, and falling prices of tobacco and wheat combined to produce a severe agricultural depression. As in Virginia, the usual reaction was to emigrate to the Southwest. One resident of the North Carolina Piedmont noted the "anxiety and confusion that pervades all ranks of people in this section of country to remove" to Alabama, and he feared that the state was losing "many of its enterprising and respectable inhabitants." [14] Among these, incidentally, was the prominent War Hawk Israel Pickens, who almost singlehandedly had given a nationalist complexion to the North Carolina contingent in Congress. Those who remained lapsed into the political particularism that had first attracted North Carolinians to Jeffersonian Democracy.

The election of 1817 in North Carolina produced nine new members in a delegation of thirteen. Old Federalists like William Gaston and John Culpeper declined to run for re-election, as did a number of nationalists like Israel Pickens, who had been elected as a War Hawk in 1811. Though two new Federalists were elected in 1817, the new Republicans tended to follow the Virginia leadership on most questions.[15] Re-elected were Lewis Williams, Daniel Forney, and Joseph Hunter Bryan, all of whom deviated from the Old Republican pattern only on the bank issue.

The election in South Carolina resulted in five new members in the South Carolina contingent of nine, but the only conservative gain was the addition of Starling Tucker to a delegation that previously had been solidly nationalist. Tucker was a militia general who distinguished himself in erecting defenses around Charleston during the war. His success in the election was due apparently to his military reputation and his opposition to the compensation law.[16] Though his political ideas were somewhat vague at the time, his election may be an early indication of the

conservative reaction in South Carolina that was to culminate in
the nullification movement a decade later. Tucker, in a congressional career that lasted until 1831, remained a consistent advocate of states' rights. In the earlier period before his state adopted
his views, he was content to follow Virginia leadership on all
issues except the bank.[17]

Four out of six members of the House from Georgia were
new in the Fifteenth Congress. The only change in the nationalist complexion of the Georgia group had been made in January,
1817, when Zadock Cook was sent to the House in a by-election.
In the spring of 1817 he had opposed Calhoun's bonus bill, and
in the succeeding years he voted consistently with the Virginia
Old Republicans.

Kentucky witnessed the greatest popular furor over the com-
pensation law, and only the popular Henry Clay, Richard M.
Johnson, and Joseph Desha were returned to the House in 1817.
The conservative Ben Hardin, opponent of Clay and friend of
Randolph, declined to run; the rest were defeated.[18] In general,
however, the War Hawks of 1811 were replaced by new nationalists, the only exceptions being Anthony New and Thomas
Speed, both of whom tended to follow the Virginia conservatives. New was a former Virginian, who had represented the Old
Dominion in the House from 1793 to 1805 and had previously
represented Kentucky in the Twelfth Congress where his war
fervor had been tempered by a distrust of the navy. The most
significant change in the Kentucky delegation was the growing
conservatism of Joseph Desha, an old Jeffersonian who had sat
in the House since 1807. A War Hawk who had occasionally
lapsed into conservatism, Desha consistently opposed the navy
during the war and supported a drastic reduction of the army in
1815. After the war he voted against the bank and the bonus bill
and followed the Old Republican pattern on every issue but the
tariff. After retiring from Congress in 1819 he served from 1824
to 1828 as an antibank, hard-money governor of Kentucky and
helped carry Kentucky into the Jackson party.

The complexion of the Tennessee delegation was complicated by the factional nature of Tennessee politics. Since 1800 the Republican party in the state had been dominated by the political machine of William Blount. The faction included most of the state's prominent men bound together by a common desire to protect their land speculation schemes. Blount's half-brother, Willie G. Blount, served as governor from 1809 to 1815 and from 1815 to 1819 was an important conservative in the House of Representatives. After the war the real leader of the faction was Judge John Overton, lawyer, planter, and land speculator from Nashville, and Overton's friend, Andrew Jackson, was its most important member.[19] In Congress the Overton faction was represented by John Rhea, an old Jeffersonian who had served in the House from 1803 to 1815. Though a nationalist who had supported the war during his first tour in Congress, Rhea grew more conservative after his return to the House in 1817, and his adherence to the Old Republicans thereafter was symptomatic of a nascent states' rights reaction in Tennessee.

The enemies of the Overton-Jackson faction were Senator John Williams of Knoxville, Newton Cannon of Middle Tennessee, and John Cocke of East Tennessee. This faction was held together by personal friendship and a common hatred of Jackson. In the elections of 1819 they finally managed several victories over the Overton faction and sent John Cocke, Newton Cannon, and Henry Hunter Bryan to the House of Representatives. All three were conservatives who enhanced the Old Republican complexion of the Tennessee delegation. Cannon had served in Congress in 1816 where he voted for the bank and the tariff, but he returned to Washington in 1819 with a decided proclivity for states' rights and fought banks, tariffs, and internal improvements through the 1820s.

The factions in Tennessee were largely a matter of personalities; neither had a monopoly on agrarian conservatism. In principle their differences centered largely on their attitudes toward banks. The Overton faction tended to be connected with various state banks in Tennessee, while their opponents supported the Bank of the United States or opposed all banks.[20] The Panic of 1819 strengthened the hand of the conservatives in the anti-Overton faction and helps to account for their election victories. Henry Hunter Bryan, for instance, was an old agrarian who campaigned in 1819 on the principle that "banking in all its forms, under every disguise, is a rank fraud upon the laboring and industrious part of society; it is in truth a schem[e], whereby in a silent and secret manner, to make idleness productive and filch from industry, the hard produce of its earnings." [21] Thus in Tennessee the conservative reaction beginning in 1817 and spurred on by the depression of 1819 cut across factional lines, but never strayed far from personalities or, in the end, presidential politics.

The beginning of Monroe's Administration also witnessed the formation of a small Old Republican faction in the Senate. In 1816 Nathaniel Macon was sent to the Senate by the legislature of North Carolina, and he was joined later in the year by William Smith of South Carolina. Described by one historian as "a persistent defender of states' rights and slavery and as persistent an opponent of banks, capitalism, internal improvements, and the tariff," Smith in a senatorial career that lasted until 1823 voted with the Old Republicans on every issue. In the early 1820s he founded an anti-Calhoun, states' rights political organization in South Carolina that backed Crawford in the election of 1824.[22] The senior senator from South Carolina, John Gaillard, was another addition to the Old Republican nucleus in the Senate. A member of the Senate since 1804, Gaillard had given loyal support to the Jefferson and Madison administrations, but his increasing opposition to the nationalistic program of Northern and Western Republicans beginning with the internal improvements debate in 1817 testifies to the growing conservatism of age and to the shifting political sentiment of South Carolina.

The remarkable aspect of the Old Republican faction by 1817 is its youth. True, the most prominent leaders in Congress like

Macon, Randolph, William A. Burwell, and Philip Barbour, as well as the members of the all-powerful Richmond Junto, had long held positions of power and influence, but at least half of the Old Republicans in Congress were relatively young conservatives who were pushed into political prominence by postwar developments. Stimulated by a depression in its staple crops, tobacco and wheat, the upper South underwent a conservative reaction, which was intensified and expanded into the lower South by the nationwide depression of 1819 and the Missouri controversy, so that by the mid-1820s the South generally had adopted the banner of states' rights in defense of cotton and slavery. And it will become evident in the course of this study that, as Southern conservatism became less a matter of the Virginia conscience and more a matter of economics, it underwent a gradual, yet perceptible, change.

The process of concentrating on a particular political faction and its ideas unfortunately results in some distortion, for several of the most important political issues after 1817 involved the Old Republicans only superficially. Such, for instance, was the question of diplomatic recognition of the new South American republics. Though one of the most divisive issues of the time, it may be treated briefly here because it did not specifically involve the Old Republicans or their philosophy. It stemmed more from the political ambitions of Henry Clay and his search for a popular issue on which he could oppose the Monroe Administration. The struggle for freedom in South America received wide sympathy in the United States, and Clay sought to capitalize on this popular feeling because neither President Monroe nor his Secretary of State, John Quincy Adams, considered the South American republics stable enough to warrant diplomatic recognition. The issue was joined in the spring of 1818 when Clay tried to tack onto an appropriation bill an amendment providing $18,000 for a minister to Buenos Aires, should the President see fit to appoint one. Most of the debate was among the nationalist Republicans—Clay, Richard M. Johnson, and Tucker on one side and Lowndes, Samuel Smith, and John Forsyth on the other.

When the Old Republicans joined the fray, they tended to side with the administration. Alexander Smyth denounced the amendment as an invasion of the Executive authority and as likely to involve the United States in war with Spain. Monroe's friend, Hugh Nelson, made the same arguments. Lacking any interest in furthering the political career of Clay, the conservatives tried to consider the issue on its merits.[23] On March 30, 1818, Clay's amendment to appropriate money for a ministry in Buenos Aires was voted down, but the vote reflected the sentiment of the House on the propriety of initiating such a move in Congress, rather than its views on recognition in general. Both nationalists and conservatives were divided.[24]

Another important issue that can be dismissed with brief notice was the debate concerning the legality of Jackson's Seminole campaign—similar to the South American question in that it was more a matter of personal politics than a clash of principle between factions of the Republican party. In the summer of 1818 General Andrew Jackson, while conducting a campaign against the Seminole Indians in southern Alabama, pursued the Indians across the border into Florida, captured the Spanish forts of St. Marks and Pensacola, and tried and hanged two British citizens, Alexander Arbuthnot and Robert Ambrister, for collusion with the Indians. The issue immediately before Congress was whether Jackson ought to be censured for a supposedly unauthorized invasion of Spanish territory and the assumption of jurisdiction over two aliens in foreign territory.

The debate revealed no clear division in the House along sectional or ideological lines. The anti-Jackson forces were led by Henry Clay and Thomas W. Cobb of Georgia, while Richard M. Johnson and John Holmes of Massachusetts conducted the defense. The Old Republicans were almost equally divided. James Johnson and John Tyler joined the attack on Jackson, while Alexander Smyth, Hugh Nelson, and Philip Barbour augmented the defense. On February 1 John Tyler argued at length that Jackson's actions had been illegal and unwarranted. Tyler's biographer attributed his criticism of Jackson to "patriotism and loyalty to principle." [25] Yet only a year before Tyler was certain that the United States had power under the Treaty of 1795 to pursue hostile Indians into Florida, and he thought this might even be used as a pretext for the conquest of Florida.[26] It seems probable that Tyler's *volte-face* was due as much to a personal distaste for Jackson's precipitate methods as to any devotion to principle. Philip Barbour was equally patriotic and principled, yet he delivered a defense of Jackson that even Jefferson considered conclusive.[27]

As the debate droned on, it became increasingly evident that the issue had become a "football" for personal factions. John Quincy Adams considered Jackson already a potential candidate for the election of 1824, and he felt that the attack on Jackson in Congress was engineered by the partisans of Crawford with the help of Clay.[28] Adams' opinion is borne out by the fact that Thomas W. Cobb and Lewis Williams, the leading Crawford men in the House, were prominent in the anti-Jackson forces. The Secretary of the Treasury himself had supported in the Cabinet the idea of repudiating Jackson. Though he took no public stand on the matter, he confided his feelings to a friend, Governor Holmes of the Mississippi Territory: "Persons so regardless of our laws as those engaged in the expedition against Pensacola deserve their severest penalties, and you may rely upon my exertions to bring them to punishment." [29]

It is quite true that the Seminole debate spurred the development of splinter groups within the Republican party, which characterized the administration of Monroe, but it should not be assumed that all those who condemned Jackson were already part of a nascent Crawford faction. The adverse reaction among many Old Republicans to Jackson's precipitate action was almost instantaneous, and it was based, even in private letters, on constitutional grounds. As early as July 28, 1818, Ritchie was condemning Jackson in the *Enquirer* on the ground that "the exercise of such powers by a *military* agent of the *executive* department" endangered the Constitution. Ritchie's reaction was due to his distrust of military power and his dislike of Jackson's peremptory methods, which Ritchie compared to Jackson's actions as commander of New Orleans. Nathaniel Macon, never connected with any personal faction, condemned Jackson on the grounds that "The Constitution gives Congress the sole authority to declare war; war has been waged and every act of sovereign power exercised without the consent of Congress—the Constitution has been violated, and I am for the Constitution rather than for war." [30] William Lee Ball of Virginia publicly denied that he was an enemy of Jackson. "My feelings were much in favor of the man," he told his constituents, "who, at New Orleans and elsewhere, had rendered such important service . . . [to] his country." Yet he had voted for the resolution of censure because he felt Jackson's actions amounted to a declaration of war without the consent of Congress. [31]

William Wyatt Bibb, governor of the Alabama Territory, hence a man with a direct interest in the Seminole threat, felt in September, 1818, that "Not a moment should have been lost in arresting the Genl. and thereby showing a just regard to the preservation of our Constitution. No man should be permitted in a free country to usurp the whole powers of the whole government and to thwart with contempt all authority except that of his own will." [32] Bibb, it will be recalled, was a former congressman from Georgia who had supported the Quids in 1808.

Only in Tennessee was the reaction to the Seminole campaign determined exclusively by personalities. The anti-Overton faction was uniformly opposed to Jackson's action, while John Rhea and the Overton men in Congress supported the general. The incident also affected the attitudes of the Tennessee factions toward the administration. Because of the supposed support given Jackson by Monroe, Adams, and Calhoun, the Overton faction thereafter supported the administration and tended to favor the presidential ambitions of Adams and Calhoun. This pushed the anti-Overton faction into the Crawford camp.[33] Hence the conservative stance of Cannon, Cocke, and Bryan in Congress after 1819 represented perhaps as much a personal regard for Crawford as a states' rights reaction in Tennessee.

Similar in their implications of factional politics but of more direct connection with the Old Republicans were the related questions of tax reduction and the standing army. The high level of wartime taxation caused some misgivings among conservatives, but the condition of the treasury prevented any reduction for several years after the war. In February, 1817, the issue was reopened when Lewis Williams offered a resolution to repeal all the internal taxes.[34] Brother of Senator John Williams of Tennessee, Lewis Williams entered the House in 1815 a pro-bank, antitariff Southern conservative. Though he eventually became one of the mainstays of the Whig party in the South in a congressional career that lasted until 1842, his early years in the House were devoted largely to efforts to reduce taxes and the size of the army.

The resolution to abolish the excises aroused immediate support from the Old Republicans. First to rise was James Johnson of Isle of Wight County, Virginia, who succeeded to the seat of Edwin Gray in 1813. His career in the House, which lasted until 1820, was marked by an absolutely consistent adherence to the "principles of '98." Apparently his demeanor as well as his politics was similar to that of John Randolph, for Monroe considered him "an honest but weak and harsh-tempered man, apt to bluster for the sake of showing his independence." [35] Johnson reminded the House that the treasury had announced a surplus of $15 million at the end of 1816. Since no great increase in expenditures was anticipated, this surplus might be expected annually and the national debt retired in a few years. Why not, Johnson suggested, stretch out the retirement of the debt and lighten the burden on the people by repealing the internal taxes.[36]

Newton Cannon of Tennessee, who had entered the House in 1813 as a "war Republican" in place of Felix Grundy, suggested that the army be reduced along with the internal taxes. This idea was elaborated by Lewis Williams, who followed Cannon on the floor. Williams felt that a reduction in taxes might induce a movement toward economy in the government, and the best place for economy was in the standing army, which Williams wished to see reduced from 10,000 to 6,000 men. Though a comparatively new addition to the conservative ranks, Williams was careful to rest his arguments on familiar Old Republican grounds, reminding the House that reducing taxes and the army were "principles which certainly at one time were deemed orthodox, and upon which the Republicans secured the confidence and support of the people of these United States." [37] John Randolph soon joined the attack and declared himself in favor of abolishing anything that could be abolished. The debate continued for three more days while opponents tried repeatedly to have the subject postponed to the following session. Finally, on February 21, 1817, a motion to postpone the resolution to March 2, a Sunday, passed 82–73.[38] Reluctant to vote against tax reduction, yet unwilling to hamstring the treasury, the House resorted to the familiar expedient of postponing a measure until it was too late to bring in a bill.

The subject, however, was not dead, and it received a new impetus the following December when President Monroe, in his first annual message to Congress, recommended the abolition of the internal taxes. A bill to accomplish this was drawn up by the Ways and Means committee and presented to the House on December 10, 1817. Although the fiscal report of the Secretary of the Treasury William H. Crawford predicted a surplus of $3 million even without the excises and there was little chance of any opposition in the House, the conservatives could not resist the opportunity to iterate their antipathy to internal taxation. Lewis Williams chided the House for waiting for an Executive recommendation before acting. Philip Barbour pronounced a requiem on the internal duties by dragging the Constitution into the debate and arguing that the framers of that instrument never intended that the government be permanently supported by excises. The excise, Barbour maintained, was to be imposed only in an emergency and abolished when not needed. Without further ado the House passed the bill on December 11 by 161–5, four Federalists and one Republican, Henry Middleton of South Carolina, in the minority.[39]

Another facet of this issue was the demand for retrenchment and a reduction of the standing army. Recurrent since the end of the war, the issue appeared again in the winter of 1818–19, but it soon became entangled in the factional maneuvering occasioned by the Seminole debate. Nothing was accomplished until the Panic of 1819 and the ensuing depression forced Congress to take a more serious look at the problem. A drastic reduction in revenue and the prospect of a Treasury deficit by the fall of 1820 revived the demand for retrenchment, which quickly focused on the War Department and the army.

Those who witnessed the battle and modern historians agree that the attack on the War Department which climaxed in the spring of 1821 was a political stratagem engineered by the partisans of Treasury Secretary Crawford. They apparently had the dual purpose of saving the treasury from a deficit and embarrassing the Secretary of War, John C. Calhoun, like Crawford a potential candidate in the presidential election of 1824. In general, this opinion seems to be justified, particularly since a similar attack on the navy failed miserably, and bills to reduce the civil expenditure were introduced almost as an afterthought, too late to be acted upon.[40]

The attack on the army was not exclusively political, however, nor were all who joined in it necessarily partisans of Crawford. Many a Northern Republican who had no apparent interest in Crawford or antipathy to Calhoun supported the reduction of the army, presumably from a genuine concern for the solvency of the government. Moreover, Old Republicans, who for the most part led the attack, had long demanded retrenchment in government expenditures in general and a reduction of the army in particular. Economy was the basic element of the Liberal creed. The depression and the treasury deficit merely gave them an opportunity which they were quick to seize. Only a few, such as Lewis Williams of North Carolina and Thomas W. Cobb of Georgia, could be identified as Crawfordites at this time.[41] On the other hand, it is true that the debate on retrenchment was the beginning of the process that eventually saw the Old Republicans merged into the pro-Crawford "Radicals."

The economy drive was revived on November 22, 1820, when Thomas W. Cobb introduced a series of resolutions to reduce the annual expenses of the government by abolishing unnecessary offices, reducing the salaries of all civil officials to the level of 1809, reducing the army to 6,000 men, and laying up half the navy. On December 12 Secretary of War Calhoun, in accordance with a resolution passed by the House in the previous spring, submitted a plan to retain the whole officer corps and reduce each company of enlisted men to half strength, so that in case of war there would be "nothing either to new model or to create." [42] Calhoun's plan was a reasonable one. It answered the demand for economy without completely mutilating the army, but it was bound to run into difficulties in the House because it proposed to retain intact the officer staff, the most dangerous part of a standing army in the view of most of the conservatives.

When the retrenchment resolutions were taken up by the House on January 5, Cobb defended his resolutions on Old Republican grounds. Though he was only sixteen-years old when Jefferson was elected President, Cobb lamented the recent departure among Republicans from the tried principles of Jefferson. The present administration, he felt, was comparable to that of John Adams in its demand for a standing army, an expensive navy, and in its tendency toward broad construction of the Constitution.[43]

Anxious to get down to specifics, the House tabled the Cobb resolutions in order to take up a bill for the reduction of the army. Reported a few days before by Alexander Smyth, chairman of the committee on military affairs, this bill proposed to reduce the peace establishment to four regiments of artillery and seven regiments of infantry —a total of 6,000 men. The bill was approved by the committee over the opposition of General Smyth, who preferred Calhoun's plan of keeping the officer staff intact.[44] After assuring the House with a bow to Jefferson, whose "principles constitute a republican text to which the legislator should often refer," that he sympathized with the idea of retrenchment, Smyth proceeded to attack any reduction in the army. Showing how many ways even a Bible can be used by a fundamentalist like Smyth, he instanced Jefferson's increase in the army in 1808 as proof that a sizable army is often needed in time of peace.[45]

The army bill had other friends, however. Lewis Williams repeated the demand for economy that he had been making annually since 1815 and dwelled at length on the dangers of a standing army. Charles Fisher, colleague of Williams from North Carolina, defended the bill on the grounds that the treasury was empty and running at a deficit of $2–$4 million, a prospect that raised the specter of a flood of treasury paper in the mind of every Republican conservative. Though only a lad of nine when the "principles of '98" were being forged, Fisher blandly reminded the House of the Republican furor over John Adams' standing army, which was only 5,000 men, half the size of the present establishment. Fisher concluded with the argument long familiar to conservatives that the militia was just as efficient as a standing army and far less dangerous to the liberties of the people.[46]

This last point was further enlarged upon by Newton Cannon, who succeeded Fisher the following day. Cannon assured the

House that it could rely on the militia, composed as it was of "the great body of the American people," and reminded the House of the effectiveness of militia at New Orleans. Cannon would reduce the army even further than the size contemplated by the bill; in time of peace, he felt, the nation needed only enough soldiers to provide guard duty for military stores and munitions. These arguments were iterated by other conservatives, Felix Walker and Hutchins Gordon Burton of North Carolina and John Floyd of Virgina, as the debate continued through most of January, 1821.[47]

A substitute bill, introduced by Alexander Smyth and embodying the recommendations of Calhoun, was rejected by the House, and on January 23 the army bill was passed by a vote of 109–48. Voting in the majority were most of the Old Republicans, but the opposition to the bill of such uniform conservatives as Hugh Nelson, a friend of Monroe, and Eldred Simkins, a friend of Calhoun, as well as the strange silence of John Randolph on an issue that normally provoked from him a lengthy diatribe, suggests that some suspected the bill to be a Crawford maneuver. The lopsidedness of the vote, however, indicates a general concern for the condition of the treasury. In the Senate the bill passed without a division. No one disagreed with it in principle; the debate centered on the details.[48]

The army was a good target. Reduction of the civil list, a move with fewer political overtones, was another story. On February 6 Thomas Culbreth of Maryland reported a bill providing a 20 percent reduction in the salaries of civil officials of the government. This received sympathetic treatment until John Campbell of Ohio offered an amendment making a comparable reduction in the salaries of members of Congress. This motion split the retrenchment forces; the bill was quietly dropped, and with it went the whole retrenchment issue.[49]

Less subject to personalities and more relevant to the philosophy of the Old Republicans were the perennial issues of the bank, tariff, and internal improvements. The last involved the most controversy because President Madison raised doubts about the constitutionality of roads and canals in his veto message of 1817. President Monroe was inclined to the same view. In his first annual message to Congress he discussed the problem at length and concluded by advocating a constitutional amendment that would give Congress power to finance roads, canals, and "seminaries of learning." To Madison, Monroe wrote that he was "fixed in the opinion that the right is not in Congress, and that it would be improper in me, after your negative, to allow them to discuss the subject & bring in a bill for me to sign, in the expectation that I would do it." [50]

On December 3, 1817, Speaker Henry Clay appointed a special committee on the subject of roads and canals in an effort to revive the subject. Headed by the nationalist Henry St. George Tucker of Virginia, the committee was loaded with Northern and Western Republicans friendly to internal improvements.[51] The report of Tucker's committee was laid before the House on December 15. After noting that the President in his annual message had not actually denied Congress a power over internal improvements, the report analyzed at length the constitutional issue. It concluded that Congress had power to appropriate money for the repair of post roads and the construction of military roads and canals, provided Congress obtained the consent of the states involved. The committee accordingly submitted a resolution that the government's annual dividend from its stock in the Bank of the United States be made into a fund for internal improvements, a repetition of the idea presented in Calhoun's bonus bill of the previous year.[52]

Tucker and his committee could predict the reaction of the Old Republicans. Tucker sent a copy of the report to Madison, and the ex-President answered that he disagreed with the report and felt that Congress had no power to deal with the subject.[53] On December 27 a writer under the pseudonym "John Hampden" in the Richmond *Enquirer* answered the House committee report. He argued that not only would the federal construction of roads and canals open a wide breach in the Constitution but it would serve as a precedent for the extension of congressional power in other directions. "The remnant of state rights will be wrested from us not on the ground of right but of precedent, and because others of them had been before assailed and carried." [54] The possibility of establishing a precedent for the extension of federal power often bothered conservatives, and with some reason, for had not Madison himself declared in 1816 that the constitutionality of the bank had been settled by precedent? The extension of federal power, moreover, was already making some Southerners fearful for the existence of slavery. Though this fear would be much more general after the Missouri debates a few years later, it was already being expressed by Nathaniel Macon, who wrote, "If Congress can make canals they can with more propriety emancipate [the slaves]." [55]

Other subjects intervened and the House did not take up the resolution of the Tucker committee until March 6, 1818. As soon as the House went into committee on the subject Lemuel Sawyer moved that the resolution be postponed indefinitely since a former President had already vetoed a similar bill on constitutional grounds. This was a sore spot for the nationalists, and Clay accused Sawyer of hiding behind Madison's veto and dared him to "get up and make a Constitutional speech on the subject." Sawyer retorted that further speeches were unnecessary. "To him it was a matter of faith and feeling, and in matters of faith, we may lay reason aside. . . . It was sufficient for him that there was no express provision in the Constitution granting this power." [56]

The nationalists responded with a defense of the resolution and the debate was on. Alexander Smyth, whose district included the "road-starved" mountainous area of southwestern Virginia, insisted that the federal government was no more than a confederation of sovereign states granted specific powers for the regulation of foreign affairs and commerce; all other matters were reserved to the states. Where the power of Congress was in doubt, as in this case, it should avoid action and leave the area to the states. Philip Barbour, who followed Smyth on the floor, argued with his usual mechanistic legalism against the growth of the Constitution by precedent. Tucker and Clay asserted that Congress by appropriating money for the Cumberland Road had established at least one precedent for its power to deal with internal improvements. Barbour answered that precedent alone cannot confer constitutional justification, for precedent is likely to change with every administration; and the Constitution itself, "which was intended to be settled upon the firmest foundation, would be subject to be whirled about, the sport of every political gust." By the time Archibald Austin of Virginia arose to denounce the resolution Clay was already complaining of the readiness of conservatives to respond to his challenge to "make a constitutional speech on the subject." No quarter was shown, however, as Austin and James Johnson of Virginia each occupied a day with lengthy speeches repeating the constitutional objections to the resolution.[57]

Since it was obvious that the opponents of internal improvements were determined to take their stand on the constitutional issue alone and to ignore the question of whether roads and canals were actually needed, William Lowndes proposed to separate the Tucker resolution so that the House could vote on the sole issue of the powers of Congress. On March 10 Lowndes offered three resolutions to the House. The first asserted that Congress had power to appropriate money for the construction of roads and canals. The second resolution, "that Congress has power, under the Constitution, to construct post roads and military roads . . . ," broached the problem of whether Congress could authorize the construction of new roads or was able only to designate already existing roads as post roads or military roads. The third resolution, "that Congress has power, under the Constitution, to construct roads and canals necessary for commerce between the states . . . ," attempted to rest internal improvements on the commerce power. To these Charles Fenton Mercer, nationalist from northern Virginia, added a fourth resolution, "that Congress has power under the Constitution, to construct canals for military purposes . . . ," which would justify internal improvements under the war power.[58]

The Lowndes resolutions only stimulated further debate, and the conservatives extended themselves for several more days on the constitutional issue. The debate thereafter was almost exclusively confined to the Virginia delegation—Hugh Nelson, Barbour, Smyth, Johnson, and Austin against Tucker and the Virginia Federalists, Mercer, Pindall, and Colston. It might be noted that the conservatives generally came from the Tidewater and Piedmont districts, except for Smyth, while the Federalists Pindall and Colston represented the tramontane counties of the West, which would naturally be more interested in roads and canals. The arguments of the conservatives followed the traditional pattern of accusing the opposition of abandoning traditional Republican principles. The apparent sympathy that this approach was getting in the House eventually forced even Clay to attempt a demonstration of his consistency with the Virginia Resolution of 1798.[59]

A few Virginians even carried the debate into the newspapers. Burwell Bassett sent a circular letter to the *Enquirer* explaining his opposition to internal improvements not so much on constitutional grounds but because they would add to the size and patronage of the federal government. An expenditure of $15–20 million a year on roads and canals, he felt, would add immensely to the number of people dependent upon the government.[60]

On March 14 the debate finally subsided, and the House proceeded to vote on the Lowndes resolutions. The first resolution that Congress had the power to appropriate money for internal improvements was passed 90–75. Voting in the minority were the Old Republicans, including some Western conservatives like Joseph Desha of Kentucky and John Rhea of Tennessee, and a few New Englanders. The House then proceeded to vote down the other three resolutions. The result of the day's work was that a majority of the House felt Congress had power to appropriate money for anything it saw fit, including roads and canals, but that it was unable to authorize the construction of roads and canals under the post roads power, the war powers, or the commerce power. The confusing vote, in which the constitutional niceties of the Virginia conservatives had had no little part, ended the debate for the time being. On April 3 the House tamely passed a compromise resolution requesting the Secretaries of War and of the Treasury to offer a plan "for the application of such means as are within the power of Congress" to the opening of roads and canals.[61]

Despite the predominantly conservative sentiment in the House on this question, the nationalists were not ready to concede defeat. They merely changed their tactics in the following year, and, paralleling Henry Clay's independent stand on the South American question, concentrated on embarrassing the administration. When a military appropriation bill came before the House in January, 1819, Clay and Tucker deliberately called the attention of the House to a section that contemplated the use of army contingent funds for the construction of military roads. This, of course, provoked cries from Barbour and Williams that such use of military funds without a specific appropriation from Congress was unconstitutional. When the nationalist David Trimble of Kentucky moved that a specific appropriation for military roads be added to the bill, Clay's object of reopening the debate on internal improvements was secured.[62]

Over the protests of Ways and Means Committee Chairman Samuel Smith the House all but lost sight of the military appropriation bill in the ensuing discussion of the authority of Congress to appropriate funds for internal improvements under the war powers. Clay's move was a shrewd one because it was customary for soldiers in peacetime to be employed in the repair and construction of roads and bridges. For this they were generally given heavy-duty pay, taken out of contingent funds appropriated by Congress. Since the contingent funds were not specifically earmarked at the time of appropriation, no constitutional objection to the system arose. But now, by Trimble's motion, the House was being asked to make a special appropriation for the extra pay of soldiers employed on the roads, thereby sanctioning the principle of internal improvements. The maneuver was also calculated to embarrass the President, for it forced him likewise to accept the principle or reject the whole military appropriation bill.

Outmaneuvered, the conservatives revealed the difficulty of applying broad principle to borderline cases. Hugh Nelson "begged that he might not be challenged to meet them on this arena—it is too narrow; let us have a fair field, such as the bill reported by the [Tucker] Committee on Internal Improvement," a bill to appropriate a general fund for roads and canals. Though outflanked, the conservatives fought the proposition, the debate being carried by Nelson, Smyth, and Barbour. On January 11 the amendment making a special appropriation passed, 90–75, which, it might be noted, was the same division by which the House passed the internal improvements resolution the previous March.[63]

In the Senate the military affairs committee struck out the Trimble amendment on the ground that Congress lacked the power to appropriate money for soldiers to construct roads. The Senate tied 18–18 in voting to sustain the committee, and the House provision was retained by the vote of the Vice-President, Daniel D. Tompkins. The President, Tompkins felt, had wide discretion in employing the army on fatigue duty, and the appropriation of extra money for heavy duty did not involve any constitutional principle.[64]

Profiting by this success the nationalists thereafter confined themselves to specific projects that could attract interested votes. Most feasible of these was the Cumberland Road, begun by the Federalists in 1796 and continued by the Republican administrations. The support given by Jefferson and Madison to this project, which furnished a valuable link between the Potomac and the Ohio Valley, indicates the flexibility of Virginia doctrine when Virginia's interests were involved. This flexibility was to cause many headaches for their disciple James Monroe.

In early 1820 the internal improvements issue was revived by two different proposals involving the extension of the Cumberland Road. The first was a section of the civil appropriation bill providing $141,000 to complete contracts undertaken in 1817 for the extension of the Cumberland Road to Wheeling, (West) Virginia. Since the contracts had already been authorized by the House, there should have been no question of honoring them, yet the section received stiff opposition from the conservatives before passing 90–66. Even so, the size of the opposition vote is deceiving. Northerners who derived no economic benefit from the road, though silent in the debate, made up most of the minority vote. Only twenty-one Southerners, all of them Old Republicans, voted against the bill.[65]

The other feature of the internal improvements issue in 1820 was a bill introduced into the Senate by the two Senators from Kentucky, Johnson and Trimble, to authorize commissioners to survey a route for the Cumberland Road from Wheeling to the Mississippi River. William Smith, in moving postponement for a year, objected that the bill proposed to finance surveys out of the treasury, rather than, as was usual, from land sales in the states concerned. Smith's motion was voted down, 27–11, with Barbour, Pleasants, Macon, Gaillard, and Smith in the minority. The House subsequently approved the bill 74–35, with nineteen Southerners, almost all of them Old Republicans, voting against it.[66]

Although both Houses tended to divide more along sectional lines on internal improvements in 1820 than they had in the vote on the bonus bill in 1817, it does not necessarily follow that the yeast of the Missouri debate was working its sectional leaven.[67] The Southern opposition to the Cumberland Road measures in 1820 was confined to new conservatives who had not had the opportunity to vote on the issue in 1817 and to Old Republicans who consistently opposed internal improvements. There is actually little evidence that Southerners were converted into an opposition to internal improvements as a result of the Missouri controversy. Senator James Barbour was the only Republican in either House who voted for the bonus bill of 1817 and against the Cumberland Road bills in 1820. The long-term effect of the Missouri debate on this issue, however, was important, for a growing Southern opposition to internal improvements in the next few years was directly related to a fear of the extension of federal power that might free the slaves as well as build roads and canals.

The revival of Republican conservatism after 1817 was more evident in the treatment accorded the Bank of the United States. Though the bank received only sporadic opposition when it was created, a shift of opinion in Congress was evident as early as the spring of 1818 when a bill was introduced authorizing the bank to appoint another vice-president to facilitate the signing of notes. Remembering the perfunctory manner in which they had overridden Randolph and his tiny band on the bank bill in 1816, the nationalists expected to push this minor alteration in the charter through the House with a minimum of discussion. The extent of the opposition took them completely by surprise. Samuel Ingham of Pennsylvania, leading defender of the bank, admitted that he was "astonished" at the vehemence of the opposition. The Old Republicans received the support of representatives of state banking interests in the North and of Westerners who had become dissatisfied with the conduct of the bank. On April 16 the bill was postponed indefinitely by a vote of 85–50. Among the conservatives who altered their opinion of the bank since 1816 were Weldon Nathaniel Edwards and Daniel Forney of North Carolina, and James Pleasants and Ballard Smith of Virginia. The new opposition to the bank, however, was primarily due to the number of new conservatives in the House.[68]

Though successful in preventing an expansion of the activities of the bank, the conservatives were unable to mount a generalized attack until the mistakes of the bank itself forced a change in public sentiment. Throughout the spring and summer of 1818 rumors of mismanagement and speculation engendered a growing public suspicion that culminated in the late summer of 1818 when the bank announced that it could no longer honor the notes of its own branches. Thomas Ritchie, who had conducted only a mild opposition to the bank in 1816, pointed out that this decision negated the strongest argument that had been made for a bank—that it would supply a national circulating medium. The commercial-minded *Norfolk and Portsmouth Herald*, recalling that it had supported the bank in 1816 because of the need for a uniform currency, asserted that if it could not perform that function, "away with it." [69]

In Congress the conservatives were quick to take up the hue and cry. On November 25, 1818, John Spencer of New York submitted a resolution to appoint a committee to examine the bank books. The resolution was agreed to, and a committee of Spencer, Lowndes, Louis McLane of Delaware, Joseph Hunter Bryan, and John Tyler was appointed. The inclusion of the conservatives Bryan and Tyler seemed to give an antibank complexion to the committee, but Tyler at least was determined to be fair. From Philadelphia he wrote in December:

As to the U. States bank I do not mean to express an opinion, particularly until we have collected all the facts we can. Many of the evils which have been ascribed to it, are incident to the system, of which it is a part, and common to all banks. For myself I would support it in all proper measures, sanctioned by its charter, and shall censure where it deserves censure.[70]

The investigation apparently convinced him that the bank conducted its affairs with dubious business ethics and violated its charter repeatedly, for he wrote to a friend a month later, "What think you of our banking gentry. Did you dream that we had been visited with so much corruption: I shall vote a scire facias and am almost willing to vote a positive repeal of the charter without awaiting a judicial decision." [71]

The report of the committee, submitted to the House on January 16, 1819, was a lengthy indictment of the activities of the bank, charging it with speculation, mismanagement, and violations of its charter. Three days later Trimble offered a resolution authorizing the Attorney General to secure a writ of *scire facias* calling on the corporation to show cause why its charter should not be forfeited in view of the violations reported by the House committee. Not content with a judicial review of the charter, James Johnson offered another resolution on February 9 to repeal the charter by law.[72]

In the meantime the affairs of the bank reached a crisis. Weakened by the incompetent management of President William Jones, by a gross overextension of loans, and by fraud in its Baltimore branch, the bank by December, 1818, was frantically calling in its outstanding debts and drawing in funds from its Southern and Western branches. In January agricultural prices dropped sharply, and that same month President Jones resigned.[73] This was the state of affairs when the House took up Trimble's resolution for a writ of *scire facias* on February 18. Johnson immediately injected his motion to repeal the charter altogether, stressing the violations of the charter reported by the committee and arguing that the bank was unconstitutional anyway. Significantly, he took care to separate himself from the state banking interests, assuring the House that he held no stock in any bank and was an opponent of the Virginia banks.[74]

Johnson failed to carry all the conservatives with him in his move for repeal. John Tyler felt legislative repeal of the charter would be a violation of a contract with the bank, an opinion undoubtedly influenced by Marshall's decision in the *Dartmouth College* case announced only a few days before. Tyler nevertheless considered the bank unconstitutional, and since it had clearly violated its charter he thought that the resolution for obtaining a writ of *scire facias* was a better way of annulling the charter "without violating the public faith." [75]

By the end of February the whole nation was in the throes of economic depression, and the House was in the midst of the debate on the Missouri question. That these two issues, which joined to give a new impetus to the states' rights movement after 1820, were already hardening Southern conservatism was shown by the argument of David Walker of Kentucky—up until this time a nationalist supporter of Clay. Walker opposed the bank because it had raised havoc with the economy of the West, and, more important, he considered it as great a threat to the rights of states as the proposal to prohibit slavery in Missouri. [76]

Despite the revelations of the investigating committee, it was unlikely that any action would be taken against the bank. William A. Burwell, who admitted that the affairs of the bank had "added but little to . . . [his] respect for monied institutions," thought the charter would stand because the government needed the bank. On February 25 the two resolutions at last came to a vote. The resolution to repeal the charter was voted down 30–121, and the resolution authorizing a writ of *scire facias* was defeated 39–116. In the minority on each vote were most of the Old Republicans and a few Westerners. Republican nationalists, Federalists, and pro-Crawford conservatives teamed up to save the bank. [77]

The protective tariff fared best in the conservative reaction of 1817, which might seem strange in view of the later Southern preoccupation with the subject. The only explanation is that attitudes were determined exclusively by economic interest, since customs duties were clearly authorized by the Constitution, and the South generally did not conceive of the tariff as a threat until after 1820. The ineffectiveness of the opposition was apparent when a bill was introduced in the spring of 1818 to increase further the duties on iron products. The conservative arguments were summarized by James S. Smith of North Carolina. He returned to the familiar charge that the bill was taxing the whole people for the benefit of the "fungus establishments" that had grown up during the war. After short debate the bill passed the House on April 15 by 88–47. Another bill to increase the duty on textiles, though opposed by Edwards, Mercer, and Rhea because it taxed agriculture for the benefit of the manufacturing interest, was steam-rollered through the House the same day, 106–34. The bills were opposed only by the most consistent of the Old Republicans. Both bills whisked through the Senate in the same fashion; neither the debate nor the division was reported.[78]

Not until 1820 did the tariff become the object of general suspicion in the South and Southwest. The economic depression renewed the demand for protection, and in Congress Speaker Clay responded by appointing a special committee on manufactures under the chairmanship of Henry Baldwin of Pittsburgh. Shortly after the first Missouri debate ended in March, 1820, Baldwin reported a bill to raise the tariff to genuinely protective levels, and the House took up the subject at the end of April.[79] The representatives of various manufacturing interests were competing for favored treatment when John Tyler moved to strike the whole first section as a means of getting a general discussion on the merits of the bill. In the ensuing debate the opposition was spearheaded by Tyler, Barbour, and Lowndes.

Tyler, who defended his motion on April 24, repeated the familiar charge that the tariff was legislation for a special interest at the expense of the people. The only novel part of his address was an attempt to answer the "home market" argument recently adopted by the protectionists in an effort to gain the support of the farmer. The growth of industry would not increase the consumption of farm products, Tyler maintained, because an increase in the industrial labor force merely represented a shift in population from farm to city and would not increase the total number of consumers. Perhaps aware of the frailty of this contention, Tyler quickly shifted to the more familiar Jeffersonian ground that the country by its vast tracts of land was destined to be predominantly agricultural. Any attempt to create manufactures by artificial means, Tyler announced somewhat pontifically, was an attempt "to subvert the ordinances of Heaven itself." [80]

Tyler's motion was negatived without a division, but it served its purpose of turning the attention of the House to the general principles of protection. The representatives from the New England seaboard joined the Old Republicans in opposition and occupied the House for the next few days. On April 27 Philip Barbour, who had voted for the tariff in 1816, sought to restate the conservative position. Tyler's speech tended to cloud the issue with disingenuous arguments, but Barbour rested his attack on Republican grounds. The proposed tariff, he pointed out, being designed to restrict imports, would reduce the revenue of the government and force it to rely on excises and direct taxes, which were not only unpopular and expensive to collect but, worst of all, were un-Republican.

Barbour then indulged in a little agrarian nostalgia. It seemed obvious to him that manufacturing, after all, was inferior to agriculture. An agricultural society was more stable, less competitive, and more likely to retain Republican institutions, while manufactures produced social classes and an unwholesome competition that resulted in the concentration of wealth in the hands of a few. Manufactures and cities were barely to be tolerated; certainly they were not to be fostered and protected. Barbour also betrayed an agrarian suspicion of capitalist business methods, similar to his suspicion of paper money and banks. Industrial enterprise was based on borrowed, or what Barbour called "fictitious," capital. He felt there was something dishonest about making a living by borrowing money to build a factory and hiring others to perform the work. Barbour, of course, had no concept of entrepreneurial wages and did not trouble himself with a distinction between investment and usury. He did, however, recognize that agriculture had its capitalistic aspects.

Though his ideal was the independent yeoman cultivating his own plot of ground, he recognized the existence of the highly capitalized Southern planter living largely on borrowed capital. But he pictured the planter as a man who habitually engaged in hard physical work, in contrast to the Northern industrialist who merely sat in his office counting his paper profits.

Barbour then began a somewhat more valid attempt to answer some of the arguments of the protectionists. To the assertion that manufacturing was prostrate as a result of the depression, Barbour answered that commerce and agriculture were also prostrate—why single out just one industry for government aid? The difficulties in which manufacturers found themselves resulted not from the depression, Barbour suggested, but from peace. Experience had shown that they could operate profitably only during a war when imports were cut off. In regard to the home market argument Barbour improved on Tyler's thesis. He admitted that the growth of an industrial labor force might increase the price of agricultural produce by diminishing the relative number of farmers and increasing the number of consumers. But he thought the vast area of free land in the West would prevent farm prices from going up much, and probably the increase would be less than the increase in the price of manufactured goods as a result of the tariff.[81] The agricultural history of the United States tends to substantiate this supposition.

On April 28 William Lowndes joined the Southern antitariff forces. A nationalist since his entrance into Congress in 1811, Lowndes had given wholehearted support to the tariff of 1816. His conversion in 1820 can be attributed in part to the Missouri debate and in part to the appearance of antitariff sentiment in South Carolina. Though expressed with his incomparable clarity Lowndes's arguments were already familiar to the House as he charged that the tariff bill was an "attempt of the manufacturing interest to lay the agricultural and commercial interests under contribution. . . ."[82]

Despite the attempt of Southerners to attract the whole agricultural interest, the West remained generally favorable to the tariff, and the Baldwin bill passed the House on April 29 by a vote of 91–78.[83] The division was much more sectional than the vote had been in 1816. Seventeen New Englanders and one Pennsylvanian voted against the bill; only nine Southerners supported it. The opposition of moderate conservatives, such as Barbour and William McCoy of Virginia, Felix Walker of North Carolina, and Newton Cannon, all of whom had supported the tariff in 1816, testifies to the effect of the Missouri debate in crystallizing the heretofore amorphous conservative group, as well as to the growing antitariff sentiment in the South.[84] In the Virginia delegation only Thomas Newton of Norfolk voted for the Baldwin bill, but his career in the House since 1801 had never involved a consistent adherence to Republican doctrine.

In the Senate James Barbour opened the debate on the Baldwin bill by moving its indefinite postponement. In the discussion that followed the attack on the bill was left to the Massachusetts Federalist Harrison Gray Otis, but Southern votes were prominent in the 22–21 decision to postpone it. Among Southerners only the two Senators from Kentucky and one from Tennessee voted for the bill. Three Senators reversed themselves since their stand in favor of the tariff in 1816—John Gaillard, John Williams of Tennessee, and James Brown of Louisiana.[85]

Of less importance but nevertheless indicative of the position of the Old Republicans was the subject of federal bankruptcy laws, which periodically troubled Congress for decades. The issue was introduced in February, 1818, when Joseph Hopkinson, a Pennsylvania Federalist, offered a bill to establish a national system of bankruptcy proceedings. The widespread demand for a uniform system of bankruptcy testified to the growing commercial maturity of the nation. Business was no longer primarily local in nature, and the need for uniformity in the regulation of bankruptcy was widely felt. State legislation varied greatly in scope and content and was generally hindered by the constitutional prohibition of laws tending to impair the obligations of contracts. Congress, moreover, was specifically empowered to pass bankruptcy legislation. The conservative opposition to this bill shows Jeffersonian agrarianism in its most regressive form.

John Tyler opened the attack on the bill on February 17. Not even Tyler could find anything unconstitutional about it, and he was forced to found his argument on the supposition that it would encourage dishonesty and irresponsibility among merchants. The honest merchant, Tyler argued somewhat irrelevantly, carefully hedged his losses and never had to avail himself of the bankruptcy laws. The irresponsible merchant, Tyler hinted, would consider this law an open invitation to contract debts in all directions for his speculative ventures and then avoid repayment by going through bankruptcy. Tyler betrayed his point of view when he referred the House to the Virginia laws on bankruptcy as a model. Under the Virginia laws a debtor never fully discharged his obligations by bankruptcy proceedings, and any future earnings remained liable for past debts.[86] Tyler was representing the creditor point of view of the wealthy planter—the same economics that insisted on hard money for its currency. The Southern planter failed to understand and instinctively feared the methods and business organization of the rising entrepreneurial class in the North.

The Old Republicans, however, did not have a monopoly on agrarian sentiments. James Pindall, Federalist from Clarksburg, (West) Virginia, denounced the bill for attempting to protect a "privileged order" of citizens—the "mercantile class." Henry St. George Tucker further developed the accusation that this bill was class legislation. It was another manifestation, he felt, of the tendency of Congress "to encourage everything: the manufacturer must be encouraged by duties; the merchant must be stimulated to mercantile enterprise by sponging his debts if he fails. And on whom do these encouragements operate as a burden? On the farmer and the planter." [87] Tucker at last was beginning to sound more like his stepbrother, John Randolph.

Philip Barbour as usual concluded the case for the opposition. The theme of his argument was that merchants ought to pay their debts in full because, in the terse phrase of another conservative a century later, "They hired the money, didn't they?" Debt, to Barbour, was a moral obligation that ought to be paid back and not be avoided with the connivance of the federal legislature. When Barbour sat down the House voted 82–70 to postpone the bill indefinitely, which killed it for the time being. The core of the majority were the Southern conservatives, and with them were the representatives from the rural areas in the North and West.[88] The issue was not dead, however, and the problem of establishing a federal system of bankruptcy continued to agitate Congress for the next decade. But the continued opposition of the Southern conservatives prevented the reform until the early 1840s.

The great Missouri controversy of 1819–21 was in a sense the climax of the conservative reaction that had begun in 1817. Yet it also marked the dividing line between the Virginia-oriented conservatism of the Old Republicans and the development of Southern sectionalism under the leadership of South Carolina in the 1820s. It was both the highpoint and the knell of Old Republicanism.

The controversy originated in an amendment offered by James Tallmadge of New York in February, 1819, to a bill enabling the territory of Missouri to form a state constitution. The Tallmadge amendment was dual in form: first, it would prohibit the further introduction of slavery into Missouri; second, it proposed to free all children of slave parents born after Missouri became a state. The debate that ensued was more sectionally than politically oriented. The Old Republicans joined other Southerners in maintaining that Congress had no right to prescribe to any state the details of its government, other than that it be republican in form. Northerners answered that Congress had a right to impose conditions of admission and that slavery was incompatible with republican institutions. The amendment was adopted, the first feature by 87–76 and the second by 82–78, in an almost completely sectional vote.[89]

The subsequent history of the Tallmadge amendment is a familiar story. The Senate rejected the amendment, and the bill died in the disagreement of the two Houses.[90] The vote in both Houses was primarily sectional and involved the Old Republicans but little, except that as the ancient spokesmen of the Southern economic and political system they were prominent in the debate. When the subject was revived the following year, they gradually assumed the leadership of the Southern defense.

As soon as the House was organized on December 6, 1819, John Scott, delegate from the Missouri Territory, moved that the memorials from Missouri be referred to a select committee. A Southern-dominated committee was appointed by Speaker Clay, and on December 9 it reported a bill for the admission of Missouri without restriction of slavery. At the same time a memorial was presented from the District of Maine seeking admission to the Union as a state. On December 30 a Maine-enabling bill was reported to the House, and after sharp debate it was sent up to the Senate a few days later.[91]

When the House took up the Missouri-enabling bill on January 26, John W. Taylor of New York immediately offered an amendment providing for the exclusion of slavery in the new state, and the debate began anew. As in the previous year the division in the House was sectional and did not specifically involve the Old Republicans, except insofar as they bore the brunt of the Southern defense. Virginia, as usual, led the way. Almost every issue of the *Enquirer* carried one or more essays on the subject filled with references to the Constitution, *The Federalist* papers, and the writings of John Taylor. All developed the proposition that was echoed by her representatives in Congress: that the regulation of slavery was vested in the states alone, that Congress could not legislate on the subject nor impose restrictions on the admission of a state that would deny its equality with the other states. The arguments, in both Virginia and Congress, were couched in the language of the states' rights doctrine. In the House debate that lasted until February 19 eighteen Southerners opposed the restriction of slavery in Missouri; nearly half were Old Republicans, including Randolph, Barbour, Smyth, Tyler, and Johnson of Virginia, Edwards of North Carolina, and Ben Hardin of Kentucky.

In the meantime the Senate judiciary committee had reported the Maine-enabling bill with an amendment that provided for the admission of Missouri without restrictions on slavery. Nathaniel Macon, who had foreseen as early as 1818 a threat to slavery in the extension of national power, warned the Senate that "the attempt to govern too much has produced every civil war that has ever been, and will probably, every one that ever may be. All governments, no matter what their form, want more power and more authority, and all the governed want less government." Not content with hinting of the possibility of civil war should Congress extend its power to include the regulation of slavery, Macon went on to make the first defense of slavery as a positive good ever to be heard on the floor of Congress.

I sincerely wish that he [James Burrill of Rhode Island] and the gentleman from Pennsylvania [Jonathan Roberts] would go home with me, or some other Southern member, and witness the meeting between the slaves and the owner, and see the glad faces and the hearty shaking of hands. . . . The owner can make more free in conversation with his slave, and be more easy in his company, than the rich man where there is no slave, with the white hireling who drives his carriage.[92]

Heretofore the Southern defense had been inhibited by the general admission that slavery was an evil. Haters of slavery like John Randolph and Charles Fenton Mercer were forced to argue that there was no reasonable alternative to the slavery system and that the regulation of slavery was beyond the constitutional powers of Congress. But the Northern attack on slavery as a moral evil produced an inevitable reaction. "These Yankees have almost reconciled me to negro slavery," wrote John Randolph. "They have produced a revulsion even on my mind; what then must be the effect on those who had no scruples on the subject?" [93]

Macon had sown the seed for the idea that slavery was in itself beneficial. William Smith of South Carolina went even further, attempting to justify it on the basis of Scripture. "Christ himself gave a sanction to slavery," Smith asserted. "He admonished them to be obedient to their masters; and there is not a word in the whole of his life which forbids it. . . . Mr. President, the Scriptures teach us that slavery was universally indulged among the holy fathers." No other member of Congress went so far, but within a month the Richmond *Enquirer* was publishing a series of articles maintaining that slavery was sanctioned by the Bible.[94] Twelve years before Thomas Roderick Dew published the classic defense of slavery the Old Republicans under the pressure of attack were defending the institution as morally justified and positively beneficial.

On February 16 the Senate passed the Maine-Missouri bill and immediately thereafter Jesse B. Thomas of Illinois offered an amendment prohibiting slavery in the Louisiana Purchase, except for Missouri, north of the line thirty-six degrees thirty minutes north latitude. This was to be the Southern concession in the compromise that otherwise admitted Missouri without restriction. The Thomas amendment was adopted the following day, 34–10. Eight of the senators opposing the amendment were Southerners, including the conservatives, Gaillard and Smith of South Carolina, James Pleasants of Virginia, and Nathaniel Macon. The Senate then passed the whole compromise to a third reading, 24–20. The South generally favored the compromise while the North opposed it; only two Northern senators voted in favor of the bill and only two Southerners voted against it.[95]

One Southerner opposing the bill was Macon, who explained to his friend Bolling Hall of Alabama that "to compromise is to acknowledge the right of Congress to interfere and to legislate on the subject. This would be acknowledging too much." To Macon the Missouri debate was but another aspect of the trend toward broad constitutional interpretation that had characterized the nationalistic legislation of the postwar period. A national bank, a protective tariff, internal improvements—with each issue the powers and rights of the states had been diminished. And now it was proposed to restrict the expansion of slavery into the West. Abolition would be the next step. It was time to call a halt; the South had retreated far enough. Southern nationalists ought to remember, Macon continued in the same letter,

that others may find as much plausibility for stretching the Constitution to cover Colonization and emancipation, as has been done to cover banks and their notes. You will I am sure recollect how often, I have told our friends that it was as easy to stretch the constitution to cover Africans as it was to cover banks.[96]

The Senate compromise reached the House on March 2. Had the House voted on the compromise as a whole it would have been defeated by a combination of Northerners who thought the compromise favored the South and Old Republicans who were unwilling to admit the power of Congress to deal with slavery at all. The tactic of the compromisers was to submit the Senate bill to the House in sections. The key provision to admit Missouri without restriction, which the Northern majority earlier refused to do, the House adopted by a vote of 90–87. Voting with the South were fourteen free-state representatives. The second part of the compromise prohibiting slavery north of thirty-six-thirty the House passed 134–42. Thirty-seven of the votes against this section of the compromise were Southern, and almost all were Old Republicans.[97]

The subterfuge of voting on the bill in sections led the Richmond *Enquirer* to wonder whether "this bill has been in fact palmed upon the nation, without having fairly the consent of its representatives." But the trickery was not yet over. On March 3 John Randolph attempted to reopen the whole debate by moving to reconsider the vote on striking out the restriction of slavery in Missouri. Speaker Clay ruled the motion out of order until the journal of the previous day's proceedings had been read. While the journal was being read Clay sent the Clerk of the House with the bills to the Senate. When Randolph renewed his motion it was too late—both bills were no longer in the possession of the House. In the phrase of John Quincy Adams the Missouri Compromise had been "smuggled through both Houses of Congress." [98]

The Old Republicans were almost uniformly unhappy with the compromise. Thomas Ritchie published a melancholy editorial announcing news of it in a spirit of mourning. They not only doubted the power of Congress to regulate slavery but approached the whole idea of such a compromise with the same fear of concession that marked their attitude toward the tariff and internal improvements.

Meet these gentlemen on the threshhold—don't encourage them to go on with their demands. Don't persuade them, that if they take similar ground again . . . they may again succeed—that they may tax us to raise up their hot-bed manufactures;—or abolish the slave representation feature in our Constitution. If we yield now beware. —They will ride us forever.[99]

The Missouri debate also cast its shadow over the presidential election of 1820. In Virginia opposition to the compromise was such that there was open talk in Richmond that if Monroe approved the compromise the legislative caucus would look elsewhere for a President.[100] When the caucus in Richmond met and adjourned without action, Henry St. George Tucker, former nationalist-turned-conservative, expressed the doubts of Virginians on Monroe's apparent approval of the compromise:

It is for fear that the President may lose his election: We are unwilling to purchase his service at such a price; still less willing to support him if *he* can with a view to his own election thus surrender the valuable rights of the South. The Caucus had adjourned accordingly. I trust in God if the President does sign a bill to that effect . . . the Southern people will be able to find some man who has not . . . [sold] himself to our foe, for such are . . . the Northern politicians.[101]

The President's son-in-law, George Hay, informed him of the concern in Richmond and urged him to veto the compromise bill. "You may be injured in the N & E states," Hay admitted, "but you will be amply repaid by the gratitude of the South." Monroe's continued silence, nevertheless, was interpreted by the politicians in Richmond as indicating a veto, and the fear of a non-Virginian President no doubt precluded any rash action. The caucus met again on the evening of February 17, and although the conservative Andrew Stevenson dominated the central committee, Hay was able to report to Monroe the next morning that "everything went on at the caucus last night as it ought to do. . . . Stevenson & . . . his lot . . . will be obliged to go right." [102]

The Virginia action, unfortunately, did not end the intrigues. When General Samuel Smith announced a congressional caucus in the *National Intelligencer* early in April, the North Carolina delegation decided not to attend. With an eye on the contest in New York between Tompkins and DeWitt Clinton the North Carolinians anticipated that "if Tompkins should be [elected] governor of New York, there . . . [would] probably be a smart scuffle for the next Vice President. . . ." [103] In view of Monroe's impartial attitude during the Missouri debate the North Carolina conservatives wished to remain uncommitted on the vice-presidential candidate so that, should Tompkins drop out of the picture, they might put forth a Southern man, preferably Nathaniel Macon. The action of the North Carolina delegation was apparently followed by a majority of the representatives of Virginia, Pennsylvania, and Massachusetts, the latter two probably from a general opposition to the caucus system, and threatened to kill Smith's idea of a caucus.[104] As it turned out, a heavy rain interfered with the scheduled meeting and Smith did not bother to call another one. Since they lacked any reasonable alternative to Monroe, the intrigues of the Virginia and North Carolina conservatives were largely wishful thinking. They may be set down as a bitter reaction to the President's approval of what they regarded as an unacceptable compromise. The party, in any case, closed ranks in support of the only available candidates, and Monroe and Tompkins were re-elected without opposition.

The second Missouri debate, which occupied the winter of 1820–21, marked a further step in the identification of the doctrine of states' rights with the defense of slavery. In accordance with the enabling bill signed by the President on March 3, the Territory of Missouri elected delegates to a convention to write a constitution for the new state. The document produced by this body during the summer of 1820, otherwise an almost verbatim copy of the Kentucky constitution, unfortunately contained a section compelling the Missouri assembly to pass any laws necessary "to prevent free negroes and mulattoes from coming into and settling in this state, under any pretext whatsoever." Since in some states free negroes were citizens and the federal Constitution stated that "the citizens of each state shall be entitled to all the privileges and immunities of citizens of the several states," it was evident that a Missouri law passed in obedience to the state constitution would be in direct conflict with the federal Constitution.

In the Senate the Missouri constitution was submitted on November 14, 1820, to a select committee, which reported a week later a resolution to admit Missouri into the Union. When the resolution was taken up for debate early in December, John Eaton of Tennessee offered as an amendment the proviso

That nothing herein contained shall be so construed as to give the assent of Congress to any provision in the Constitution of Missouri . . . which contravenes that clause in the Constitution of the United States which declares that "the citizens of each state shall be entitled to all the privileges and immunities of citizens of the several states."

In effect affirming that Congress could admit a state to the Union while withholding complete assent to its constitution, the amendment was intended to avoid the central issue of whether Missouri could constitutionally exclude citizens of other states. As a compromise intended to avoid a sectional debate it was temporarily successful, and a week later the Senate passed the resolution with the proviso attached. The only Southerner to vote against the resolution was the uncompromising Nathaniel Macon, who objected to it because of the Eaton amendment. Macon wanted Missouri admitted without any provisos.[105]

In the meantime the House also took up the Missouri constitution, which had been referred to a select committee headed by William Lowndes. On November 23 Lowndes reported a resolution admitting Missouri into the Union. The defense of the resolution was conducted primarily by Lowndes and the Virginia Old Republicans—Philip Pendleton Barbour, Alexander Smyth, and William S. Archer. Each based his remarks on the theory that Missouri, having been authorized to create a constitution and having done so, was already a state and that a congressional declaration to that effect was unnecessary. Even if it wanted to, Congress could not attach conditions to its declaratory resolution admitting Missouri because Missouri was already a sovereign state, the equal of the other states. Thus the doctrine of states' rights, long used by the Old Republicans as a barrier to the tyranny of centralized power, was now wedded to the defense of slavery, a tyranny of individual power that was equally reprehensible. This argument was predictably unacceptable to the Northern majority, and on December 13 the House defeated the Lowndes resolution in a sectional vote.[106]

The House then took up the Senate resolution with its proviso regarding the potential conflict with the federal Constitution.

The Southerners continued to maintain that Missouri was already an independent state or nation having drawn up a constitution and was merely awaiting admission to the federal compact. Any conditions placed on her constitution would make her an inferior, second-class state. On February 12 the House voted down, 83–80, an attempted compromise by Henry Clay to admit Missouri provided her legislature agreed not to implement the objectionable provision in the state constitution. Most of the opposition votes were Northern because the Clay resolution did not require Missouri to expunge the obnoxious section from its constitution, but the deciding votes were those of John Randolph, Weldon Nathaniel Edwards, and William Terrell of Georgia. These three Old Republicans steadfastly refused to allow Congress to impose conditions on the admission of a state that might encroach on its sovereignty.[107]

Despite this temporary defeat, Speaker Clay managed to obtain the permission of the House for a new select committee to work out a compromise. This committee reported a new resolution, substantially the same as the one rejected on February 12; and on February 26, with the need for compromise evident, it was carried 87–81. The only Southerner to vote against it was John Randolph, though Robert S. Garnett and Severn E. Parker of Virginia refrained from voting because of the condition on the admission of Missouri. The other Old Republicans voted for the resolution because, as Hugh Nelson expressed it, they "thought it better to make some sacrifice to form, than to lose the substance." In the Senate the Clay compromise was adopted by a vote of 28–14. The only Southerners in opposition were Macon and William Smith, neither of whom was willing to compromise the form of state sovereignty for the substance of an additional slave state.[108]

One of the most interesting results of the Missouri controversy was the increased popularity of the conservative "principles of '98." Repeated references to them by Republicans too young to remember the political battles of the 1790s reveals the growth of a new states' rights party in the South careful to identify itself with the Republican doctrines that had proved so successful in 1800. The related doctrines of strict construction and states' rights had always been, to some extent, a defensive maneuver by those dissatisfied with the conduct of the government. But, more than that, they were a symbol of freedom against the tyranny of centralized government. With the rejuvenation of the doctrines in the 1820s, unfortunately, they not only lost some of the broad, theoretical character they had had in the hands of the Old Republicans but they tended to become a political stratagem to be adopted or discarded at will. The St. Louis *Enquirer*, for instance, at the same time that it was defending the sovereignty of the state of Missouri against a conditional admission to the Union, was demanding an extensive federal program of internal improvements. The states of Ohio and Kentucky violently denied the power of Congress to create a bank, yet both thought it had power to undertake roads and canals or to restrict slavery in the territories.

Though affected by the slavery issue and the economic depression the states' rights movement in Virginia tended to retain its theoretical character. Two Supreme Court decisions—*McCulloch v. Maryland* in 1819 and *Cohens v. Virginia* in 1821—probably contributed as much as the Missouri debate to the conservative reaction in Virginia. John Marshall's decision in the first case, which held a state tax invalid as contrary to the implied power of Congress to create a bank, provided a good departure for legalistic Virginians to re-examine the nature of the Constitution. In a series of legalistic essays, under the pseudonym of "Hampden," Judge Spencer Roane defended the strict constructionist view, maintaining that the Union was no more than a league of sovereign states that had delegated only certain specific powers to the central government. Roane's authorship was an open secret; he sent copies to Jefferson, Madison, Barbour, and other prominent figures. Jefferson returned the essays with the observation that they "contain the true principles of the revolution of 1800." [109] Backed by the prestige of Roane's name and the approval of the Richmond Junto, the Hampden essays became the official creed of Virginia Republicans, in Congress as well as in the state legislature.

Another response to Marshall's opinion in *McCulloch v. Maryland* was John Taylor's *Construction Construed and Constitutions Vindicated*, a lengthy plea for strict construction in Taylor's prosaic and incredibly complicated style. Exorcized by the threat to the South implicit in Marshall's expansion of federal powers and by the antislavery sentiments expressed by the Northern majority in the Missouri debate, the Virginia prophet again emerged from obscurity to voice his timeworn prediction that unlimited government would eventually destroy the republic.

The restriction of slavery in Louisiana, north of thirty-six-thirty, Taylor considered an unconstitutional interference with the right of private property. The assumption by Congress of this dubious power to legislate on slavery seemed to Taylor conclusive evidence of the extent to which the limitations of the Constitution had been abandoned. Making full use of the ever-popular "conspiracy theory of history," Taylor argued that this erosion of the Constitution was the work of the "monied interest . . . , which is gradually obtaining an influence over the federal government. . . ." He had a ready example of this subversive influence in the bank decision, to which he devoted the better part of the work. Agreeing with Spencer Roane, he regarded the federal government as nothing more than "a league of nations." The only solution was for the Supreme Court to recognize that only a very "limited power . . . over persons and property was given to the representatives of the united nations." [110] Jefferson, growing more conservative with the years, thought it "the most effectual retraction of our government to its original principles which has ever yet been sent by heaven to our aid. Every state in the Union should give a copy to every member they elect, as a standing instruction. . . ."[111]

In the spring of 1821 a decision by the Supreme Court in the case of *Cohens v. Virginia* stimulated a new wave of states' rights sentiment. Cohens, who had been selling lottery tickets under an act of Congress authorizing a lottery for the District of Columbia, was convicted by a state court in Norfolk for a violation of Virginia's antilottery laws. The conviction was appealed directly to the Supreme Court of the United States on the ground that an act of Congress was involved. The major issue, involving the jurisdiction of the Supreme Court, should have been governed by the decision in *Martin v. Hunter's Lessee*, five years before, but Alexander Smyth and Philip Barbour, counsels for the state, distinguished the earlier case. The *Cohens* case, they argued, was a criminal suit and therefore a matter for state jurisdiction; the appeal, moreover, in effect made the state a party to a suit in a federal court without her consent and hence was barred by the Eleventh Amendment. Marshall's decision in favor of the state on the ground that the act of Congress was intended to apply only to the District of Columbia in no way mitigated the adverse effect in Virginia of his assumption of jurisdiction.

Spencer Roane again dashed into print with a series of articles signed "Algernon Sidney," which appeared in the Richmond *Enquirer* in the summer of 1821. Roane argued that the section of the Judiciary Act of 1789 permitting appeals from state to federal courts was unconstitutional because the Constitution did not confer appellate jurisdiction on the Supreme Court in criminal cases. Roane unfortunately was allowing his political instinct to prevail over his legal judgment, for the Constitution specifically grants Congress the power to establish the appellate jurisdiction of the court. Roane also maintained with Smyth and Barbour that the Eleventh Amendment barred the suit, an assertion equally ridiculous because that amendment was not intended to apply to cases in which the state initiated the suit and the defendant appealed to a federal court. Roane's conclusion that the decision in effect reduced the state courts to a secondary status was somewhat more reasonable. Despite the deficiencies in Roane's logic, the attack on *Cohens v. Virginia* seemed to Jefferson "to pulverize every word which had been delivered by Judge Marshall. . . ." [112]

One of the most striking results of the conservative reaction in Virginia that began in 1817 was the restoration to popular favor of the twin apostates John Randolph and John Taylor of Caroline. The surprise and skepticism with which the old Quids viewed this convolution in popular sentiment was expressed by James M. Garnett in a letter to Randolph:

One symptom of the times, I confess, surprised me not a little, altho I am getting somewhat too old for surprises of almost any kind, but especially for those occasioned by the eternal inconsistencies of man. *You* were actually toasted lately at a public meeting in Prince George where there were some men present who, but a few short years before, would probably have seen you *roasted* almost as soon as drink your health. . . . [John Taylor] too is now eulogised to the skies by many who not long since would have thought it a national blessing for him to be hanged. Master Enquirer, I hear does not hesitate to express openly an anxious desire that the old Gentleman should either once more come into public life; or illuminate our benighted citizens with some of the good old doctrines of '98. [113]

Shortly thereafter Ritchie and Taylor patched up the feud that had begun in 1808, and in November, 1820, Ritchie published Taylor's *Construction Construed*. In the spring of 1820 a reconciliation between Randolph and Monroe was effected by Hugh Nelson and George F. Strother, and Monroe invited Randolph to dinner. The reinstatement of Randolph and his ideas was such that soon even Jefferson was boasting that he had "as companions in sentiments, the Madisons, the Monroes, the Randolphs, the Macons, all good men and true, of primitive principles." [114]

The restoration of the "principles of '98" came too late for some. Many of the Old Republicans had retired from politics; others were dead. In the Congress the states' rights movement was being carried on largely by new men. On February 16, 1821, John Quincy Adams recorded in his diary the death of William A. Burwell, former private secretary to President Jefferson and member of Congress from 1806 until his death. Adams added a note that was at once an epitaph for Burwell and for Old Republicanism:

Jealousy of State rights and jealousy of the Executive were the two pillars of Burwell's political fabric, because they are the prevailing popular doctrines in Virginia. He floated down the stream of time with the current, and always had the satisfaction of being in his own eyes a pure and incorruptible patriot. Virginia teems with his breed more than any other state in the Union, and they are far from being the worst men among us. Such men occasionally render service to the nation by preventing harm; but they are quite as apt to prevent good, and they never do any.[115]

The Old Republicans, to be sure, had always been sectionally oriented, in the sense that most of them came from Virginia and the South, but their program had been concerned primarily with matters of national policy, that is, small government, a weak executive, and low taxes. The Old Republicans had been the conservative wing of a party in power; the states' rights party of the early 1820s, though it absorbed the Old Republicans and paid lip-service to their ideas, was primarily concerned with local economic problems—with the tariff in South Carolina, with the Indians in Georgia, with the bank in Kentucky—and insofar as it became identified with the "Radical" party it was devoted to gaining power by the election of its presidential candidate, William Harris Crawford.

VIII

The Radicals

The election of 1824 cast a long shadow over the politics of the second term of President James Monroe. To Monroe the presidency was a logical reward for a long life of public service. Though a strong partisan in his youth, he had little taste for party politics in old age; indeed, he hopefully foresaw the gradual elimination of all political factions. With the demise of the Federalist party as a political entity, after 1816, Monroe's Administration might have been truly an "era of good feelings" free from party warfare, but this unfortunately was not the case. His Cabinet, the ablest since the first administration of Jefferson, contained a number of young, ambitious men who were inclined to cast covetous eyes on the presidential succession. As a result, instead of two great parties, there were by 1820 a number of personal factions devoted to furthering the interests of Secretary of State Adams, Secretary of the Treasury Crawford, Secretary of War Calhoun, House Speaker Henry Clay, and somewhat later of Andrew Jackson, governor of the Florida Territory and after 1823 senator from Tennessee.

As each faction struggled for advantage, politics became increasingly personal and each issue seemed to become entangled with the paramount subject of the approaching election. As early as February, 1822, it was evident to a discerning observer like Justice Joseph Story "that all public business is colored with the hues borrowed from this subject. Every measure is watched with a jealous regard to its bearing on this point." [1]

The outstanding candidate since 1816 when a sizable minority of the Republican congressional caucus had voted for him was William Harris Crawford. By 1821 he commanded what approached a nationwide political machine, centered in the South, but with strong branches in New York, Pennsylvania, and the Northwest. Crawford was also the most successful of the candidates in identifying himself with the principles of the Virginia dynasty. He entered Congress in 1807 as a senator from Georgia a friend of John Randolph, and in Congress his only deviation from the conservative pattern was a strong defense of the bank in 1811. The period when he was a strong nationalist came, fortunately, while he was a member of the Cabinet, first under Madison and then Monroe; and in his administrative position he was free from the necessity of recording any potentially embarrassing votes. Crawford could thus pose as a nationalist or a conservative as the occasion demanded, and the faction that grouped itself around him was as heterogeneous as his politics.

This party, known eventually as the "Radicals," managed to absorb the new economic liberals of the North, the post-Missouri states' rights party of the South, and, gradually, the Old Republicans. The faction took its name, according to John Taylor of Caroline, from the Radical party in France, which was founded to defend the charter granted the people by King Louis XVIII. The constitutionalism of the American Radical party, however, was largely veneer. Taylor and other Old Republicans noticed that their Radical friends too often abandoned their constitutional doctrines, and, "dictated by local interest or prejudice," joined their adversaries in passing such measures as internal improvements and the protective tariff.[2]

All Radicals were not Old Republicans, though nearly all the Old Republicans eventually settled on Crawford as the candidate most likely to carry on the "principles of '98" and thus became Radicals. In the personal politics of the early 1820s it is quite difficult to distinguish the Old Republicans from their Radical friends. The problem is illustrated by the political career of the leading New York Radical, Martin Van Buren. Elected to the Senate in 1821, Van Buren came to Washington determined to revive the party spirit of the 1790s. Within a month after his arrival he was accusing Monroe, with some justice, of trying to integrate the two parties by making no distinction between Republicans and Federalists in the distribution of patronage.

The disjointed state of parties here, the distractions which are produced by the approaching contest for President, and the general conviction in the minds of honest and prudent men, that a radical reform in the political feelings of this place has become necessary, render this the proper moment to commence the work of a general resuscitation of the old democratic party.

He even suggested that the New York legislature pass a resolution protesting the appointment of Federalists and appoint a committee of correspondence to communicate with the legislatures of the other states.[3]

Van Buren evidently viewed Monroe as a latter-day version of President Washington and compared himself to Jefferson in his efforts to found a new party based on old Republican principles. But it does not necessarily follow from this, as his most recent biographer seems to think, that Van Buren was an Old Republican primarily concerned with reviving the doctrines of 1798.[4] His career in Congress evidences no doctrinaire dislike for the bank, the protective tariff, or federally sponsored internal improvements. He voted for the Cumberland Road bill in 1823 and the tariff in 1824. To be sure, by 1826 he was denouncing federal internal improvements as unconstitutional, but by then New York had built its Erie Canal and the internal improvements issue was a popular ground for opposition to the Adams Administration. As in his advice to President Jackson to veto the Maysville Road bill in 1830, Van Buren's Old Republicanism always seemed to have a political flavor. In his dislike for Monroe's policy of appointing Federalists can be seen a desire for more patronage as much as a hatred of Federalists. Van Buren may have wanted to "resuscitate" the Republican party, but he was more concerned with the party than with its doctrines. Such political faith as he had seems to have been a laissez-faire Liberalism, which blended well with the agrarian Liberalism of his Southern cohorts.

Whatever his motives, Van Buren succeeded in reviving the old New York–Virginia alliance and made it the basis of the Crawford faction. Within a few months after his arrival in Washington he made friends with John Randolph.[5] Then in March, 1822, Van Buren made the first of a series of trips to the South to begin his "general resuscitation" of the Republican party. In Richmond he talked to Spencer Roane, "a hearty and bold Republican of the old School," who was highly critical of "the course pursued by Mr. Monroe. . . ."[6] It is uncertain whether he met Ritchie on this trip, but in 1838 Ritchie told him that from "the first moment of my acquaintance with you, I have been your personal and political friend."[7] By January, 1823, Ritchie in the *Enquirer* was referring to Van Buren and his friends as "statesmen and patriots."

The first evidence of this new alliance appeared in the election of a Speaker of the House when Congress assembled in December, 1821. The Speaker in the previous Congress, John W. Taylor of New York, had made many enemies. As a supporter of the restriction of slavery in Missouri he was hated in the South, and as an Adams man he was opposed by the Crawfordites. In New York politics he was generally supposed to be a Clintonian, and it was the Van Buren "Bucktails" in the New York delegation that swung the majority away from Taylor and elected Philip Pendleton Barbour.[8] It is uncertain whether Barbour was a Crawford partisan at this time, but his election was a triumph for the Southern conservatives, who now controlled the House committee system for the first time since Macon was ousted as Speaker in 1807.

The outstanding issue of the spring of 1822 was a renewal of the great retrenchment debate, which saw the reappearance of that strange alliance between the forces of Crawford and Clay in Congress against the War Department and its secretary, John C. Calhoun. Though stimulated by the depression and the treasury deficit, the debate had major implications for the coming election since Calhoun was a potential candidate. That the Old Republicans would join in the attack was to be expected, though it does not necessarily mean that they were already in the Crawford camp.[9] Long-time advocates of economy and simplicity in government, their reaction to the financial difficulties of the government, as expressed by Jefferson, was "to cease borrowing money & pay off the national debt. If this cannot be done without dismissing the army & putting the ships out of commission, haul them up high and dry, and reduce the army to the lowest point at which it was ever established." [10] Such a reaction was neither politically inspired nor personally antagonistic to Calhoun.

The attack on the War Department in the spring of 1822 got under way slowly with some preliminary skirmishing over a bill to supplement the reduced military appropriation of the previous year, made necessary by the inability of the War Department to put economies into immediate effect. The real battle developed over a bill reported by William Eustis, chairman of the military affairs committee, to force economies on the army by reducing the size of the officer staff.[11] Eustis, a former Secretary of War under Madison, was able to give only a halfhearted defense of the bill. He tried to persuade the House that the changes would increase efficiency by placing more jobs in fewer hands, but he admitted frankly that he would not be unhappy if the bill were defeated.[12]

The burden of defending the bill thus fell on the leading retrencher in the House, John Cocke of Tennessee. Cocke pointed out that the number of enlisted men in the army had been reduced several times since 1815; it was only logical that the size and rank of the officer staff should also be reduced. Assigning a major general to command the handful of men that garrisoned such posts as Sackets Harbor and Council Bluffs was absurd. The economies contemplated by the bill would save the government $110,000 a year, Cocke estimated; should the House adopt certain amendments to be proposed by his friend from New York, even greater savings might be effected. With this introduction David Woodcock of New York followed Cocke on the floor. Admitting that he was a Radical and interested solely in the condition of the treasury, Woodcock proposed a series of amendments that would further emasculate the officer staff in the name of economy. Woodcock's amendments were adopted "by a large majority." [13]

Always ready to preside over the demise of the army, the Old Republicans soon joined the fray. John Rhea of Tennessee iterated the familiar arguments against a standing army. The nation, he pointed out, was under no threat from abroad, and the preservation of domestic order was a problem of the states and their militia.

The Constitution of the United States does not contemplate a regular army, except in time of war; the constitutions of the respective states declare standing armies dangerous in time of peace; that principle ought not to be contradicted. Admit the contrary to prevail, and the liberties of the people will ultimately be prostrated.

To the oft-repeated thesis that the nation ought to prepare for war in time of peace Rhea answered, "To provide effectually for the extinguishment of the debt of the United States, is the preparation for war." [14]

The lengthy appeals to Old Republican doctrine were largely superfluous, for the determining factor in the division of the House was the strength of the personal factions. In the end the forces of Adams and Calhoun imposed a series of amendments that modified the more severe features of the bill. With its teeth removed the retrenchers lost interest in the bill, and it was quietly abandoned.[15]

This by no means ended the economy debate, however. In February the Radicals obtained the appointment of a special committee on retrenchment headed by Ben Hardin of Kentucky.[16] Though the committee contained only one Old Republican, Lewis Williams, the willingness of the Radicals to take over the litany of Old Republicanism was made strikingly evident when the committee reported to the House on April 15. Recommending a "return to good old principles, which, for some years past, have been lost sight of," the committee thought the government ought to live within its income and provide for the reduction of the national debt. This could be accomplished by revising the tariff with a view to revenue, dispensing with "useless expenditures," and by reducing the salaries of government officials "to what they were during the Administrations of former Presidents." Finally the committee proposed that "in the great and good work of retrenchment, Congress ought to be the first to set an example to the balance of the nation, and begin with themselves. . . ."[17]

Political "hay" was always to be made in a move to reduce the compensation of congressmen, and a bill was accordingly brought in. Alexander Smyth promptly added an amendment to reduce the salaries of all government officials by 20 percent, which was adopted without a recorded division. The retrenchment forces were riding high and no one dared oppose the bill, but few were sincerely willing to take such a drastic step for the sake of economy. On May 3 the bill was laid on the table "without a division, by a large majority," and it was not heard from again.[18]

The retrenchment debate illustrates the difficulty of identfying the Old Republicans after 1820. Their litany and to some extent their dogma were adopted by the Radicals. Indeed, a few of the Old Republicans, such as Lewis Williams, John Cocke, and John Floyd were already partisans of Crawford. But that there was still a distinction to be made can be shown by the debate on the bankruptcy bill in this session of Congress. The agitation among mercantile interests for a uniform federal system of bankruptcy was sharpened by the depression, and in response the House judiciary committee reported a bankruptcy bill on December 11, 1821. In defending the bill John Sergeant of Pennsylvania, former Federalist and one of the leading spokesmen for business in Congress, told the House that the growth of business on a national scale demanded a uniform system of bankruptcy.[19]

On January 22, 1822, Andrew Stevenson of Virginia moved to strike out the first section in order to secure a debate on the principle of the bill. He was a member of the Richmond Junto, brother-in-law of Dr. John Brockenbrough, and Speaker of the Virgina House of Delegates since 1812. Stevenson, an Old Republican, was elected in 1821 to the seat of John Tyler from the Richmond district. As a lieutenant of Spencer Roane he secured from the Virginia Assembly a pair of resolutions condemning the decision in *McCulloch v. Maryland* in 1819, and shortly after his entrance into Congress he submitted a bill to repeal the twenty-fifth section of the Judiciary Act providing for appeals from state courts to the Supreme Court.[20]

The grounds for Stevenson's opposition to the bankruptcy bill show the extent to which the spirit of strict construction was being carried in the South. Stevenson admitted that the Constitution gave Congress specific power to pass bankruptcy legislation, but he contended that the proposed law was nevertheless contrary to the spirit of the Constitution. Ironically enough, he founded his argument on Marshall's decision in *Sturges v. Crowninshield* (1819), which by declaring unconstitutional a state bankruptcy law for tending to impair the obligations of prior contracts had given new impetus to the demand for federal legislation. As a result of the restriction on the states imposed by the Constitution as interpreted in *Sturges v. Crowninshield*, Stevenson argued, there is an "implied moral prohibition" on the impairment of a contract by Congress.[21] This, of course, was strict construction by implication. The states, it seems, had certain implied rights, one of which was that Congress had no power to do anything the states could not do, even when that power was specifically delegated.

Like sheep following a familiar leader into a familiar fold, the Virginians adopted Stevenson's constitutional arguments. William S. Archer maintained that the power to pass bankruptcy laws was circumscribed by "the inherent limitations on political authority," one of which was the sanctity of contracts. Though the Constitution appeared to grant the power to pass bankruptcy laws, "both the grant and exercise of such a power, stood inhibited by an authority which was paramount to the Constitution, in conflict with which, the Constitution stood, to the extent of the collision, superceded and annulled." [22] This argument, reminiscent of the later stand of William Lloyd Garrison, confirms the suspicion that the strict constructionist respected the Constitution only when it served his interests.

The Old Republicans were joined by agrarians, Northern and Southern, who developed the less esoteric argument that no landowner could benefit by the bill because by going through bankruptcy he lost his land and thus his means of subsistence. The property of a merchant, on the other hand, was largely in easily liquidated assets, and he could afford to take bankruptcy in stride. No representative of agrarian interests was willing to give this additional advantage to the mercantile segment of the economy. This bill, moreover, differed from earlier bankruptcy bills in that it applied to everyone and not just to merchants. For this reason James Buchanan of Pennsylvania thought it particularly pernicious because, instead of being confined to merchants, it would teach everyone "to disregard the faith of contracts." [23]

The agrarian forces were too strong, and the bill was rejected on the second reading, March 12, by a vote of 90–72. The division is an interesting one, for it enables one to distinguish between agrarian Liberals like the Old Republicans and their allies among the Northern Radicals, who might be described as commercial Liberals. The number of Old Republicans, excluding the newly elected states' rights men from the lower South, declined somewhat from the high point reached in 1820 to about twenty-five, largely as a result of deaths and resignations.[24]

The annual debate provoked by the perennial issues of internal improvements and the tariff is of further aid in identifying the Old Republicans after 1820. The subject of federally financed internal improvements reappeared in April, 1822, as an appropriation for repairs on the Cumberland Road, a minor section of a bill appropriating money for the various Executive departments. Sanctioned by the annual appropriations of more than two decades, the Cumberland Road was normally the target of only the staunchest opponents of internal improvements. But in 1822 it encountered new difficulties as the Old Republicans were joined by retrenchers and representatives of state interests. Silas Wood, leading New York Radical, denied that an appropriation for the road was constitutional, while James Buchanan pointed out that Pennsylvania had turnpikes of her own and disliked the idea of having a competing road maintained at the national expense. With the help of Old Republicans like John Rhea of Tennessee, whose constitutional scruples were frequently contrary to the economic interests of his state, the appropriation was struck out, 105–58.[25]

In the meantime a proposal to erect tollgates on the Cumberland Road in order to make the users pay for repairs was introduced into the Senate by Richard M. Johnson. Walter Lowrie of Pennsylvania and Nathaniel Macon objected that it was a money bill, and on this ground the bill was laid on the table. Two weeks later, Joseph Hemphill of Pennsylvania reported the same measure to the House.[26] When the appropriation for the maintenance of the road was lost, the tollgate bill was taken up.

The toll bill received the usual Virginia bombardment, but the alliance with the New York and Pennsylvania interests was broken by the prospect of levying a toll on the users of the national road. Amendments that would transfer the road to the states were beaten down, and the bill was quickly passed to a third reading. On April 29 John Taylor of New York, who never before had shown any concern for constitutional niceties, considered the bill "such a violation of the Constitution" that he ordered the yeas and nays recorded on the final passage; the bill passed anyway, 87–68. The Senate concurred three days later with no discussion and only seven negative votes.[27]

On Saturday, May 4, 1822, Congress received President Monroe's veto. In his opinion, "a power to establish turnpikes with gates and tolls, and to enforce the collection of tolls by penalties, implies a power to adopt and execute a complete system of internal improvement." Monroe conceded that Congress had power to appropriate money for certain specific projects, but he denied the power to undertake a general system of roads and canals. The exercise of "jurisdiction and sovereignty" within the states by means of tollgates on the national road was beyond the constitutional power of Congress, even if it had the consent of the states involved.[28]

The following Monday the House voted 72–68 to sustain the President's veto. As in 1817 the Speaker descended from the rostrum to have his vote recorded first. Only this time the Speaker was not Henry Clay but Philip Barbour, and his vote was in the President's favor.[29] The Old Republicans were, of course, overjoyed to hear this reaffirmation of their doctrines from the Executive chair itself. But there were some reservations. After all, the pure orthodoxy of the message contained a trace of alloy in the concession that Congress had power to appropriate money for specific projects. Spencer Roane, to whom Monroe sent a copy of the veto message, noted this immediately and warned Monroe that this, in effect, negated the rest of his argument. Congress had no general power of appropriation, Roane reminded him; it could appropriate money only to carry out some specifically delegated power. Roane also disapproved of Monroe's admission that precedent can make a matter constitutional unless the people object—an argument Madison used in approving the bank in 1816. "On that ground," Roane pointed out, "the true construction of the Constitution would be made to depend upon the persistence of error of those representatives on the one hand, and upon the relative promptitude or tardiness by which that error might be put down, by the people, on the other." [30]

Though discouraged by the President's obvious distaste for a comprehensive program of internal improvements, the nationalists decided to probe his theoretical stand by appropriating money for a series of specific projects. In January, 1823, Senator Talbot of Kentucky appended to a routine appropriation bill an amendment providing funds for the repair of the Cumberland Road. It was pushed through the Senate with the assistance of Van Buren, who felt that unless the road were repaired the money already expended on it would be wasted. This was Van Buren's only vote in favor of internal improvements, and he later regretted it. In his *Autobiography* he recorded that his vote was given "rather on the ground of its paternity . . . than from an examination of the subject." [31] The only verbal opposition to the bill in the Senate came from John Taylor of Caroline, who for the third time in his career consented to a brief tour of duty in the Senate when James Pleasants resigned in December, 1822, to become governor of Virginia. Taylor's speech was unfortunately not reported, but his opposition meant that Monroe's interpretation of the appropriation power had been rejected by another Old Republican.

A month later, February 19, 1823, the House took up the Senate amendment providing $25,000 for the maintenance of the Cumberland Road, but the subject was treated to little discussion. After years of debate no one could say anything new on the issue, and few tried. The bill passed to a third reading by a vote of 89–66 and received the final approval without a division. The Old Republicans made up nearly half the minority; most of the rest were New Englanders who had no economic interest in the project. Many Northern Radicals voted with the nationalists.[32] As a simple appropriation it was tailored to meet the constitutional scruples of the President, and it was signed a week later.

Heartened by this success, the nationalists a year later initiated a bill to appropriate money for surveys of a general system of roads and canals. This was the sort of bill Spencer Roane and Taylor of Caroline had feared in questioning Monroe's veto message. The bill was an appropriation for a specific project, surveys; but its passage would imply approval of a nationwide system of roads and canals. Nor were their fears allayed when the author of the bill, Joseph Hemphill of Kentucky, who sponsored the tollgate bill of 1822, assumed that the President would agree to the survey bill since it was in accord with his doctrine of appropriation.[33]

Philip Barbour led off for the opposition with his customary motion to strike out the enacting clause. In general his constitutional arguments were those he had advanced in earlier debates. He started with the general proposition that all governmental functions that related "to matters of internal regulation, all that might be denominated municipal powers, were reserved to the States." Municipal powers had been defined in Number 45 of *The Federalist* as pertaining to "measures to promote internal order, improvement, and prosperity," a category which surely included a system of roads and canals. Barbour rested this hypothesis on the most altruistic argument that can be made for the states' rights theory—the assumption that these "municipal powers" could not be exercised by the federal government on a basis equally fair to all states, for they "bear directly on the internal affairs of a people almost infinitely diversified in situation, circumstances, and local interests." Turning to the President's veto message of 1822 he noted that Monroe conceded the power of Congress to appropriate money for internal improvements while denying any right of jurisdiction over them. But, said Barbour, "I deny both." [34]

In answer Speaker Clay belittled the constitutional objections of Barbour, appealed for a broad national outlook, and affirmed:

The system contemplated . . . looks to great national objects and proposes the ultimate application . . . of the only means by which they can be effected, the means of the nation—means, which if they be withheld from such objects, the Union, I do most solemnly believe, of these now happy and promising States, may at some distant (I trust a far, far distant) day, be endangered and shaken at its center.

Under the spell of Clay's eloquence the House voted down Barbour's motion to strike out the enacting clause and approved an appropriation of $30,000.[35]

Andrew Stevenson, who took the floor when the House again took up the bill on January 29, 1824, sought to answer Clay's imputation that only the friends of internal improvements were concerned with the national interest. The subject, said Stevenson, "was of local rather than a national character," and the "schemes" of the bill's supporters "had . . . their origin in local views." Virginia held aloof from such views. Though she herself was engaged in building roads and canals, "she asks not the aid of this government, and would scorn to receive it, by a sacrifice of her principles, or an abandonment of duty." No sir, "Virginia has maintained too long her worship at the altar of the Constitution, pure and undefiled, to be seduced from her allegiance by golden considerations, or alarmed by any mistaken apprehensions of disunion or disaffection." Throughout his address Stevenson evidenced a type of thinking that distinguished the Old Republican from the more recent adherents of the states' rights school. "The Constitution," he insisted, "cannot shift and change with circumstances and our notions of expediency. What was unconstitutional on yesterday, will be so today, tomorrow, and forever, until the Constitution is amended." [36]

The next day, January 30, was John Randolph's, and in his discursive way he threw random shots at Clay, the West, Madison, and the whole loose system of constitutional construction.

But his most startling point came toward the end of his discourse when he told the House, "If Congress possesses the power to do what is proposed by this bill, they may not only enact a sedition law—for that there is precedent—but they may emancipate every slave in the United States—and with stronger colour of reason. . . ." Nathaniel Macon had long since come to the conclusion that "if Congress can make banks, roads, and canals under the Constitution they can free any slave in the United States. . . ." But this was the first time the thought had been uttered on the floor of Congress, and it reflected the growing fear among conservatives of the uses to which loose construction and the doctrine of precedent might be put. Should Congress be disposed to free the slaves, Randolph argued, it need only

follow the example of the gentlemen who have preceded me, and hook the power upon the first loop they find in the Constitution; they might take the preamble—perhaps the war-making power—or they might take a greater sweep, and say, with some gentlemen, that it is not to be found in this or that of the granted powers, but results from all of them—which is not only a dangerous, but *the most* dangerous doctrine.[37]

The only effect of Randolph's speech was to bring Henry Clay back to the floor. After defending himself against Randolph's various insinuations, he begged the House to broaden its vision, to look to the future:

Sir, a new world has come into being since the Constitution was adopted. Are the narrow, limited necessities of the old thirteen states, of indeed parts only of the old thirteen states, as they existed at the formation of the present Constitution, forever to remain a rule of its interpretation? Are we to forget the wants of our country? Are we to neglect and refuse the redemption of that wilderness which once stretched beyond the Allegheny? I trust not, sir. I hope for better and nobler things.[38]

The rest of the debate was like small-arms fire after an artillery barrage. George Tucker advanced the laissez-faire argument that roads and canals ought to be built by private initiative.

William Cabell Rives, who succeeded Hugh Nelson, minister to Spain, as representative from Monroe's own district, presented in his maiden speech to the House an able summary of the states' rights position. On February 10, 1824, the House at last brought itself to a vote and passed the survey bill 115–86. Southern conservatives and New York Radicals made up most of the opposition.[39]

As in the year before, the main opponent of internal improvements in the Senate was John Taylor of Caroline. After examining and dismissing, one by one, the various constitutional provisions on which the power to construct roads and canals was based, Taylor warned the Senate that the economic and social welfare of the people was best left in the hands of the states. "Congress, acting by a majority, without local fellow feeling, can never constitute a representation of the geographical interests and climates at the extremities of the Union." Neither the public buildings in Washington nor the Cumberland Road inspired Taylor with much confidence in the capacity of Congress to direct internal improvements. He remained convinced "that the policy of leaving individuals, partnerships, and States, as much as possible to pursue their own interest, in their own way, is the only good evidence that the Government is founded in reason and justice, and not in error and fraud." [40]

Nathaniel Macon added his pleas to those of Taylor, but without avail. The Senate passed the survey bill on April 24 by a vote of 24–18. Van Buren had already altered his stand and voted against the bill on the third reading, though he was missing from the final division. Voting in favor of the bill, on the other hand, was the new senator from Tennessee, Andrew Jackson, who only two years before told Monroe that his "opinion" had "always been that the Federal Government did not possess the constitutional right." [41]

The fears expressed by Randolph and Macon that an extension of federal power might lead to emancipation were not yet common among Southern conservatives, but nearly all of them linked internal improvements with the tariff as evidence of the growing paternalism of the government. Henry Clay linked them too, but the reverse of the bold relief of the American System was the cavity of conservative fears. Early in 1824 Burwell Bassett wrote: "We have not only gone back to all the old federal doctrines of '98 but have taken up others. . . . The internal improvement system is to double at least the Presidential patronage and the tariff which is to take from one for the benefit [of] another and the poor for the rich, will both be forced on us." [42]

The question of a protective tariff had been put off from year to year, but a demand for one had been rising steadily in volume since the panic of 1819. Protectionist meetings were held annually in Pittsburgh, Harrisburg, Philadelphia, or Albany, and the enticing arguments of Hezekiah Niles and Mathew Carey, backed up by statistics largely of their own making, added to the clamor. In January, 1823, the protectionists sought to test the temper of the House by introducing a bill to increase the duties on textiles and finished iron products, but they encountered a stiffening Southern resistance led by the Old Republicans. Alexander Smyth of Virginia, lead-off man for the opposition, adopted the position that the protective tariff was unconstitutional. The Old Republicans had been approaching this idea for several years, but this was the first time it was openly asserted on the floor of the House. Smyth maintained that the power to lay and collect taxes was for purposes of revenue only; Congress had no power to protect domestic manufactures.[43]

A little later John Rhea of Tennessee enlarged further on the constitutional objection. The power to levy taxes, he told the House, was to raise revenue to pay the nation's debts, provide for the common defense and general welfare, "and for no other use or purpose whatever." The phrase "general welfare," moreover, meant exactly what it said—Congress had no power to tax for the benefit of a special group. To those, like President Monroe, who thought that certain industries ought to be protected because the country might need them in time of war, Rhea answered with the physiocratic argument that "domestic manu-facturers" working in their homes could supply the country's needs in an emergency. The nation did not need huge factories that had to be protected from competition.[44]

The extent to which the Virginia doctrines had spread over the South by 1823 became evident when Thomas Montgomery of Kentucky spoke for two days against the bill. Kentucky had long been overwhelmingly in favor of the tariff, and Mont-gomery had been a nationalist since he entered the House in 1813. Yet on February 11 he blandly told the House that the protective tariff was contrary to the Constitution. The govern-ment had no power to protect manufactures, he asserted; its sole functions were to protect the rights of individuals, prevent crime, and administer justice. Apparently none of Montgomery's constituents grew hemp, for he argued that the tariff was harm-ful to agriculture; it tended to aggregate the people into fac-tories and workshops to the detriment of energy and virtue, and it abetted the tendency for wealth to accumulate in the hands of a few great capitalists.[45]

In the lengthy debate the Southerners received support from some of the Northern Radicals, notably Churchill C. Cambre-leng of New York, Van Buren's chief lieutenant in the House. The position taken by Cambreleng, however, can be explained on personal grounds and does not signify a reversal in the politi-cal outlook of New York. Cambreleng himself was president of an importing firm and represented the shipping interests of New York City, much as Daniel Webster represented the commercial interests of New England in opposition to the tariff. A motion to strike out the enacting clause was lost, but the bill was dropped shortly thereafter.[46]

When Congress reassembled in December, 1823, Henry Clay was back in his old seat after a two-year absence from the House, and he was easily elected Speaker by 139 votes to Barbour's 42. Though the selection of Clay was more an indication of his personal influence in the House than a forecast of party strength, it was nevertheless clear that a revision of the tariff could be put off no longer.[47] Equally important was the growing nationalism of the Monroe Administration. The announcement in the President's annual message of December 2, 1823, that the United States would view as an unfriendly act any interference by Europe in Latin America, "whatever else it may have been, was not agrarian at all." It was an announcement of America's commercial maturity, and it was a nationalistic answer to the Liberal Toryism of William Huskisson and George Canning. In the same message to Congress President Monroe recommended "additional protection to those articles which we are prepared to manufacture, or which are more immediately connected with the defense and independence of the country." If not a carte blanche for protectionism this was sufficient encouragement to the leaders of the House, and on January 9, 1824, John Tod of the committee on manufactures reported a bill to raise the tariff: on woolens to 33 percent and on other textiles, raw wool, and metal goods to 25 percent.[48]

When the House took up the tariff on February 11, the day after it passed the survey bill, Philip Barbour announced that he would forego his customary motion to strike out the enacting clause so that debate might proceed to the details. The opposition then proceeded to bring up every detail of the bill with the object of deleting it or reducing the duty. This new tactic met the protectionists on their own ground. The usual protectionist strategy was to promise benefits to enough special interests to insure a majority in the House. The opposition now clearly intended to align special interests in opposition to each particular duty. The tactic was generally unsuccessful, but it served to prolong the debate, and it began to seem as if the bill might be talked to death. Finally on February 24, after two weeks of discussion, the protectionist Henry C. Martindale of New York moved to strike out the enacting clause in order to secure a debate on the principle of protection. This maneuver satisfied neither side and was quickly negatived.[49]

As the debate resumed it soon became evident that the leading opponents were not the Old Republicans, heretofore the most vociferous opponents of the tariff, but the representatives from the lower South, from South Carolina, Alabama, Mississippi, and Louisiana. Typical of these was the brilliant George McDuffie, close friend of Calhoun, who had taken the seat vacated by the conservative Eldred Simkins. A former nationalist who had written a pamphlet in "Defense of a Liberal Construction of the Powers of Congress," McDuffie bent sufficiently to the sentiment of South Carolina to oppose the tariff. But he was unable to condemn it as unconstitutional and was forced to confine his arguments to the injustice of the tariff in its operation on the Southern planter.[50]

After a contest of ten weeks the bill was carried in the House by the lean majority of five votes, 107–102. In opposition were the Old Republicans and Northern shipping interests represented by Webster and Cambreleng, but the closeness of the vote was due primarily to a growing opposition in the lower South, an opposition that was noticeable in 1820, but which had hardened considerably by 1824.[51]

In the Senate the most vocal opposition again came from the lower South, though John Taylor of Caroline and Nathaniel Macon fought every provision. On May 4 Taylor occupied most of the day with a speech on the tariff. Taylor began with his usual appeal to history showing how the Hamiltonian system, with its bank, its paper money, and its excises tended to create a "legislated pecuniary aristocracy." He then produced a long series of statistics designed to prove that the current nationalist system that combined a bank with a protective tariff benefited only the nine Northern states and injured the other seventeen states of the South and West. If nothing else, the statistics proved that advocates of the American System, such as Mathew Carey and Hezekiah Niles, did not have a monopoly on the use of figures. Taylor then drove home his point:

> For, in truth, this is not a tariff bill to encourage manufactures. It is a bill of bargains, to enrich a pecuniary aristocracy. This aristocracy is a polygamist, and is, by this bill, courting a number of local interests, with a design to marry them for the sake of their fortunes; and as Spindle attempted with Lady Truman, it proposes to bribe them with small portions of their own estates, to get the rest for itself.

This unholy series of bargains did more, unfortunately, than injure the South and West—it tended to wreck the whole representative system. "Under our Constitution neither territories nor representation were intended to be consolidated; or law, geographically partial, to be enacted." The authors of the Constitution, Taylor apparently felt, intended members of Congress to represent only their localities and not economic interests of national scope. Taylor had apparently never read, or chose to ignore, Madison's issue number ten of *The Federalist*.[52] This was Taylor's last speech in Congress—three months later, August 21, 1824, the conservative conscience of Virginia was dead.

Free trade sentiment in the Senate was strong enough to amend the bill severely before it passed on May 13, by 25–21. Northern Radicals, including Van Buren, voted for the measure. The South, except for Tennessee and Kentucky, was solidly opposed. Voting in favor was the unpredictable Andrew Jackson and his friend and disciple from Tennessee, John Henry Eaton.[53]

"James Monroe's signature to a protective tariff was an obituary in itself. The Virginia dynasty was dead. There would be no more Old Republicanism in high places." [54] With these words a modern historian pronounces the end of the Virginia dynasty and the doctrines of government associated with it. But if Old Republicanism was dead it was not because Monroe had signed a tariff bill—Madison too had signed into law a tariff—but because it had been swallowed up. Its constitutional doctrines were taken over by the lower South for the defense of economic and sectional interests. And its adherents were absorbed into the broad-based political movement devoted to the election of William Harris Crawford.

Crawford himself was an Old Republican only in point of age. His career as senator from Georgia from 1807 to 1813 was conservative enough, except for his support of the bank in 1811. As Secretary of the Treasury he tended toward nationalism, giving general, if vague, support for the bank and the protective tariff. On the vexing question of internal improvements he made no public statements, but his private letters, particularly to Northerners, indicate that he considered them constitutional and inevitable.[55] All that could be said for Crawford as a conservative was that he seemed to believe in economy and simplicity of government. Yet he remained high in the estimation of the Old Republicans. Nathaniel Macon, for instance, favored him on the basis of his career in Congress.

His talents, independence, firmness, and honesty, I never heard doubted by a single member who served with him; his republicanism was not then questioned, nor do I now recollect but one vote of his, which was at variance with the old republican doctrine, and that was to renew the charter of the first bank of the U.S., and that certainly would have been better than establishing the present one. . . .[56]

Yet his politics was sufficiently obscure to attract a following of varied interests, geographical and economic. Van Buren, already recognized as the leading opponent of the nationalists in New York, narrowed his choice of candidates down to Crawford early in 1823. Van Buren's commercial Liberalism seemed to blend with Crawford's public views, but, equally important, by 1823 Crawford was the leading candidate and Van Buren was always primarily concerned with party unity.[57] Even in the South Crawford attracted not only the states' rights advocates but many nationalists. Thomas W. Cobb of Georgia, an early supporter of Crawford, favored both the bank and internal improvements in his congressional career. Samuel Smith, a nationalist as senator and representative from Maryland since 1793, favored Crawford as early as the summer of 1823.[58]

The Old Republicans, on the other hand, only slowly took up the cause of Crawford. Many of them, particularly the Virginians Thomas Ritchie and John Randolph, favored at first the archparticularist, Judge Spencer Roane. In the *Enquirer* Ritchie lauded Roane as a man who "comprehends the true intent and meaning of our political institutions." [59] The death of Roane on September 4, 1822, nipped this idea in the bud, and Virginia conservatives gradually moved into the Crawford camp. By early 1823 Ritchie was explaining away Crawford's occasional lapses from conservative doctrine. As Secretary of the Treasury, explained Ritchie, Crawford had been forced to approve the tariff because it would bring in revenue, and he had given support to the bank only in his official capacity and not from personal preference.[60]

The general attitude toward Crawford among Virginia conservatives was summed up by "Constitution" in the *Enquirer* in May, 1823, who supported Crawford only because his opinions were less "unconstitutional" than those of the other candidates. As late as February, 1824, Burwell Bassett was only a lukewarm supporter of Crawford and placed his name on the list of those calling for a congressional caucus largely at the insistence of his friends. John Randolph, still highly critical of Crawford in January, 1824, did not come out publicly in his favor until the following May.[61]

Nathaniel Macon became a partisan of Crawford as early as the spring of 1822, and in the congressional delegation from North Carolina there was a solid Crawford majority, headed by the Old Republicans Lewis Williams and Thomas Hall. The election of Willie P. Mangum to the House in 1823 was another victory for the Crawford cause. A youthful conservative steeped in the litany of the states' rights doctrine, Mangum identified himself with the Republicans of the "old school" and began working actively for Crawford, whom he considered "decidedly preferable on the score of being a sounder constitutionalist. . . ." [62] In the state legislature Bartlett Yancey, friend and confidant of Nathaniel Macon and member of Congress during the War of 1812, presided over a Crawford majority from his position as Speaker of the Senate.

Crawford's support, however, was confined largely to the conservative planters of the Roanoke Valley, who had long dominated the politics of North Carolina through the Warren Junto. The small farmers of the West supported Calhoun at first and later turned to Jackson, while Adams' strength lay largely in the commercial centers, Fayetteville and Hillsboro. The division was further complicated by a popular demand for reform of the state constitution, a widening of the suffrage, and state internal improvements, all of which were opposed by the Eastern planters. In the spring of 1824 the Jacksonian leaders organized a "Peoples' Ticket" designed to promote the candidacy of Jackson and Calhoun with vague promises of reform. This fusion of interests carried the state for Jackson in the election, but the conservatives managed to salvage the governorship when the Assembly elected the Old Republican, Hutchins Gordon Burton.[63]

The two South Carolina Old Republicans, Senators John Gaillard and William Smith, favored Crawford as early as 1820, but the state was still predominantly nationalist-minded. In an anti-Crawford move a legislative caucus in December, 1821, nominated William Lowndes for President; the nominating speech made it clear that South Carolina regarded the "principles of state sovereignty" and the "unrelenting economy" associated with Crawford as dangerous to the nation.[64] When Lowndes declined the nomination the South Carolina nationalists naturally turned to Calhoun.

Calhoun's first task was to undermine the position of the leading spokesman of the Crawford forces in the state, Senator

William Smith. Accusing Smith of being "wedded to Georgia politicians," Calhoun engineered his defeat for re-election to the Senate in 1823 on the grounds that Smith's states' rights particularism did not "fairly represent the state." [65] Smith returned from Washington and opened an extensive newspaper campaign against Calhoun that lasted into the summer of 1824. And the other Old Republicans in the state fell into line behind him. Dr. Thomas Cooper, Republican of '98 and a victim of the Sedition Law, re-entered the political stage to write a number of pamphlets and articles denouncing Adams, Clay, Calhoun, and Jackson as consolidationists and praising Crawford as the only true representative of the states' rights school. Two relics of the Jeffersonian era, John Taylor and D. R. Williams, also threw their political influence to Crawford.[66] The Old Republicans in South Carolina, however, remained a negligible minority, and when Calhoun threw his influence to the popular Jackson the cause was lost. Judge Smith, at least, gained a personal victory in his election to the legislature in 1824 where he was to engineer the spectacular "revolution of 1825."

By the beginning of 1824 Crawford, with the best organization, had easily the largest following in Congress—Macon estimated it at between 80 and 100 members.[67] With Crawford thus virtually assured of the nomination if the traditional caucus method were followed, the supporters of the other candidates began an intensive campaign against the caucus system, labeling it unrepresentative and undemocratic. Their recommendations varied from national conventions to state legislative caucuses. Early in February, 1824, more than half the members of Congress signed a statement that they would not attend a caucus. Undaunted, Van Buren, who had taken over the Crawford campaign in Congress, issued a call in the *National Intelligencer* for a caucus to meet on February 14 in the chamber of the House of Representatives. The result was a dismal showing for the Radicals. Only 66 Congressmen showed up, most of them from New York, Virginia, North Carolina, and Georgia. A number of conservatives such as Taylor, Randolph, and Garnett of Virginia and Macon and Mangum of North Carolina, all of whom eventually supported Crawford, refused to attend because they disliked the caucus system of nomination. In the meeting Crawford received 62 votes; there were two for Adams and one apiece for Jackson and Macon.[68]

For Vice-President the caucus nominated Albert Gallatin, recently returned from Paris. Van Buren preferred Clay for Vice-President and had approached him through Thomas Hart Benton, but Clay refused. Van Buren was then persuaded to accept Gallatin because of the influence it might have on Pennsylvania.[69] Crawford, on the other hand, favored Gallatin all along, and so did most of the Old Republicans. Gallatin himself attributed his selection to an attempt to unify the party on its old principles. "Almost all the old Republicans (Mr. Jefferson & Mr. Madison amongst them) think as I do," he wrote,

but they were aware that Mr. Crawford was not very popular and that the bond of party . . . being nearly dissolved, neither of the other candidates would withdraw, and they were at a loss whom to unite to him as V. Pres[iden]t. I advised to nominate nobody for that office, or if anybody some person from N. York or New England. The last was attached to Adams; there were contentions in N. York. The friends of Mr. Crawford thought the persons proposed there too obscure, & that my name would serve as a banner & show their nomination to be that of the old Republican party.[70]

The Crawford campaign was under a severe handicap before it even got under way. Returning from Washington in the summer of 1823 the Secretary of the Treasury had become feverish and found his skin inflamed. He took to his bed and summoned a local physician, who gave him a drug—possibly lobeline or calomel—to combat what was apparently a case of erysipelas. The treatment evidently caused a paralytic stroke that rendered the Secretary blind and dumb. Though Crawford recovered slowly through the winter, which encouraged his friends enough to nominate him in the caucus, it was evident by the summer of

1824 when he was still partially paralyzed that his recovery might not be complete. "Our friends begin to feel uneasy about Mr. Crawford," George M. Troup, governor of Georgia and former nationalist, wrote to Macon.

They fear that his disease may prove fatal or otherwise disqualify him for the office which we so much hoped to see him fill. In this unfortunate event, I know of no person who would unite so extensively the public sentiment of the Southern Country as yourself. . . . Unless you forbid it I will take the liberty to propagate my opinions as diffusively as I can. In the administration of the general government we want virtue, virtue, virtue.[71]

In the meantime the Crawford campaign was running into trouble in other sections. When Gallatin's home state of Pennsylvania declared for Jackson, it became evident that Gallatin was politically useless to the Radical ticket. At Van Buren's instigation Gallatin was asked to resign, and the Radical Party allowed each state to write in its own favorite for Vice-President.[72] Significantly enough, Virginia delivered hers to Nathaniel Macon.

In the election Crawford received a majority of the electoral votes in only two states, Virginia and Georgia. The rest of the South and Pennsylvania went to Jackson. Adams carried New England and New York, and Clay the Northwest. Nearly a year before Calhoun had retired from the campaign to run for the vice-presidency. Though Jackson had a plurality of both the popular and the electoral vote, no candidate had a majority, and the contest among the three top candidates, Jackson, Adams, and Crawford, was thrown into the House of Representatives.

In the contest in the House the Old Republicans stuck with Crawford, though next to him they were divided in their preferences. Thomas Ritchie and the Richmond Junto favored Clay, while Jefferson and most of the Virginia Assembly preferred Adams. None of them could abide Jackson. The election of Adams and the rumor of a "corrupt bargain" with Clay were the first steps in the conversion of the Old Republicans from

Radicals to Jacksonians, and, as such, it is part of another story. During the contest in the House, Nathaniel Macon wrote:

New parties will I suspect rise in the U.S. not founded, like the old, on the construction of the constitution, though that may in part divide them. They may I fear be like the parties in a few of the states, rather the followers of men than principle; principle however may be mixed with the admiration of the men, but the love of a snug office is apt to attach to such parties.[73]

This was more than a prophecy—it was a commentary on the immediate past.

IX

The Jacksonians

"The great majority of Mr. Crawford's friends in Virginia are so decidedly opposed to Jackson, that under no circumstances whatever could they be induced to favor his election; put Mr. Crawford out of the question to the people of Virginia, J. Q. Adams would be President without a doubt." [1]

Though coming from an Adams paper, the *Norfolk and Portsmouth Herald,* this statement reflected with reasonable accuracy the feelings of the political leaders of Virginia. The Old Republicans respected the ability and integrity of Adams, and his nationalist political beliefs were generally obscured by the election campaign. Adams himself made overtures toward gaining Old Republican support. Early in 1823 he wrote a letter to Alexander Smyth that was published in the *Enquirer,* in which he tried to convince Virginians that he was a true friend of the "principles of '98." He also made it known that he would like to have Nathaniel Macon as vice-presidential candidate on his ticket. [2]

Shortly after his inauguration Adams tendered the post of Secretary of War to a leading Virginia Crawfordite, James Barbour. A senator from Virginia since 1814, James Barbour, unlike his brother, Philip, was not an Old Republican. A nationalist during his early years in Congress, he had become an opponent of the tariff and internal improvements only after 1820. Barbour wrote to Andrew Stevenson in Richmond to find out the reaction of the Richmond Junto to the appointment. Stevenson answered that Virginia was still neutral on Adams and that opinion in Richmond was divided on the propriety of Barbour's accepting a post in the Cabinet. For himself, Stevenson expected to remain open-minded toward the administration: "Principles and not men, has heretofore and will continue to be my motto." [3]

With Crawford at least temporarily out of the political picture on account of his health, the conservatives had at first no obvious alternative to Adams. Despite his popularity, many of them were suspicious of Jackson, remembering his arbitrary actions in New Orleans in 1814 and his disregard of authority and proper legal procedure in Florida in 1818. Gallatin, who considered Jackson "an honest man and the idol of the worshippers of military glory, but from incapacity, military habits, and habitual disregard of laws and constitutional provisions, altogether unfit for office," expressed the general fears.[4] Gallatin was one of the few Old Republicans who remained friendly to the Adams Administration, accepting in 1826 an appointment to the Court of St. James's.

The first nail hammered into the coffin of Adams' popularity was the appointment of Henry Clay as Secretary of State. After Clay had thrown his support to Adams in the House of Representatives to ensure his election, this action easily led to the charge, though somewhat unjustly, of a "corrupt bargain." The effect among Virginia conservatives that this news produced was revealed by Betsy Coles when she wrote to her brother Andrew Stevenson,

The good people are run mad here about the presidential election. I was with some of our great men at Dr. Brockenbrough's the other night and found them all universally denouncing Clay and Adams. They (Mr. Nicholas, Dr. & Judge S. Rone [sic], Campbell, etc. etc.) said that they would take Jackson and anybody now in preference to Adams.[5]

The "corrupt bargain" made a lasting impression and led to serious doubts about the integrity of the administration. Within a year it had become a rallying cry and a propaganda weapon, as is shown by a letter of Willie P. Mangum, a North Carolina conservative elected in 1823:

Sir, this administration I verily believe will be conducted upon as corrupt principles indeed more corrupt, than any that has preceded it. Bargain & compromise will be the order of the day—I came here hoping that I might be able to lend it a frank support—The Crawford party will have to stand aloof, they will not be able I fear to support this administration.[6]

The second nail was the President's first annual message to Congress, December 6, 1825. The message not only assumed the power to undertake but positively recommended a national university, the financing of scientific explorations, the building of an astronomical observatory (a "lighthouse of the sky"), the creation of a Department of the Interior, and the inception of a program of internal improvements on a vast scale. Under the "necessary and proper" clause Adams felt Congress could pass "laws promoting the improvement of agriculture, commerce, and manufactures, the cultivation and encouragement of the mechanic and of the elegant arts, the advancement of literature, and the progress of the sciences, ornamental and profound."[7] Such a vast extension of government paternalism, a century ahead of its time, was bound to produce as a reaction an alliance between the Southern conservatives and the laissez-faire Liberals of the North.

Nathaniel Macon noted that the message seemed "to claim all the power to the federal government, which has heretofore produced so much debate, and which the election of Mr. Jefferson was supposed to have settled." Jefferson himself saw it as a revival of Federalism. "Their younger recruits," he wrote to William Branch Giles,

having nothing in them of the feelings or principles of '76, now look to a single and splendid government of an aristocracy, founded on banking institutions, and moneyed incorporations under the guise and cloak of their favorite branches of manufactures, commerce, and navigation, riding and ruling over the plundered ploughman and beggared yeomanry. This will be to them a next best blessing to the monarchy of their first aim, and perhaps the surest stepping stone to it.[8]

Jefferson frequently overstated his case when he had a sympathetic listener, and Giles was certainly sympathetic. As senator an "invisible" opponent of the Madison Administration and a nationalist, Giles by 1825 was in the thick of the states' rights reaction in Virginia. He denounced the President's message in a series of articles in the *Enquirer* under the title "Political Disquisitions," an action that brought him back into political favor in Virginia and in 1827 earned him the governorship. Ritchie, too, bitterly assailed the message in the *Enquirer*.[9]

The House of Representatives in 1825 was controlled by the administration, and it elected as Speaker an Adams partisan, John W. Taylor of New York, by a majority of five votes. The Old Republican ranks had thinned considerably. Though the Virginia delegation retained its conservative character, only a handful were familiar names.[10] In North Carolina, where the people had voted for Jackson and the state's congressional delegation had stuck with Crawford, a popular revolt in the election of 1825 defeated five Radicals, among them the Old Republicans Charles Hooks and Thomas Hall. Conservatives Willie P. Mangum, Lewis Williams, Romulus Saunders, and Weldon N. Edwards survived the holocaust, but Williams was soon found in the Adams camp because of his ancient antipathy to Jackson.[11] Elsewhere in the House only John Cocke of Tennessee and Starling Tucker of South Carolina can be legitimately considered Old Republicans.

In the Senate neither the administration nor the friends of Jackson had a majority; the balance of power lay with the Crawfordites. For this reason the first indication of the coalition that was to ruin John Quincy Adams appeared not in the House but in the Senate early in 1826. The important figures were Martin Van Buren and his new ally, John Randolph, who was elected to the Senate in 1825. Both were already unhappy with

the President's annual message and with his policy of appointments. Van Buren, whose only dispute with Adams in principle
was internal improvements, might have backed the administration, but he was alienated by the President's friendliness with the
Clintonians in New York, and he was disgusted with the appointment of the former Federalist Rufus King as minister to
Great Britain in 1825. John Randolph, who considered the administration forces to be composed of "old Sedition Law federalists & soi-disant republicans who had abjured their old principles
for the 'Law of Circumstances,' " linked the annual message with
the appointment of former Federalists and concluded that this
was "the second four years of John Adams' administration." [12]

The breach came into the open when the President accepted
an invitation to the Congress of American Republics soon to
assemble in Panama. The documents on the matter that Adams
sent to the Senate indicated that the Latin Americans had in
mind an extension of the Monroe Doctrine into a defensive alliance. Van Buren, who considered the action possibly unconstitutional and certainly at variance with the isolationist foreign
policy established by Washington and Jefferson, offered two
rather mischievous resolutions in the Senate on February 15,
1826, asking the President whether any or all of the documents
relating to the mission could be made public. Adams retorted
that the publication of such documents was contrary to precedent and he would leave to the Senate a decision "upon the
motives of which . . . I do not feel myself competent to decide." [13] Although the Senate's motives were indeed questionable,
it was hardly politic for the President to raise the point. The
imputation was immediately seized upon by John Randolph,
who declared in the Senate that the moment he heard the President question its motives, "That moment did I put, like Hanni-
bal, my hand on the altar, and swear eternal enmity against him
and his politically. . . . Here I plant my foot—here I fling defiance
right into his teeth before the American people." Randolph went
on to denounce the Adams-Clay alliance, with a reference to

Fielding's *Tom Jones,* as "the coalition of Blifil and Black George—the combination, unheard of till then, of the puritan and the blackleg." [14]

In the ensuing debate the new coalition of Jacksonians and Radicals argued that the President should never have accepted the invitation without asking the advice and consent of the Senate and that the United States should not send delegates to a conference that would probably result in a multilateral alliance. Macon's opinion was that the agreement to send delegates without the consent of the Senate smacked of Executive prerogative and was probably based on the precedent of the Monroe Doctrine, which "was a strong measure and of a prerogative nature." Littleton Waller Tazewell, former Quid who had taken John Taylor's seat in the Senate in 1824, similarly regarded the President's failure to seek the advice of the Senate as an attempt to break down the constitutional principle of separation of powers, the basis of the whole institutional framework of the government. The coalition, however, did not yet have a majority, and on March 14 the Senate consented to the nomination of Richard C. Anderson and John Sergeant as envoys by votes of 27–17 and 28–18. On April 22 the House voted 134–60 to appropriate $4,000 to finance the mission.[15] Among the Old Republicans only Lewis Williams voted for the Panama Mission, and he remained a staunch supporter of the Adams Administration.

Toward the end of the session Nathaniel Macon summed up his opinion of the Adams Administration after its first year in office. "The administration," he felt, "might have got along probably tolerable well, had it have been content to have traveled a plain and known road. But the Panama trip, and the visit to the sky, and the attempt to make the constitutional way as wide as the world, has and will embarrass it." However, Macon, less willing than Randolph to accept Van Buren's verbal assurances that he was an Old Republican, was not yet ready to join the opposition camp. "It seems to me," he added in the same letter, "that the two parties now contending for power have the same political principles; the contest is whether A[dams] or J[ackson] shall be the next President." [16]

By the following November, however, when Congress again assembled in Washington, Macon and most of the other Old Republicans had concluded that Jackson was their man, if only "because he cannot do worse for us." [17] The connection between Jackson and the Old Republicans, if never very close, was at least an old one. Macon's correspondence with Jackson began even before Jackson became the first congressman from Tennessee in 1796, and after Jackson resigned from the Senate in 1798 Macon continued to keep him informed of events in Congress and of the progress in the election campaign of Jefferson. In 1806 Jackson sympathized with the stand of John Randolph and the Quids in Congress, and a little later his sympathy for Burr tended to ally him with the antiadministration Republicans. In 1808 he supported the presidential candidacy of Monroe against Madison. As early as 1810 Jackson corresponded with Randolph in connection with Randolph's efforts to have General Wilkinson dismissed and brought to trial. Considering Randolph "a man of talents and firmness," Jackson furnished him with information.[18]

That seems to have ended the connection until Jackson returned to politics as senator from Tennessee in 1823. His actions as senator, in voting for both internal improvements and the tariff in 1824, bespoke no doctrinaire conservatism and probably contributed to the suspicions of the Old Republicans. Indeed, even Van Buren, no doctrinaire himself, when he finally decided in the fall of 1826 to join the Jackson camp, wanted a guarantee that the campaign would be based "on old party grounds [and] preserve the old systems." [19]

By early 1827 John Randolph, who had admitted two years before that "the first requisite with me in a candidate is the capacity to get a majority of the votes," joined the campaign for Jackson largely through lack of an alternative. With a political pragmatism that was novel for him, he wrote to his cousin:

Practical men know that of all the qualifications for the Presidency that of being able to obtain the votes is not the least essential. There is but one man who can unite them & the question is not whether that man is preferred over every other but whether we shall take him or the present incumbents. We have no other choice. I think too that his character has in many respects been undervalued. There are great and valuable points in it.[20]

More important than the gradual movement of men like Randolph and Macon into the Jackson camp was the rapid expansion of the states' rights movement in the lower South, a movement that Van Buren sought to harness to the Jacksonian wagon. In this he was aided by his connections among the Old Republicans, for it was they who taught the younger generation of Southern statesmen the almost forgotten language of strict construction.

Most spectacular was the political revolution in South Carolina managed by the old enemy of Calhoun, Judge William Smith. Though the Jackson-Calhoun alliance had carried the state in the presidential election, the Radicals were generally successful in the elections to the state legislature in the summer of 1824. A Radical majority, led by Smith, former Senator John Taylor, and the old Quid David R. Williams, was determined to stem the tide of nationalism in the state.[21] Their opportunity came when President Monroe presented a plan for a new national road to extend from Washington to New Orleans in his annual message to Congress in December, 1824. In the South Carolina Senate Stephen D. Miller, a conservative who had served in the Fifteenth Congress, introduced a series of resolutions denying the power of Congress to authorize a system of internal improvements or a protective tariff. Though the nationalists succeeded in postponing the resolutions temporarily, Judge Smith reintroduced them in the following session and pushed them through the legislature in December, 1825.[22]

Smith's victory in the "revolution of 1825" presaged a three-year period of Radical supremacy in the state. When the Old Republican John Gaillard died in the summer of 1826, the legislature sent Smith to take his seat in the Senate, and the same year it elected John Taylor governor. When the Calhoun forces regained control of the state in 1828, they succeeded only by adopting the particularist ideas of their opponents.

The change in leadership in South Carolina, however, made little difference to the Jacksonian presidential campaign. In the summer of 1825 Judge Smith took a tour through the Northeast and met Van Buren in Boston. According to Van Buren's account of the meeting, Smith was persuaded to join the Jacksonian bandwagon. When Calhoun formed an alliance with Van Buren in 1826, the state was virtually unanimous for Jackson, although the Old Republicans Williams, Taylor, and Thomas Cooper remained suspicious of Calhoun and refused to support him as Jackson's running mate.[23]

A parallel reaction toward states' rights in Georgia, though it embarrassed the Adams Administration and furthered the Jacksonian cause, had less connection with the Old Republicans. Governor George M. Troup, former War Hawk and nationalist Republican, was the leader in Georgia politics of the Crawford faction, whose main support came from the seaboard planters. Responding to the planters' need for new cotton lands in the Piedmont, Troup demanded the forced removal of the Cherokees by the federal government. When the Adams Administration refused to violate its treaty obligations, he resurrected the doctrine of states' rights and asserted the jurisdiction of Georgia over the Indians within its limits. In the hands of Troup, however, the concept of states' rights was a useful weapon rather than an eternal truth. While defying the Adams Administration on the Indian matter, he continued to champion federal internal improvements and not till 1827 did he declare his opposition to a protective tariff.[24]

The opposition faction in Georgia politics, led by John Clarke, governor from 1819 to 1823, found its main strength among the small farmers of the interior. No basic difference in principle divided the parties, however; the contest was almost exclusively personal. They differed on a national issue on only one occasion—when Troup supported Crawford and Clarke tended toward Jackson in 1824. Both were in agreement on the necessity for Indian removal, and by 1826 each was trying to outshine the other in its support of Jackson.[25] In the election of 1828 the Troup faction retained its Crawfordite suspicion of Calhoun, and seven of Georgia's vice-presidential electoral votes were cast for Senator William Smith of South Carolina.

The conservative reaction in Alabama in the mid-1820s also borrowed from the Old Republican heritage. Until 1820 the politics of the territory and the state were dominated by Georgia planters who had moved into the "black belt" of Alabama, led by an old Quid, William Wyatt Bibb. After Bibb's death in 1820 the conservative, Crawfordite party disintegrated, and in 1821 Israel Pickens, the former North Carolina nationalist, was elected governor. Representing the small farmers of the northern hill country, Pickens campaigned for a state-owned bank and carried the state for Jackson in 1824. The vote reflected the numerical superiority of the small farmers, for the large planters generally voted for Crawford. After the election Dixon H. Lewis assumed control of the Crawford party in Alabama. A former Virginian who had moved first to Georgia and then to Alabama, Lewis' political ideas were influenced largely by his uncle, Bolling Hall, though he was also a friend of Nathaniel Macon and John Taylor of Caroline. Elected to the legislature in 1826, Lewis pushed through a series of resolutions condemning the Adams Administration for its use of implied powers. Then, embracing Jackson as the states' rights candidate, he led the Alabama Radicals into the Democratic camp.[26]

In Washington, Van Buren was quick to see the political implications of the states' rights reaction in the lower South. He turned first to Calhoun, whose nationalist ideas were already undergoing a profound change. In December, 1826, the two agreed to join forces in support of the Jackson campaign. Van Buren then made another tour of the South in the spring of 1827. In

Charleston he spent a few days talking to supporters of Calhoun and then pushed on to Georgia to see Crawford. The Georgia leader refused to join the new party, probably from a distrust of Calhoun, but Van Buren continued to make headway among the Southern conservatives. On his return journey he stopped to visit D. R. Williams in western South Carolina, and he spent several days in Raleigh with Macon and Governor Burton.[27]

As part of his understanding with Calhoun, Van Buren promised to write to Thomas Ritchie in order to secure the adherence to the coalition of the Virginia Radicals. In this letter Van Buren made clear his intention to form a new party based on the principles of the Republican party of the 1790s and on the old alliance between "the planters of the South and the plain Republicans of the North. The country," he added, "has once flourished under a party thus constituted & may again." [28] Ritchie hesitated for some months, and Van Buren turned his powers of persuasion on other Virginians.

In the spring of 1827 Senator Tazewell wrote to Ritchie that he had discussed with Van Buren the possibility of establishing a new journal in Washington "to keep alive by frequent repetition and argument, the great principles of the Republican party, as they were manifested and expressed prior to 1801." Tazewell distrusted Van Buren and wanted to ensure a strong Old Republican influence in any new political combination that was formed. "For my part," he continued,

I look forward beyond the 4th of March, 1829. Should we be defeated then, it would be necessary to take a new departure. Should we then succeed (of which I have no doubt) it is possible, nay probable, that our party will soon be in danger of separating from the very fact of its overwhelming force and unmanagable numbers. Then will arise a new crisis, for the occurrence of which timely preparation should be made; & I feel solicitous that a Southern Editor should have acquired and established the reputation of the proposed journal before that day arrives. What may be Mr. Van Buren's views upon this point of the subject I know not, nor does he know mine. In your reply, therefore, to this letter (which I shall be compelled to show him) you will not of course notice this.[29]

In Tazewell's mind the alliance with the Van Buren forces was a temporary coalition dependent upon the behavior of the party after it succeeded in electing Jackson. Foreseeing that it might succumb to the Northern entrepreneurial interests in the same way that the Republican party had, he wished to ensure that a strong voice of conservatism would continue to exist. Tazewell was a better prophet than politician.

Within a month after he received Tazewell's letter, April 27, 1827, Ritchie endorsed publicly the candidacy of Jackson. Admitting that there were objections to him—his votes for a tariff and internal improvements—Ritchie nevertheless insisted that Jackson's letters showed him to be "opposed to the dangerous doctrine of implication, opposed to foreign political connections, opposed to the system of loans." [30] Strict construction, small government, isolation, and hard money—Jackson, it would seem, had become an Old Republican.

When Ritchie fell into line, the Jacksonians turned their attention on another influential Old Republican, John Tyler. Governor of Virginia since 1825, Tyler in 1827 was a candidate for the Senate seat formerly held by James Barbour and filled since 1825 by John Randolph. The fact that Randolph and Tyler were the only candidates for the seat indicates the extent to which the Old Republicans, indeed even the Quids, had returned to popular favor in Virginia. Despite a warning from Andrew Stevenson, a Jacksonian by late 1826, that the defeat of Randolph might "produce . . . an impression that Virginia is wavering," there was general agreement in the Assembly that both candidates held the same political beliefs. Tyler was elected by a combination of Adams men and Jacksonians unhappy with the eccentric conduct of Randolph in the Senate.[31]

It is true that Tyler and Randolph were of the same political hue, but Tyler was not yet a partisan of Jackson. In the fall of 1826 he told James Barbour that it was "a matter of indifference" to him "whether the man at the head of affairs shall come from this or that side of the Tweed. . . ." What was important was that the government

be administered on correct principles. In interpreting the constitution I would neither be liberal or parsimonious, but would take the instrument as I find it written—giving to its terms their ordinary acceptation in their plain and obvious meaning. So far as the government is administered on this principle it shall have my support— and of consequence my opposition when upon any other.[32]

Almost a year later Tyler still thought the choice between Adams and Jackson a tossup. He considered them both "latitudinarians" in the construction of the Constitution. Tyler at this time preferred DeWitt Clinton largely because the construction of the Erie Canal had demonstrated the feasibility of state-financed internal improvements, and Clinton, the patron of the Erie Canal, could also be the patron of states' rights.[33] With this same line of reasoning he might have backed Daniel Webster, who had sympathized with the states' rights Hartford Convention, but, after all, party meant something even to a man of principle. By December, 1827, he was safely ensconced in the Jackson camp, and he explained his conversion in the following way:

From having heretofore felt some indifference touching the matter, I am now most earnestly solicitous for Jackson's success. I do believe it to be loudly called for by the present state of things. The President, you may rest assured, is as confirmed a federalist now as at any preceding day of his life. His principles as given in his first message are entirely ultra—and the mere fact that Daniel Webster (a Hartford Conventionist) has been his mouth piece from the beginning has always been with me enough to damn him. To his opponent Genl Jackson I have entertained the strongest objections— there are even *now* many others whom I would prefer—but every day that passes inspires me with the strong hope that his administration will be characterized by simplicity—I mean republican simplicity. This contest has chastened and improved his temper, and when you look to the men from among whom he must select his cabinet, his course may already be anticipated. Who are they: Clinton, Van Buren, Tazewell, White, P. P. Barbour, etc. all agreeing with Virginia in principle, or approximating very closely to her.[34]

Tyler might be excused for being a poorer prognosticator than Tazewell, but in supposing that both Clinton and Van Buren held "Virginia principles" or even that they would serve in the same Cabinet Tyler was being incredibly naïve.

That Van Buren was more concerned with party organization than with doctrine should have been evident to Tyler a few months later when the question of the tariff again appeared before Congress. Van Buren's own attitude toward the tariff was determined strictly by party necessity. In the summer of 1828 he told a protectionist meeting in Albany that he favored a tariff which would be "temperate and wise and therefore salutary" in promoting "every branch of domestic production and industry," which is about as ambiguous as Jackson's famous letter to Littleton H. Coleman of April, 1824, in which he favored a "judicious" tariff.[35]

The tariff of 1828 was steered through Congress by Van Buren for political reasons. He had to silence the opposition to him in New York, and he wished to lend aid to the areas that Jackson needed most—Pennsylvania and the Northwest. The Southern conservatives fought the tariff every inch of the way, but, as Van Buren had predicted, they remained in the Jackson party for lack of an alternative.[36] John Randolph denounced it because it was designed to promote "manufactures of no sort, but the manufacture of a President of the United States," but there is no record that he ever blamed Van Buren for the measure. Even John Tyler it seems swallowed the assurances of someone, probably Van Buren, that the purpose of the bill was to make the rates so high as to produce a "reaction in the North which may ultimately enable us to get back to safe principles." [37]

It was thus with an almost blind faith that the Old Republicans followed Andrew Jackson into the presidency. The tariff of 1828 was an accurate forecast of the relative importance of the Southern conservatives in the new political coalition formed by Van Buren. Despite Tyler's hopes, not a single Old Republican was included in the Cabinet of the new President. Calhoun, a new friend of the Old Republicans, pleaded for the appointment of Tazewell as Secretary of State, trying to convince Jackson of the importance of cultivating Virginia. Jackson retorted that it was equally important to keep the support of New York and appointed Van Buren instead.[38] Of the members appointed who had previously sat in Congress not one could point to a conservative record. The Secretary of the Treasury, Samuel D. Ingham of Pennsylvania, had had a long career in the House serving from 1813 to 1818 and again from 1822 to 1829. A friend and protégé of Calhoun, Ingham entered Congress a strong nationalist. He consistently supported the bank, the tariff, and internal improvements, even in the latter years when he followed Calhoun into the Jackson party. When Ingham resigned from the Treasury in 1831, he was succeeded by Louis McLane, a former Federalist-turned-Republican who had supported the bank, tariff, and internal improvements in Congress since 1817. Another former Federalist in the Cabinet was Attorney General John M. Berrien of Georgia, whom William Coleman, editor of the Federalist New York *Post*, described as a member of "the old Hamilton school." [39]

John Henry Eaton, the new Secretary of War, was an old friend of Jackson's from Franklin, Tennessee. He had entered the Senate in 1818 a nationalist, voting for the tariff in 1820 and internal improvements two years later, though after 1824 his votes adhered more closely to the Van Buren line. William T. Barry, Postmaster General, as a senator from Kentucky from 1814 to 1816, had supported both bank and tariff.

If the composition of the Cabinet is any indication, it was not the conservative Southern agrarian, but the Northern or West-

ern businessman—mercantilist or Liberal as it suited his interests—
who triumphed in the election of Andrew Jackson.[40] To be sure,
this new ruling class used the slogans and symbols of Old Republicanism often and to great advantage. Jackson, for instance,
informed Randolph that the bank, "besides being unconstitutional . . . [was] dangerous to liberty, and therefore, worthy of
the denunciation which it has received from the disciples of the
old republican school." [41] Amos Kendall's famous slogan, "The
World is governed too much," appealed to the Liberal mind,
whether it be Southern agrarian or Northern businessman. The
Maysville veto, moreover, though partly a political slap at Henry
Clay, served to place the Jackson Administration in line with
the conservative position of Madison and Monroe on this issue
and helped to reassure the Old Republicans that all was not lost.
Ritchie admitted that "it does not come up to our Virginia doctrine, but it does a great deal by arresting those . . . local appropriations . . . which were wasting the public funds and bribing
members of Congress out of their Constitutional principles." To
Randolph the veto fell "upon the ear like the music of other
days." [42]

The only political concession to the Old Republicans in the
new administration was the appointment of John Randolph as
minister to Russia in the spring of 1830. "I do not consider that
I am identifying myself with the admin[istration]," Randolph
wrote his cousin in explanation of his acceptance,

although I have no hesitation in saying that the same motives which
induced me to support the election of Gen J[ackson] are equally
strong in prompting me to sustain him against a most unprincipled
opposition; the object of which is to bring back the Stuarts & the
Bourbons whom we have expelled. Many of the acts of the present
Adm[inistration]—viz.: the formation of the Cabinet; some re-
movals; & several appointments have my decided disapprobation—
but I have the highest confidence in the ability & firmness of the
Chief, who is liable like other men to err, from misinformation
sometimes—sometimes from passion. But where am I to find a faultless man of any description.[43]

Where indeed! But it is comforting that after searching for the "faultless man" for over thirty years Randolph was at last gaining some political *savoir-faire*. More important, this letter reveals that some Old Republicans still considered the Jacksonians only the best of a bad lot and supported the administration largely for lack of any alternative.

That alternative, for a few of the Old Republicans at least, was not long in coming. Indeed, the schism predicted by Tazewell had begun in 1828 with the publication of a small pamphlet, *The South Carolina Exposition and Protest*, published anonymously, but written by Vice-President John C. Calhoun. Calhoun had now come full circle, following his native state from an active nationalism in 1820 to a reactionary sectionalism in 1828. Temporarily removed from active politics by his position as Vice-President under Adams, Calhoun quietly reshaped his political thought to conform to the militant states' rights position of South Carolina. The *Exposition* was a reincarnation of the Kentucky Resolution of 1798 in more extreme form. Calhoun maintained that a single state might nullify a law that it regarded as unconstitutional, such as the protective tariff, until three-fourths of the states justified the law by making it an amendment to the Constitution. With the publication of the *Exposition* the leadership of the states' rights movement passed from the moderation of Virginia to the extremism of South Carolina.

The irony of the nullification movement in South Carolina is that it was led primarily by the formerly nationalist followers of Calhoun. Though initiated by a sharp drop in cotton prices in 1826 and the tariff of 1828, it also represented an attempt by the Calhoun forces to regain control of the state by adopting and extending the ideas of their Radical opponents.[44] The maneuver was quite successful, for the Calhoun forces regained control of the state legislature in 1828. The Radicals split on the issue of summoning a nullification convention because the Old Republican leaders among the Radicals were unable, in the end, to carry their Virginia doctrines to the extreme of nullification. Governor John Taylor, in a Fourth of July address in 1828, opposed any hasty action and suggested resisting the tariff by cooperating with the other Southern states in nonconsumption pacts. In a message to the legislature the following November he asked it to declare the tariff unconstitutional and adopt measures that would bring the issue before the federal courts.[45]

D. R. Williams too opposed hasty and ill-considered action in 1828. He came out of retirement temporarily to recommend that the people acquiesce in the will of the majority of the nation despite the unconstitutionality of the tariff. As a temporary recourse he suggested a nonconsumption agreement and an effort to increase home manufactures, but in the end he felt the only solution lay in "the good sense of the people at large." Nullification would end only in disunion and bloodshed.[46]

The only South Carolina Old Republicans left in Congress, Starling Tucker and William Smith, also opposed the idea of a nullification convention. Tucker felt that such a move would undermine the efforts of the Jackson Administration to reduce the tariff; he remained loyal to the administration until his retirement from the House in 1831. Smith, as usual, bore the brunt of the opposition to the Calhoun forces, and in 1830 he was forced from his seat in the Senate by the nullifiers in the legislature.[47] Prodded by the Calhounites to explain the apparent inconsistency between his states' rights views and his opposition to nullification, Smith published his position in a letter to his hometown newspaper, the Yorkville *Pioneer*. Though he carefully reaffirmed his faith in Virginia doctrine, Smith nevertheless denied that nullification was based on the Virginia and Kentucky resolutions. Those resolutions, he explained, were "merely intended to recommend a convention to amend the Constitution . . . so as to restrain the operations of Congress. . . ." They were not intended actually to nullify the Alien and Sedition laws. Smith's interpretation was very similar to the attempt of Madison in 1830 to distinguish between the purpose of the Virginia

and Kentucky resolutions and the Calhoun philosophy of nullification. Smith reminded the people of South Carolina that no
other Southern state had as yet embraced nullification and recommended that they endure the tariff with patience until some
compromise could be worked out in Congress.[48]

Defeated in his bid for re-election to the Senate, Smith then
ran for a seat in the State Senate where he planned to carry
on his battle against the nullifiers in the legislature. When the
nullification convention was finally summoned in 1832, he retired in disgust and moved to his plantation in Alabama. On leaving, he issued a parting shot at his enemies in a letter to the
Richmond *Enquirer*. He defended his consistency and expressed
his pleasure at being united in opposition to nullification with
his Old Republican friends, Crawford and Macon.[49]

Judge Smith was generally correct in his assertion that a number of Old Republicans shared his opposition to nullification, but
for others the states' rights crisis in South Carolina and the purge
of Calhoun influence in Washington brought into focus a latent
distrust of the Jackson Administration. John Floyd, for instance,
had taken an active part in the Jackson campaign in Virginia.
After Jackson's victory he resigned his seat in Congress in the
expectation of receiving a cabinet post and was keenly disappointed when neither he nor any other Old Republican was rewarded with a seat in the Cabinet. Elected governor of Virginia
in January, 1830, by the states' rights element in the Assembly,
Floyd promulgated in messages to the legislature the doctrine of
state sovereignty as elaborated by Calhoun. The split between
Jackson and Calhoun in 1830, the subsequent purge of Calhoun
influence in the administration, and the failure of Jackson to
lower the tariff further alienated Floyd, and in December, 1830,
he declared war on the administration in a letter to Jackson's old
enemy, former Senator John Williams of Tennessee.[50]

Along with Floyd into opposition went Senator Tazewell,
who had anticipated the schism several years before. In April,
1831, Tazewell informed Floyd that he considered "Jackson

wholly incompetent to administer the government and that his cabinet is more incompetent than he." But finding himself opposed by the predominantly pro-Jackson sentiment in Virginia, Tazewell resigned his seat in the Senate in July, 1832. To his friend Floyd he explained that

Jackson has abandoned all his principles and ignorant and vicious as his mind is there is no hope for maintaining the struggle for States Rights, and it would be worse than useless for me to spend my time in the Senate in fruitless attempts to sustain the States Rights principles alone or in a hopeless minority.[51]

He was replaced by the equally conservative William Cabell Rives, newly returned from the Paris embassy and a more loyal supporter of the administration.

Floyd and Tazewell were soon joined in opposition by another Old Republican, James Pleasants, a War Hawk of 1811 who had reacted against the postwar nationalism and served as governor from 1822 to 1825. This trio formed the nucleus of the antiadministration party in Virginia, and Floyd's announcement in 1832 that he was "a sort of Clay man" was the first step in their transformation into Southern Whigs.[52]

It is not surprising, of course, to find a number of Old Republicans following Calhoun out of the party, for he had at last swung around to their views. After his break with Jackson, moreover, Calhoun made a determined effort to reopen friendly relations with Old Republicans whom he had known years before in Congress. To Bolling Hall of Alabama, friend of Crawford and Macon, he wrote in the summer of 1831, "We are at least now agreed in the great principles of '98...." And a month later he added: "If my experience has taught me thoroughly one truth, it is the extreme danger of departing from those principles. A rigid adherence to them I believe to be the Rock of our political salvation." Despite these efforts, however, Calhoun remained suspect to most of the Old Republicans; his swift conversion to the faith had about it the aroma of a political maneuver. His alliance with the nationalists Clay and Webster, moreover, offered no particular attraction. "Save us, my dear Sir," wrote John Randolph to the New Hampshire Democrat Levi Woodbury, "from *ultra* federal, ultra Bank & ultra Tariff men of the one part—& ultra *Bank* & anti Tariff, state-right Nullifiers of the other. This [coalition] beats Horace's womanfish." [53]

As the election of 1832 approached, some Southern Democrats, unable to accept Van Buren, started a movement to place Philip Barbour on the Jackson ticket as Vice-President. Though appointed by Jackson a federal judge for the Eastern District of Virginia, Barbour had put himself back into the political limelight by serving as chairman of a national antitariff convention that met in Philadelphia in September, 1831. In the spring of 1832 Barbour was nominated as Jackson's running mate by the Alabama legislature and by Democratic meetings in Raleigh, North Carolina, and Charlottesville, Virginia. The maneuver evidently was initiated by followers of Calhoun anxious to gain Old Republican support in a move to stop Van Buren, and it met with little success. In a meeting of the party in Baltimore in May, 1832, Barbour received all of Virginia's 23 votes, all of South Carolina's 11, 6 each from North Carolina and Alabama, and 3 from Maryland. Although Old Republicans Peter V. Daniel and William S. Archer headed the Virginia delegation, the Virginia ballots represented more a "favorite son" vote than a rejection of Van Buren. Most of the Old Republicans no doubt agreed with Ritchie, who wrote in June to assure Van Buren that he still considered him "a friend of State rights & of the old Republican School." On the eve of the election Barbour himself sought to halt the movement by publishing a letter in the Richmond *Whig* affirming his support for the Jackson-Van Buren ticket. [54]

At the same time, Calhoun was considering an effort to court the Old Republicans by placing Barbour on the National Republican ticket with Clay. Governor Floyd of Virginia apparently entertained the same hope. This possibility dismayed John Randolph. "I fear," he wrote the President, "that our friend P.P.B. will do himself no service by permitting his name to be used by the coalition, of which I now consider Mr. Calhoun to be a regularly installed member." [55] Barbour nevertheless remained loyal to the Jackson Administration, and in 1836 he was elevated to the Supreme Court.

The bank war and the climax of the nullification movement in the fall and winter of 1832–33 created new difficulties for the Old Republicans still loyal to the Jackson Administration. Senator John Tyler, lifelong opponent of the tariff, tended to sympathize with the nullification movement in South Carolina and was an outspoken opponent of the administration's Force Bill in December, 1832. At the height of the crisis Tyler wrote to Governor Floyd that

If South Carolina be put down, then may each of the states yield all pretensions to sovereignty. We have a consolidated government, and a master will soon arise. This is inevitable. How idle to talk of preserving a republic for any length of time with an uncontrolled power over the military, exercised at pleasure by the President.

Already unhappy with Jackson's precipitate action toward South Carolina, Tyler broke openly with the administration on the bank issue. He voted against the bill to recharter the bank, and he voted to sustain the President's veto in 1832, but he opposed killing the bank immediately by removing the government deposits. In the fall of 1833 he joined the Clay-Calhoun coalition. [56]

John Randolph, now at the end of his life, mentally unbalanced and ill much of the time, also lost faith in Jackson. Though in most ways willing to carry the doctrine of state sovereignty to its logical extremes, he never sanctioned the principle of nullification as expounded by Calhoun. But Jackson's proclamation of December, 1832, in which he threatened to use force against South Carolina, was another matter. On December 4 Randolph served as chairman of a meeting, at Charlotte Court

House, that passed a series of resolutions condemning the action of the President. While the resolutions reprobated "the doctrine of nullification as equally weak and mischievous," they upheld the rights of Virginia as a "free, sovereign and independent state," including the right to "secede from the confederacy," and they concluded by endorsing the mission of Benjamin Watkins Leigh, who had been sent to South Carolina as a sympathetic observer.[57]

Two days later Randolph wrote to President Jackson urging him to move cautiously toward South Carolina. Given time, he thought, South Carolina would retreat from her extreme states' rights position. His pleas unfortunately had no effect on the impetuous Jackson, and Randolph later broke with the President completely and asked for the return of the letters he had written in opposition to nullification.[58] That unfortunate incident was the last of his long political career; six months later Virginia's Jeremiah was dead.

A few other Old Republicans joined the coalition that was soon to be known as the Whig party. Lewis Williams, whose career in Congress lasted until his death in 1842, remained a staunch foe of Jackson, and, along with Willie P. Mangum, who broke with Jackson on the bank issue, helped to organize the Whig party in North Carolina.[59] Newton Cannon, enemy of Jackson in Tennessee politics since 1816, ran for governor of Tennessee in 1834 on an anti-Jackson ticket and was elected with the support of the planters, merchants, and bankers of Eastern Tennessee. Though Cannon's victory was based largely on local issues and represented primarily a rebellion against the domination of the state by the Overton-Jackson faction, Cannon and his following gradually migrated into the Whig party. These various anti-Jackson groups in the South coalesced around the candidacy of the Tennessee planter Hugh Lawson White in the election of 1836.[60]

Even in the Southern wing of the Whig party the Old Republicans and their states' rights disciples were in a minority.

The Southern Whigs were primarily commercial, middle class in background, nationalist in outlook.[61] Few Old Republicans found this environment congenial, and most preferred the more agrarian-centered atmosphere of the Democratic party. Their nostalgia for the "principles of '98," in the end, differed very little from the attempt of the Jacksonians to regain the "pristine purity" of the early republic.[62] The essential negativism of Jacksonian Democracy, exemplified in the Maysville veto and the bank veto, also had its appeal to the conservative, agrarian conscience.

In Virginia, for instance, the "Richmond Junto"—Thomas Ritchie, Dr. John Brockenbrough, Philip Norborne Nicholas, and Peter V. Daniel—remained loyal to Jackson. Ritchie, its accustomed spokesman, kept the *Enquirer* squarely behind the President even in the nullification crisis. Privately, however, Ritchie, Dr. John Brockenbrough, Philip Norborne Nicholas, He urged Senator Rives to prevent Congress from adopting extreme measures and warned that if the President resorted to force, the whole South would rally to the support of South Carolina.[63] After Jackson's retirement Ritchie supported Van Buren, and finally in 1846 his influence in the Democratic party was recognized when President Polk summoned him to Washington to establish a new administration paper, the *Constitutional Union*.

In North Carolina the center of Jacksonian strength continued to be the conservative Roanoke Valley where the aging Nathaniel Macon still held sway. Macon, of course, was delighted with the war on the bank, and even the nullification issue failed to shake his allegiance. He opposed alike the South Carolina ordinance of nullification and President Jackson's proclamation against it because each threatened the Union. He seems to have regarded the right of secession as a stronger defense than nullification against the unconstitutional actions of the federal government. Yet, like Randolph, he felt that right ought to be exercised only under the most extreme provocation. In the end he re-

mained loyal to Jackson, and in 1836 pledged his support to Van
Buren. That same year—the year of his death—he was able to pay
a powerful tribute to Jackson's accomplishments: "If the wisest
man living had have predicted that Jackson would have done
half the good he has for the people, no one would have believed
him; his doings are known to everybody and need not be repeated. . . ." [64] Thomas Hall and Weldon Nathaniel Edwards
also remained firm in their support of Jackson and Van Buren.
Edwards, himself a protégé of Nathaniel Macon, was the only
Old Republican to live into the Civil War era. In 1861 he presided over the convention in which North Carolina seceded
from the Union.

In Georgia, William Harris Crawford never publicly supported Jackson or Clay. In the detachment that comes from
retirement he felt that the doctrine of nullification "carries ab-
surdity on its face," but he also disapproved of Jackson's proclamation against it. [65] Crawford failed to outlive the Jackson
Administration. His death in 1834, coupled with Randolph's the
year before and the deaths of Macon and Monroe in 1836, stilled
the last faint echoes of the Virginia school.

The division among the Old Republicans during the Jackson
period contributed to the dual impression their ideas made on
the next generation. On the one hand, as "keepers of the Virginia conscience" they kept alive the defensive doctrines of the
Republican party of the 1790s and passed them on to the Southern states' rights politicians of the 1840s and 50s. And, on the
other hand, the slogans and symbols of their agrarian Liberalism
proved admirably adaptable to the political purposes of the new
entrepreneurial Liberalism that triumphed with the election
of Andrew Jackson. Amos Kendall, Kentucky editor-turned-
banker, intimate adviser of Jackson, and later a business agent of
Samuel F. B. Morse, reflected the fusion of the doctrines of
aristocratic agrarianism and middle-class Liberalism in his *Autobiography*. He wrote that government ought to leave the economic life of the country alone because Americans had always

demanded "that their governments shall content themselves with protecting their persons and property, leaving them to direct their labor and capital as they please, within the moral law; getting rich or remaining poor as may result from their own management or fortune." [66] These words could just as easily have come from the pen of William Graham Sumner or Calvin Coolidge, but behind them all are the spirits of John Randolph and Nathaniel Macon and John Taylor of Caroline.

Yet the legacy of Old Republicanism was more than this. The Jeffersonian assumption—that centralized power represents an ever-present threat to individual liberty and that human liberty in America is best protected by the diffusion of power among the several states in exercising their reserved rights—remains an important part of the American political tradition. The preservation of this tradition was the most important contribution of the Old Republicans. They both reflected and contributed to the suspicion of governmental power and its potential influence over the lives of individuals, which still lingers in the American conscience.

Notes

Notes to Introduction

1. This view is supported by Auerbach, pp. 71–72, 83–84; and Wickwar, p. 1107. It is also the central thesis of Hartz, *The Liberal Tradition in America*.

2. Kirk, *The Conservative Mind*, pp. 136–46; and *Randolph of Roanoke*, pp. 9–12, emphasizes this connection.

Notes to Chapter I: Prelude: 1798

1. Jefferson, "Thoughts on Lotteries," February, 1826, in Washington, ed., *Writings*, IX, 507.

2. Jefferson to Lewis, May 9, 1798, in Ford, ed., *Writings*, VII, 250.

3. *Annals of Cong.*, 5th Cong., II, 1465, 1545, 1522, 1553–54.

4. *Ibid.*, pp. 1526–27, 1537, 1700, 1729, 1772.

5. Thomas Cooper, "Political Arithmetic," 1798, reprinted in *Political Essays* (Philadelphia, 1800), p. 36.

6. *Annals of Cong.*, 5th Cong., II, 1848–53, 1922–23, 1925, 2048–49.

7. Jefferson to Taylor, June 1, 1798, in Ford, ed., *Writings*, VII, 263–66.

8. For a detailed account of these laws, see J. M. Smith, chaps. 3–8 *passim*.

9. *Annals of Cong.*, 5th Cong., II, 2013, 2028–29, 2103, 2111, 2171.

10. Jefferson, in Ford, ed., *Writings*, VII, 289–308. On the Antifederalist fear of governmental power, see Main, *The Antifederalists*, pp. 9–10.

11. *The Virginia Report of 1799–1800*, pp. 22–23.

12. For the origin and influence of the Virginia and Kentucky resolutions, see Adrienne Koch and Harry Ammon, "The Virginia and Kentucky Resolutions: An Episode in Jefferson's and Madison's Defense of Civil Liberties," *William and Mary Quarterly*, 3d series, V (1948), 145–76; and Koch, pp. 174–211.

Notes to Chapter II: The Conservative Wing

1. Page to Tucker, February 25, 1801, Tucker-Coleman Papers, Colonial Williamsburg.

2. Randolph to Nicholson, July 26, 1801, Nicholson Papers, LC.

3. *Annals of Cong.*, 12th Cong., 2d sess., 782. The closest approach to a formal party "platform" was printed in the Philadelphia *Aurora*, October 14, 1800, but it is much too long to warrant quotation here. See Cunningham, *The Jeffersonian Republicans*, pp. 213–14.

4. H. Adams, *History of the United States*, I, 185–217; Hofstadter, pp. 26–39; Koch, pp. 212–20.

5. Quoted by Binkley, pp. 86–87.

6. Dawson to Monroe, February 23, 1801, Monroe Papers, LC; Monroe to Jefferson, March 18, 1801, Monroe, III, 262.

7. Cunningham, *The Jeffersonian Republicans in Power*, pp. 12–13, 29.

8. *Ibid.*, p. 63; Macon to Nicholson, September 5, 1803, Nicholson Papers, LC.

9. Jefferson to Gallatin, July 12, 1803, in Ford, ed., *Writings*, VIII, 252.

10. Jefferson to Gallatin, December 24, 1808, Jefferson Papers, LC.

11. Randolph to Tucker, January 15, 1802, Randolph Papers (microfilm), UVA. Lib.

12. Jefferson to John B. Colvin, September 20, 1810, in Ford, ed., *Writings*, IX, 279–82.

13. Savelle, *Seeds of Liberty*, pp. 556 ff.; Shafer, pp. 106–7; Savelle, "Nationalism and Other Loyalties," pp. 901–23.

14. Snyder, pp. 61–62, 80–81.

15. Taylor to Nicholas, September 16, 1802, Wilson Cary Nicholas Papers, LC.

16. Mays, II, 332–36; Taylor to Nicholas, August 3 and September 5, 1801, Coolidge Papers, Mass. Hist. Soc.

17. Taylor to Monroe, October 26, 1810, Monroe Papers, LC.

18. Main, "Sections and Politics in Virginia, 1781–1787," pp. 96–112; Abernethy, *South in the New Nation, 1789–1819*, pp. 24–25 and map on p. 30.

19. Craven, "John Taylor and Southern Agriculture," p. 146.

20. Kirk, *Randolph of Roanoke*, pp. 86–87.

21. The disciple of Taylor and Garnett, Edmund Ruffin, carried the tradition into the Civil War era.

22. Abernethy, *South in the New Nation*, p. 435.

23. St. George Tucker, ed., *Blackstone's Commentaries on the Laws of England* (Philadelphia, 1803), I, Appendix, 187.

24. Gates, p. 110; Abernethy, *South in the New Nation*, pp. 40–41.

25. Bowers, *Jefferson and Hamilton*, p. 45.

26. Foster, pp. 144, 184, 188–89.

27. *Ibid.*, p. 145.

28. Cunningham, *The Jeffersonian Republicans in Power*, pp. 203–15.

29. *Ibid.*, pp. 215–20.

30. Randolph to Gallatin, October 25, 1805, quoted by H. Adams, *Gallatin*, p. 332; Macon to Nicholson, September 7, 1804, Nicholson Papers, LC; Taylor to Nicholas, June 14, 1805, Edgehill-Randolph Papers, UVA Lib.

31. Private Memoir of William A. Burwell, *ca.* 1809, Burwell Papers, LC; Jefferson to Randolph, December 1, 1803, in Ford, ed., *Writings*, VIII, 281–82.

32. Tucker, II, 190; see also Bruce, I, 265–66.

33. Brant, *Madison, Secretary of State*, p. 232.

34. Taylor to Nicholas, February 5, 1808, Edgehill-Randolph Papers, UVA Lib.

35. Randolph to Nicholson, December 17, 1800, January 1, 1801, Nicholson Papers, LC.

36. Randolph to Tucker, January 15, 1802, Randolph Papers (microfilm), UVA Lib.

37. Randolph to Monroe, January 3, 1803, Monroe Papers, LC.

38. Taylor to Nicholas, June 10, 1806, Edgehill-Randolph Papers, UVA Lib.

39. Taylor to Nicholas, February 5, 1808, Edgehill-Randolph Papers, UVA Lib.

40. Randolph to Monroe, June 15, 1803, November 7, 1803, February 28, 1804, July 20, 1804; Macon to Monroe, November 15,

1803; Taylor to Monroe, November 12, 1803, February 27, 1806, Monroe Papers, LC.

41. Tazewell to Monroe, October 8, 1808, Monroe Papers, LC.

Notes to Chapter III: The Quid Schism

1. Cunningham, "Who Were the Quids?" pp. 252–63, makes an important distinction between the Randolphites in Virginia and the splinter factions in New York and Pennsylvania, who, being in the middle of the road politically, can more properly be called "Quids." So long as the distinction among these various state factions is kept clearly in mind, it would seem that the question of whether the Randolph faction deserved the name Quids is largely a semantic one. The term is used here and in the next chapter because it is a convenient tool for distinguishing the rather tiny group of Randolphites from the larger body of Old Republicans who never accepted Randolph's leadership.

2. H. Adams, *History of the United States*, I, 303–6, II, 210–17; Abernethy, *South in the New Nation*, chap. VI; Haskins, V, 395–440.

3. *Annals of Cong.*, 8th Cong., 1st sess., 1039–40.

4. *Ibid.*, 1031–32, 1173–74.

5. Brant, *Madison, Secretary of State*, p. 250; Macon to Nicholson, August 6, 1803, Nicholson Papers, LC.

6. Randolph to Nicholson, March 29, 1805, Nicholson Papers, LC.

7. Randolph to Gallatin, October 25, 1805. H. Adams, *Randolph*, p. 160.

8. Brant, *Madison, Secretary of State*, p. 270; see also Cox, chap. 3 *passim*.

9. Brant, *Madison, Secretary of State*, pp. 259–60.

10. Jefferson to Madison, September 16, 1805; Gallatin to Jefferson, September 12, 1805, Jefferson Papers, LC.

11. Cabinet memorandum on Spain, November 12, 1805, Jefferson Papers, LC.

12. Armstrong to Madison, September 10, 1805, Diplomatic Dispatches, France, National Archives; memorandum of proposed treaty, undated, Jefferson Papers, No. 26862, LC.

13. Draft of Jefferson's Fifth annual message with Madison's comments appended, in Ford, ed., *Writings*, VIII, 384–96.

14. *Messages and Papers of the Presidents*, I, 390.

15. Cunningham, *The Jeffersonian Republicans in Power*, p. 94.

16. Randolph to Monroe, December 5, 1806, Monroe Papers, LC.

17. "Decius" No. 1, Richmond *Enquirer*, August 15, 1806; *Annals of Cong.*, 9th Cong., 1st sess., 985.

18. *Annals of Cong.*, 9th Cong., 1st sess., 1117; Randolph to Hay, January 3, 1806, Randolph Papers, uva Lib.

19. Jefferson, in Ford, ed., *Writings*, VIII, 398–400 (note); Nicholson to Gallatin, December 8, 1805, Gallatin Papers, nypl; "Decius" No. 1, Richmond *Enquirer*, August 15, 1806; Cunningham, *The Jeffersonian Republicans in Power*, p. 88.

20. *Annals of Cong.*, 9th Cong., 1st sess., 1117–19, 1120–26; H. Adams, *History of the United States*, III, 138.

21. *Annals of Cong.*, 9th Cong., 1st sess., 957–58, 1135–36; Randolph to Monroe, March 20, 1806, Monroe Papers, lc.

22. *Annals of Cong.*, 9th Cong., 1st sess., 771.

23. The four Republicans were John Adair (Ky.), Nicholas Gilman (N.H.), David Stone (N.C.), and Thomas Sumter (S.C.), *ibid.*, pp. 87–88; Plumer, *Memorandum*, p. 425; Tolles, p. 267.

24. Logan to Jefferson, March 12, 1806; Jefferson to Logan, March 12, 1806, George Logan Papers, Hist. Soc. of Penn.

25. Jefferson to Cooper, February 18, 1806, Jefferson Papers, lc.

26. J. Adams, I, 408.

27. *Annals of Cong.*, 9th Cong., 1st sess., 255.

28. Brant, *Madison, Secretary of State*, p. 313; Macon to Nicholson, April 21, 1806, Nicholson Papers, lc.

29. *Annals of Cong.*, 9th Cong., 1st sess., 409–13, 441–42.

30. *Ibid.*, pp. 449–51.

31. Brant, *Madison, Secretary of State*, p. 312; H. Adams, *History of the United States*, III, 154–55.

32. References to the debate on the Gregg resolution on pp. 55–57 are from *Annals of Cong.*, 9th Cong., 1st sess., 555–74.

33. Quoted by Brant, *Madison, Secretary of State*, p. 316.

34. Plumer, *Memorandum*, p. 446; Smith to Nicholas, March 11, 1806. For Smith's private support of Randolph, see Smith to Nicholas, May 24, 1806, Edgehill-Randolph Papers, uva. Lib.

35. Cook, pp. 70–71.

36. *Annals of Cong.*, 9th Cong., 1st sess., 643–50.

37. *Ibid.*, 660–66.

38. *Ibid.*, 671–86, 686–98.

39. *Ibid.*, 767–69, 823; Jefferson to Monroe, March 16 and 18, 1806, Monroe Papers, lc.

40. *Annals of Cong.*, 9th Cong., 1st sess., 240. Tolles, p. 274. Tolles errs in stating that Logan was the only Republican to vote against the bill in the Senate.

41. E. Merton Coulter, "John Adair," *Dictionary of American Biography*, I, 34–35; J. G. DeR. Hamilton, "David Stone," *ibid.*, XVIII, 72–73.

42. Gregorie, pp. 221–22, 229, 231; Randolph quote is from obituary of Thomas Sumter in Sumterville (South Carolina) *Gazette*, June 9, 1832.

43. For Bryan's political views, see Bryan to Randolph, March 18 and April 23, 1806, Randolph Papers, UVA. Lib.

44. Randolph to Garnett, May 11, 1806, Randolph-Garnett Letterbook, UVA. Lib.

45. Jefferson to Monroe, March 16, 1806, Monroe Papers, LC.

46. Jefferson to Duane, March 22, 1806, in Ford, ed., *Writings*, VIII, 431–33.

47. Jefferson to Cooper, February 18, 1806, Jefferson Papers, LC.

48. Randolph to Garnett, June 4, 1806, Randolph-Garnett Letterbook, UVA. Lib.

49. Jefferson to Macon, March 26, 1806, in Ford, ed., *Writings*, VIII, 439.

50. Williams to Jefferson [received January 29, 1806], cited by Cunningham, *Jeffersonian Republicans in Power*, p. 95.

51. Macon to Nicholson, April 15, 1806, Nicholson Papers, LC; Taylor to Nicholas, April 14, 1806, Edgehill-Randolph Papers, UVA. Lib; Jefferson to Nicholas, April 13, 1806, in Ford, ed., *Writings*, VIII, 434–35.

52. Tucker to Randolph, December 26, 1805; Bryan to Randolph, June 3, 1806, Randolph Papers, UVA. Lib.

53. *Annals of Cong.*, 9th Cong., 1st sess., 566; Plumer, *Memorandum*, pp. 464–65.

54. *Annals of Cong.*, 9th Cong., 1st sess., 508–9.

55. *Ibid.*, 891–92, 924, 928, 935–36, 1015; Plumer, *Memorandum*, pp. 392–93.

56. *Annals of Cong.*, 9th Cong., 1st sess., 998–99.

57. *Ibid.*, 1029–52, 1078.

58. *Ibid.*, 1107–15.

59. Taylor to Nicholas, April 14, 1806, Edgehill-Randolph Papers, UVA. Lib.

Notes to Chapter IV: Isolation and Defeat, 1806–1808

1. Jefferson to Nicholas, April 13, 1806, in Ford, ed., *Writings*, VIII, 434–35; Randolph to Nicholson, July 7, 1806, Nicholson

Papers, LC; Randolph to Monroe, July 3, 1806, Monroe Papers, LC; Anderson, p. 102.

2. Ammon, "James Monroe and the Election of 1808 in Virginia," pp. 38–39.

3. Randolph to Garnett, May, 1806, June 4, 1806, Randolph-Garnett Letterbook, UVA Lib.; Ambler, *Thomas Ritchie*, pp. 36–37; Richmond *Enquirer*, September 2, 1806.

4. Cunningham, *The Jeffersonian Republicans in Power*, p. 223; Leib to Rodney, February 8, 1806, Gratz Collection, Hist. Soc. of Penn.; Randolph to Garnett, June 4, 1806, Randolph-Garnett Letterbook, UVA Lib.

5. Nicholson to Monroe, May 5, 1806, Monroe Papers, LC.

6. Monroe to Jefferson, June 15, 1806, Monroe Papers, LC; Jefferson to Monroe, May 4, 1806, Monroe Papers, LC; Monroe, IV, 477.

7. Beckley to Monroe, July 13, 1806, Monroe Papers, NYPL.

8. Monroe to Randolph, June 16, 1806, Monroe Papers, LC.

9. *Annals of Cong.*, 9th Cong., 2d sess., 110–15; Plumer, *Memorandum*, pp. 525–26; Macon to Nicholson, December 2, 1806, Nicholson Papers, LC.

10. *Messages and Papers of the Presidents*, I, 405–10; Randolph to Nicholson, December 10, 1806, Nicholson Papers, LC.

11. *Annals of Cong.*, 9th Cong., 2d sess., 114–27, 319–20; Macon to Nicholson, December 26, 1806, Nicholson Papers, LC.

12. Randolph to Nicholson, December 10, 1806, Nicholson Papers, LC; Taylor to [Nicholas], February 5, 1807, Edgehill-Randolph Papers, UVA Lib.

13. Jefferson to Nicholas, February 28, 1807, in Ford, ed., *Writings*, IX, 32.

14. Randolph to Nicholson, December 21, 1806, Nicholson Papers, LC; *Annals of Cong.*, 9th Cong., 2d sess., 458–59, 610.

15. *Annals of Cong.*, 9th Cong., 2d sess., 334–36, 424–25; Randolph to Major Joseph Scott, February 3, 1807, Randolph Papers, UVA Lib.

16. Taylor to Nicholas, August 22, 1807, Edgehill-Randolph Papers, UVA Lib.

17. Randolph to Garnett, August 31, 1807, Randolph-Garnett Letterbook, UVA Lib.; *Annals of Cong.*, 10th Cong., 1st sess., 830; H. Adams, *Gallatin*, pp. 360–61, 363.

18. *Annals of Cong.*, 10th Cong., 1st sess., 782–94; Gallatin to his wife, October 30, 1807, H. Adams, *Gallatin*, p. 363.

19. Randolph to Nicholson, March 25, 1808, Nicholson Papers, LC.

20. Phillips, pp. 94–97.

21. *Messages and Papers of the Presidents*, I, 425–30; Jefferson to Martha Jefferson Randolph, November 23, 1807, Jefferson Papers, LC.

22. *Annals of Cong.*, 10th Cong., 1st sess., 1133–37, 1156, 1167–72.

23. Taylor to Nicholas, November 30, 1807, Edgehill-Randolph Papers, UVA Lib.

24. *Annals of Cong.*, 10th Cong., 1st sess., 1216, 1217–22; Jefferson to Thomas Mann Randolph, December 22, 1807, Jefferson Papers, LC.

25. Randolph to Nicholson, December 24, 1807, Nicholson Papers, LC; Gallatin to Jefferson, December 18, 1807, Jefferson Papers, LC.

26. Taylor to Garnett, December 17, 1807, James M. Garnett Papers, Duke Lib.; Macon to Nicholson, April 4, 1808, Nicholson Papers, LC.

27. *Annals of Cong.*, 10th Cong., 1st sess., 1904–12, 1922–24, 1939–52; Macon to Nicholson, April 6, 1808, Nicholson Papers, LC.

28. *Annals of Cong.*, 10th Cong., 1st sess., 2062–63.

29. Macon to Nicholson, April 11, 12, 1808, Nicholson Papers, LC.

30. *Ibid.*, June 14, 1808; Randolph to Nicholson, May 27, 1808, Nicholson Papers, LC.

31. Brant, *Madison, Secretary of State*, p. 421.

32. Monroe to Randolph, June 16, 1806; Randolph to Monroe, September 16, 1806; Monroe to Randolph, November 12, 1806. Monroe Papers, LC.

33. Perkins, chap. 4, takes a friendlier view of the treaty than most historians. It is true that it might have resulted in a temporary rapprochement in Anglo-American relations, but it also might have had the same domestic political repercussions as the Jay Treaty.

34. Cresson, p. 236; Ammon, "James Monroe and the Election of 1808 in Virginia," pp. 42–43.

35. McRae to Monroe, December 31, 1807, Monroe Papers, NYPL; "Address of the Monroe Corresponding Committee," Raleigh *Minerva*, October 6, 1808, which outlined the Monroe platform of better relations with England and an end to the embargo, was signed by George Hay, John Clarke, Edward C. Stannard, William Robertson, and John Brockenbrough, all prominent in the "Richmond Junto."

36. Randolph to Garnett, May 8, 27, 1808, Randolph-Garnett Let-

terbook, uva Lib.; Gilpatrick, p. 163; Macon to Nicholson, March 29, April 6, 1808, Nicholson Papers, lc.

37. Randolph to Major Joseph Scott, February 18, 1808, Randolph Papers, uva Lib.; Walters, *Alexander James Dallas*, pp. 143–44; Cunningham, *The Jeffersonian Republicans in Power*, p. 165.

38. Brant, *Madison, Secretary of State*, pp. 423–24; John Nicholas to Wilson Cary Nicholas, January 28, 1807, Wilson Cary Nicholas Papers, uva Lib.; Taylor to Monroe, March 20, 1808, Monroe Papers, lc.

39. Richmond *Enquirer*, January 26, 1808.

40. Brant, *Madison, Secretary of State*, pp. 425–26; Nathaniel Beverley Tucker to Randolph, January 27, 1808, Tucker Papers, uva Lib.; Creed Taylor to ———, December 21, 1807, Creed Taylor Papers, uva Lib.; John Clopton to Alexander McRae, December 25, 1807, Monroe Papers, lc; Randolph to Nicholson, January 5, 1808, Shippen Family Papers, lc; Randolph to Major Joseph Scott, January 25, 1808, Randolph Papers, uva Lib.

41. *National Intelligencer*, March 7, 1808; Brant, *Madison, Secretary of State*, p. 433, lists only four followers of Randolph, but he probably considers Joseph Clay a member of the "Leib-Maclay" faction in Pennsylvania.

42. Jones to Monroe, January 20, 1808; Clay to Monroe, February 29, 1808. Monroe Papers, lc.

43. Taylor to Monroe, February 22, 1808; Randolph to Monroe, March 9, 1808, Monroe Papers, lc.

44. Ammon, "James Monroe and the Election of 1808 in Virginia," p. 47.

45. Monroe to Jefferson, February 27, 1808; Monroe to Randolph, March 23, 1808; Randolph to Monroe, March 26, 1808, Monroe Papers, lc. Monroe to Tazewell, October 30, 1808, Monroe, V, 70.

46. Randolph to Nicholson, March 28, 1808, Nicholson Papers, lc; Randolph to Monroe, March 26, 1808, Monroe Papers, lc; Taylor to Wilson Cary Nicholas, May 10, 1808, Edgehill-Randolph Papers, uva Lib.

47. Randolph to Garnett, August 31, 1808, Randolph-Garnett Letterbook, uva Lib.

48. Monroe to [John Taylor?], July 19, 1808, Monroe Papers, nypl.

49. Monroe to Nicholson, September 24, 1808, Nicholson Papers, lc; Monroe to Tazewell, September 25, 1808, Monroe Papers, lc.

50. Simms, *John Taylor*, pp. 124–26.

51. Richmond, *The Spirit of '76,* October 11, 1808; Richmond *Enquirer,* October 18, November 18, 1808; Brant, *Madison, Secretary of State,* p. 467; Ambler, *Sectionalism in Virginia,* p. 90.

Notes to Chapter V: Conservatives and War Hawks

1. Brant, *Madison, President,* p. 27, speaks incorrectly of "Randolph and his Third Party Quids" as if they were a third party rivaling the Federalists for leadership of the opposition.

2. Taylor to Monroe, October 26, 1810, Monroe Papers, LC; Cresson, p. 243.

3. An able, but somewhat dated, survey of the historiography of the war is Goodman, pp. 171–86. The impact of the price depression on the West and South is explored by G. R. Taylor, "Agrarian Discontent in the Mississippi Valley," pp. 471–505; and "Prices in the Mississippi Valley," pp. 148–63; Latimer, pp. 914–29; and Horsman, "Western War Aims, 1811–1812," pp. 1–18. See Risjord, "1812: Conservatives, War Hawks, and the Nation's Honor," pp. 196–210, for a more detailed criticism of the economic interpretations.

4. Perkins, pp. 434–37; Horsman, *Causes of the War of 1812,* pp. 156–57, 264–67.

5. Brown pp. 44–66, 186–91.

6. Horsman, *Causes of the War of 1812,* pp. 156–57, 266–67; Perkins, pp. 267, 373–74, 392, 415.

7. Brown, p. 66. For a more detailed explanation of this thesis and my comments upon it see *The Indiana Magazine of History,* LX, No. 2 (June, 1964) pp. 137–51, 155–158.

8. Shafer, pp. 135–136; Snyder, pp. 96–97.

9. Handman, pp. 107–14; Snyder, p. 123.

10. H. Adams, *History of the United States,* Book V, pp. 176–99 *passim.*

11. William Anderson (Pa.), David Bard (Pa.), John Brown (Md.), Joseph Calhoun (S.C.), William Crawford (Pa.), William Findley (Pa.), Alexander McKim (Md.), Pleasant M. Miller (Tenn.), John Nicholson (N.Y.), John Roane (Va.), and Ebenezer Sage (N.Y.). For an explanation of the procedure used for determining the extent of war sentiment in the Eleventh Congress, see Risjord, "The War Hawks and the War of 1812," p. 157*n.*

12. Stanford to Logan, January 13, 1810, Logan Papers, Hist. Soc. of Penn.

13. Jenkin Whiteside to John Overton, February 1, 1810, John

Overton Papers (microfilm), UNC Lib.; see also William A. Burwell to William Dickerson, March 10, 1810, William A. Burwell Papers, LC.

14. *Annals of Cong.*, 11th Cong., 2d sess., 754–755.

15. *Ibid.*, pp. 1161–63, 1276.

16. *Ibid.*, pp. 1168–70; editorial from *The Spirit of '76* reprinted in the Fredericksburg *Virginia Herald*, January 13, 1810.

17. Philadelphia *Aurora*, May 26, 1810; Richmond *Enquirer*, December 23, 1809; *Annals of Cong.*, 11th Cong., 2d sess., 1328–29.

18. *Annals of Cong.*, 11th Cong., 2d sess., 1354; Taggart to the Rev. John Taylor, January 26, 1810, "Letters of Samuel Taggart," p. 342.

19. *Annals of Cong.*, 11th Cong., 2d sess., 577, 579–82, 602–11.

20. Randolph to Nicholson, December 4, 1809, Nicholson Papers, LC; *Annals of Cong.*, 11th Cong., 2d sess., 1646–50, 1701.

21. *Annals of Cong.*, 11th Cong., 2d sess., 1703, 1711–12.

22. *Ibid.*, pp. 1482–84, 1789–90.

23. Macon to Nicholson, April 25, 1810, Nicholson Papers, LC; *Annals of Cong.*, 11th Cong., 2d sess., 1763.

24. Macon to Nicholson, April 28, 1810, Nicholson Papers, LC; Philadelphia *Aurora*, May 26, 1810; Washington *The Spirit of '76*, April 6, 1810.

25. Brant, *Madison, President*, pp. 42–43; Robert Weakley to John Overton, April 22, 1810, John Overton Papers (microfilm), UNC Lib.

26. *Annals of Cong.*, 11th Cong., 2d sess., 1772–81.

27. *Ibid.*, pp. 1887, 1931.

28. *Ibid.*, pp. 664, 666–67, 673–74, 678–80.

29. *Ibid.*, pp. 1609–13.

30. Taylor to Monroe, October 26, 1810, Monroe Papers, LC; Macon to Nicholson, April 3, 1810, Nicholson Papers, LC; *Annals of Cong.*, 11th Cong., 2d sess., 1863.

31. *Annals of Cong.*, 11th Cong., 2d sess., 1866–75, 1883–85.

32. *Ibid.*, pp. 1933–34, 1950–54, 1977–82.

33. B. Hammond, pp. 146, 211–12; Walters, *Albert Gallatin*, pp. 237–40; Anderson, *William Branch Giles*, pp. 161–62; *Annals of Cong.*, 11th Cong., 3d sess., 675–85, 749–55.

34. *Annals of Cong.*, 11th Cong., 3d sess., 580–95, 687; John Clopton to John Clopton, Jr., February 20, 1811, John Clopton Papers, Duke Univ. Lib.

35. *Annals of Cong.*, 11th Cong., 3d sess., 491; Macon to Nicholson, February 2, 20, 1811, Nicholson Papers, LC.

36. *Annals of Cong.*, 11th Cong., 3d sess., 826; Taggart, pp. 352–53.

37. *Annals of Cong.*, 11th Cong., 3d sess., 134–50; Macon to Nicholson, February 11, 1811, Nicholson Papers, LC.

38. *Annals of Cong.*, 11th Cong., 3d sess., 175–208; Randolph to Nicholson, February 14, 1811, Nicholson Papers, LC.

39. *Annals of Cong.*, 11th Cong., 3d sess., 209–19.

40. Mayo, pp. 158 ff., 375.

41. *Annals of Cong.*, 11th Cong., 3d sess., 346.

42. Gallatin to Nicholas Biddle, August 14, 1830; Gallatin to R. Potter, December 3, 1830; Gallatin, II, 435, 441; J. Hammond, I, 578.

43. Worthington was an official of a state bank in Ohio, but he also owned stock in the Bank of the United States. His biographer apparently thinks that the two economic interests canceled each other, for he attributes Worthington's stand to party regularity. A. Sears, pp. 161–62.

44. Brant, *Madison, President*, p. 25; Anderson, *William Branch Giles*, pp. 148–49, 155–56; Pancake, "The 'Invisibles,'" pp. 17–37, makes an unconvincing effort to demonstrate that the Smith faction had a consistent and worthwhile program.

45. Jefferson to William Wirt, March 30, 1811 (copy), William Wirt Papers, Md. Hist. Soc.; Macon to Nicholson, May 23, 1809, April 26, 1810, Nicholson Papers, LC; Randolph to Garnett, August 14, 1810, Randolph-Garnett Letterbook, UVA Lib.; Washington *The Spirit of '76*, April 6, 1810.

46. Macon to Nicholson, February 9, 11, 15, 1811, Nicholson Papers, LC; Walters, *Albert Gallatin*, p. 241.

47. Monroe to Wirt, December 20, 1808, William Wirt Papers, Md. Hist. Soc.; Jefferson to Madison, March 30, 1809, Jefferson Papers, LC; Jefferson to Madison, November 30, 1809, in Ford, ed., *Writings*, IX, 265–67.

48. Taylor to Monroe, October 26, November 25, 1810; Randolph to Monroe, January 14, 1811, Monroe Papers, LC.

49. Randolph to Garnett, March 19, 25, April 11, 1811, Randolph-Garnett Letterbook, UVA Lib.; Monroe to Tazewell, March 14, 1811; Tazewell to Monroe, March 17, 1811; Taylor to Monroe, March 21 and 24, 1811, Monroe Papers, LC.

50. Monroe to Madison, March 23, 1811; Madison to Monroe, March 26, 1811, Madison Papers, LC.

51. By 1811 only two former Quids remained in the Virginia House of Delegates—Benjamin Watkins Leigh and William Daniel—and both followed Monroe back into the party fold. Steiner, pp. 91–93.

52. Tucker to Garnett, May 25, 1811, Henry St. George Tucker Papers, Duke Univ. Lib.; Garnett to Randolph, April 15, 1811, Randolph-Garnett Letterbook, UVA Lib.; Jefferson to Madison, April 7, 1811, Madison Papers, LC.

53. Burwell to Jefferson, May 27, 1808, Jefferson Papers, LC; Jefferson to James Bowdoin, May 27, 1808, Jefferson Papers, LC; Nicholas to Jefferson, December 22, 1809, Carter-Smith Papers, UVA Lib.; Jordan, pp. 66–67.

54. Ambler, *Thomas Ritchie*, p. 45; Philadelphia *Aurora*, March 4, July 21, and December 14, 1809.

55. Thomas Law to George Logan, January 17, 1810, George Logan Papers, Hist. Soc. of Penn.

56. Adams, *History of the United States*, Book V, pp. 316–17; Book VI, pp. 122–23.

57. Brant, *Madison, President*, p. 379.

58. Washington *National Intelligencer*, September 28, 1810.

59. *Ibid.*, October 5, 8, and 12, 1810. Maryland's three new Republicans in the Twelfth Congress were Joseph Kent of Bladensburg, Peter Little of Baltimore, and Stephenson Archer from the Eastern Shore. They replaced Nicholas R. Moore, a member of the war party in the Eleventh Congress, Archibald Van Horne, who had generally supported stronger measures, and John Montgomery, who resigned his seat after being re-elected to the Twelfth Congress.

60. See "Corvus," Richmond *Virginia Argus*, January 29, 1811.

61. Richmond *Enquirer*, April 25 and 30, May 3 and 10, 1811.

62. Richmond *Virginia Argus*, March 28, April 4, 1811; Richmond *Enquirer*, March 26, April 2, 1811.

63. Raleigh *Star*, August 16 and 23, 1810; Gilpatrick, pp. 241–44.

64. Wolfe, p. 241; Wiltse, p. 51; Cook p. 84; Taggart to the Rev. John Taylor, May 9, 1812, "Letters of Samuel Taggart," p. 399.

65. Perkins, pp. 262–67, has reached similar conclusions on the significance of the election of 1810–11 in the West and South.

66. Franklin to Thomas Ruffin, November 14, 1813, Ruffin, I, 136.

67. See Risjord, "1812: Conservatives, War Hawks, and the Nation's Honor," pp. 196–210, for an elaboration of this thesis.

68. Taggart to Rev. John Taylor, May 9, 1812, "Letters of Samuel Taggart," p. 398.

69. Randolph to Richard Kidder Randolph [November, 1811], Randolph Papers, LC; *Annals of Cong.*, 12th Cong., 1st sess., 333, 342–43.

70. *Annals of Cong.*, 12th Cong., 1st sess., 373–77, 414–17. Calhoun later admitted that Randolph at least had opposed the resolutions in committee, *ibid.*, p. 476.

71. See Shulim, *passim.*

72. *Annals of Cong.*, 12th Cong., 1st sess., 441–55.

73. *Ibid.*, pp. 492–95.

74. Taggart to the Rev. John Taylor, December 14, 1811, "Letters of Samuel Taggart," p. 369; Joseph C. Cabell to Henry St. George Tucker, December 18, 1806, Tucker-Coleman Papers, Colonial Williamsburg; Nelson to Dr. Charles Everett, December 4, 1811, Hugh Nelson Papers, LC.

75. *Annals of Cong.*, 12th Cong., 1st sess., 497–99.

76. *Ibid.*, pp. 545–48.

77. "All idea of war is abandoned and there is no doubt but the idea that has got hold of the friends of the administration is that . . . the orders in council are or soon will be withdrawn." Taggart to the Rev. John Taylor, December 30, 1811, "Letters of Samuel Taggart," p. 372; Brant, *Madison, President*, pp. 372–74.

78. *Annals of Cong.*, 12th Cong., 1st sess., 29–30, 34–86; Monroe to John Taylor, June 13, 1812, Monroe, V, 206–8.

79. *Annals of Cong.*, 12th Cong., 1st sess., 660–64, 665–75.

80. *Ibid.*, pp. 691, 709.

81. *Ibid.*, pp. 815–16; Taggart to the Rev. John Taylor, January 22, 1812, "Letters of Samuel Taggart," p. 379.

82. *Annals of Cong.*, 12th Cong., 1st sess., 823–33, 999–1005.

83. *Ibid.*, pp. 848–58.

84. *Ibid.*, pp. 1054–56.

85. *Ibid.*, pp. 1114–15, 1126–27, 1147–55, 1558–59.

86. Taggart to the Rev. John Taylor, January 20, 1812. "Letters of Samuel Taggart," p. 377.

87. H. Adams, *Gallatin*, p. 455; Madison, II, 530; Randolph to Richard Kidder Randolph, March 10, 1812, John Randolph Papers, LC.

88. John Clopton to Sarah Clopton, March 30, 1812, John Clopton Papers, Duke Univ. Lib.

89. *Annals of Cong.*, 12th Cong., 1st sess., 1265–66, 1593.

90. *Ibid.*, pp. 1588–89, 1592.

91. *Ibid.*, pp. 1593–94.

92. *Ibid.*, pp. 1594–98.

93. Samuel Smith's Memorandum of March 31, 1812, quoted by Pancake, "The General from Baltimore," p. 219; *Annals of Cong.*, 12th Cong., 1st sess., 189.

94. *Annals of Cong.*, 12th Cong., 1st sess., 1266.

95. *Ibid.*, pp. 1356–59.

96. *Ibid.*, pp. 1368–69, 1375–76.

97. *Ibid.*, pp. 1451–61.

98. *Ibid.*, pp. 1461–68; see also Randolph to his constituents, Georgetown, *Spirit of Seventy-six*, June 9, 1812.

99. *Annals of Cong.*, 12th Cong., 1st sess., 1630–37.

100. *Ibid.* pp. 265–71; Taggart to the Rev. John Taylor, June 12, 1812, "Letters of Samuel Taggart," p. 404.

101. *Annals of Cong.*, 12th Cong., 1st sess., 271–84, 297; A. Sears, pp. 168, 177.

102. White, p. 217.

103. Taylor to James M. Garnett, December 14, 1807, John Taylor Papers, Duke Univ. Lib.

Notes to Chapter VI: "This Metaphysical War"

1. Randolph to Key, September 12, 1813, Randolph-Key Letterbook, Md. Hist. Soc.

2. Randolph even respected the ability of the War Hawks: "By the way, this Mr. Cheves and his colleague Lowndes have risen high in my esteem." Randolph to Garnett, December 7, 1812, Randolph-Garnett Letterbook, UVA Lib.

3. Garnett to Randolph, May 20, 1813, April 8, 1814, *ibid.*; Philip N. Nicholas to Wilson Cary Nicholas, March 3, 1810, Wilson Cary Nicholas Papers, UVA Lib.

4. Tolles, p. 304; Garnett to Randolph, April 8, 1814, Randolph-Garnett Letterbook, UVA Lib.

5. *Annals of Cong.*, 12th Cong., 2d sess., 908; Randolph to Quincy, January 29, 1814, Randolph-Quincy Letters, LC.

6. Randolph to Richard Kidder Randolph, February 15, 1814, John Randolph Papers, LC; Randolph to Quincy, February 8, 1814, Randolph-Quincy Letters, LC.

7. John Steele to Joseph Pearson, August 31, 1812. Steele, II, 68.

8. Macon to Nicholson, November 21, 1812, Nicholson Papers, LC.

9. See Henry St. George Tucker to Garnett, August 3, 1811, Henry St. George Tucker Papers, Duke Univ. Lib.

10. Georgetown *Spirit of Seventy-six*, September 8, 15, 18, and December 22, 1812.

11. J. Taylor, *Inquiry into the Principles and Policy*, p. 61.

12. Wright, p. 892.

13. *Annals of Cong.*, 13th Cong., 2d sess., 873–74. On the Ways and Means committee were Eppes (Va.), Taylor (N.Y.), Roberts (Pa.), Creighton (Ohio), Alston (N.C.), McKim (Md.), and Cox (New Jersey Federalist). Eppes and Creighton were the only ones to vote against the bank when it was finally brought to a vote in October, 1814, indicating that some of the members of the committee subsequently lost their constitutional scruples.

14. *Annals of Cong.*, 13th Cong., 2d sess., 1235, 1578–85, 1861.

15. *Ibid.*, pp. 1941–42, 1956, 2002, 2023.

16. *Ibid.*, pp. 1269–74, 1782, 1798.

17. Nelson to Dr. Charles Everett, January 3, 1815, Hugh Nelson Papers, LC; Macon to Nicholson, October 27, 1814, Nicholson Papers, LC.

18. *Annals of Cong.*, 13th Cong., 3d sess., 324, 335–39.

19. *Ibid.*, pp. 378–79.

20. *Ibid.*, pp. 408–9, 437, 496–99; see also John Clopton to Andrew Stevenson, January 16, 1815, Andrew Stevenson Papers, LC.

21. The nineteen were: Philip P. Barbour (Va.), David Bard (Pa.), John Bowen (Tenn.), William A. Burwell (Va.), William Crawford (Pa.), John W. Eppes (Va.), David Evans (S.C.), Meshack Franklin (N.C.), Thomas Gholson (Va.), Hugh Glasgow (Pa.), Peterson Goodwyn (Va.), Bolling Hall (Ga.), Parry W. Humphreys (Tenn.), John G. Jackson (Va.), Nathaniel Macon (N.C.), Thomas Newton (Va.), James Pleasants (Va.), John Rhea (Tenn.), and John Smith (Va.).

22. *Annals of Cong.*, 13th Cong., 3d sess., 126.

23. *Ibid.*, pp. 976–88.

24. Randolph to Harmannus Bleecker, January 2, 1815, Randolph-Bleecker Letterbook, UVA Lib.

25. *Annals of Cong.*, 13th Cong., 3d sess., 1044–45; Taggart to the Rev. John Taylor, November 22, 1814, "Letters of Samuel Taggart," p. 434.

26. Philip Pendleton Barbour to James Barbour, November 17, 1814, Barbour Papers, UVA Lib.

27. *Messages and Papers of the Presidents*, I, 555–57; *Annals of Cong.*, 13th Cong., 3d sess., 226, 232, 1168.

28. Jefferson to Monroe, October 16, 1814, in Ford, ed., *Writings*, IX, 492.

29. Monroe to Giles, October 17, 1814, *American State Papers*, I, 514.

30. Macon to Nicholson, November 5, 1814, March 3, 1816, Nicholson Papers, LC.

31. *Annals of Cong.*, 13th Cong., 3d sess., 38, 109, 705, 775, 869–70, 928–29.

32. *Ibid.*, pp. 992–93, 1130.

33. *Ibid.*, pp. 255–56, 1177–78; Monroe to Giles, February 22, 1815, Monroe, V, 321–27.

34. *Annals of Cong.*, 13th Cong., 3d sess., 1200–1.

35. *Ibid.*, pp. 1229–31, 1251–52.

36. *Ibid.*, pp. 286–87, 297, 1271–73.

37. Snyder, pp. 133–46; Williams, pp. 419–37.

38. *Annals of Cong.*, 14th Cong., 1st sess., 844.

39. Randolph to George Logan, April 27, 1816, George Logan Papers, Hist. Soc. of Penn.

40. *Annals of Cong.*, 14th Cong., 1st sess., 842.

41. *Ibid.*, pp. 1316–20, 1328–29, 1352.

42. Abernethy, *South in the New Nation*, pp. 428–30.

43. Macon to Nicholson, March 25, 1816, Nicholson Papers, LC; *Annals of Cong.*, 14th Cong., 1st sess., 326–31.

44. *Annals of Cong.*, 14th Cong., 1st sess., 494–505, 1110–13; B. Hammond, pp. 242–43.

45. *Messages and Papers of the Presidents*, I, 555.

46. *Annals of Cong.*, 14th Cong., 1st sess., 1217–19; Macon to Nicholson, March 3, 1816, Nicholson Papers, LC.

47. *Annals of Cong.*, 14th Cong., 1st sess., 1219; Randolph to Richard Kidder Randolph, March 22, 1816, Randolph Papers, LC.

48. *Annals of Cong.*, 14th Cong., 1st sess., 250, 281; the four Republicans were Macon, Gaillard, Benjamin Ruggles, (Ohio), and James J. Wilson (N.J.).

49. *Ibid.*, pp. 1338, 1340.

50. *Annals of Cong.*, 14th Cong., 2d sess., 11–17, 296, 361.

51. *Ibid.*, pp. 862–66, 868–69, 870.

52. Barbour's view on this clause was similar to that adopted by the Supreme Court in *United States v. Butler* in 1935 (297 US Reports 1).

53. *Annals of Cong.*, 14th Cong., 2d sess., 893–99.

54. *Ibid.*, pp. 918, 922, 934.

55. Harrison, pp. 372–73.

56. Abernethy, *South in the New Nation*, pp. 431–32.

57. *Annals of Cong.*, 14th Cong., 2d sess., 165, 177–179.

58. *Ibid.*, pp. 180, 191.

59. *Messages and Papers of the Presidents*, I, 584–85; Richmond *Enquirer*, March 11, 1817; see also Fredericksburg *Virginia Herald*, March 15, 1817.

60. *Annals of Cong.*, 15th Cong., 1st sess., 1371.

61. Clinton to Rufus King, December 13, 1817, DeWitt Clinton Papers, Columbia Univ. Lib.

62. H. Adams, *History of the United States*, Book IX, p. 113.

63. Willie G. Blount (Tenn.), Joseph Hunter Bryan (N.C.), William A. Burwell (Va.), John Clopton (Va., retired in 1816), Peterson Goodwyn (Va.), Benjamin Hardin (Ky.), James Johnson (Va.), John Randolph (Va.), William Roane (Va.), Erastus Root (N.Y.).

Notes to Chapter VII: "This Era of Good Feelings and Bad Principles"

1. "High prerogative doctrines are at present too fashionable and prevalent among the sycophants and courtiers of this era of good feelings and bad principles." Richmond *Enquirer*, December 16, 1824.

2. Richmond *Enquirer*, January 9, 1817; Fredericksburg *Virginia Herald*, March 15, 1817.

3. Gates, pp. 4–5; Craven, *Soil Exhaustion*, pp. 77–79, 81.

4. Carpenter, p. 69; Dodd, "Chief Justice John Marshall," pp. 776–87.

5. The other members of the court, William H. Cabell and Francis T. Brooke, were Old Republicans who had served in the state legislature in the 1790s. Cabell had been elected governor in 1805 and was re-elected in 1806 and 1807 with the support of the conservative "minority."

6. Ambler, *Thomas Ritchie*, pp. 63–64.

7. Ammon, "The Richmond Junto, 1800–1824," pp. 404–5.

8. Ambler, *Thomas Ritchie*, pp. 72–74.

9. Ammon, "The Richmond Junto, 1800–1824," pp. 399–400.

10. See "Robert S. Garnett to the Freeholders of the Congressional District composed of the Counties of Caroline, Essex, King & Queen, and King William," Fredericksburg *Virginia Herald*, March 22 and 26, 1817, in which Garnett links his campaign to the compensation law by promising not to be corrupted by power or patronage and weaves this in with an isolationism in foreign affairs, a demand for a low tariff, and a defense of the Republican "Minority."

11. Ambler, *John Floyd*, pp. 34–37.

12. Richmond *Enquirer*, May 6, 1817. Ambler, *Sectionalism in Virginia*, pp. 100–6, errs in saying that no Federalist was elected. Edward Colston and James Pindall, elected from tramontane districts in 1817, were both considered Federalists; Charles Fenton Mercer of the northern Piedmont, elected in 1817 to replace the Federalist Joseph Lewis, Jr., was a Federalist at the time of the election, though he eventually became a nationalist Republican.

13. Nelson to Dr. Charles Everett, December 2 [1817], Hugh Nelson Papers, LC.

14. Gates, p. 7; James Graham to Thomas Ruffin, August 10, 1817, Ruffin, I, 194–95.

15. Thomas Hall was consistently conservative. Thomas Settle, James Owen, and J. S. Smith voted with the conservatives in the Fifteenth Congress on all issues except the bank.

16. Charleston *Southern Patriot*, September 16, 1816.

17. A number of Southern conservatives outside of Virginia supported the bank. Men like Tucker and Eldred Simkins of South Carolina, Lewis Williams of North Carolina, and John Williams of Tennessee helped to form in the 1830s the Southern wing of the Whig Party, which was probank, antitariff, and anti-internal improvements.

18. Little, p. 66.

19. Sellers, "Banking and Politics in Jackson's Tennessee, 1817–1827," pp. 62–63.

20. *Ibid.*, pp. 64–65.

21. Nashville *Whig*, July 3, 1819.

22. J. G. deR. Hamilton, "William Smith," *Dictionary of American Biography*, XVII, 359–60.

23. *Annals of Cong.*, 15th Cong., 1st sess., 1569–79, 1596–1604;

John Tyler to Dr. Henry Curtis, January 19, 1818, John Tyler Papers, LC.

24. *Annals of Cong.*, 15th Cong., 1st sess., 1655.

25. *Annals of Cong.*, 15th Cong., 2d sess., 925–35; Chitwood, pp. 39–40.

26. "As to Amelia I do hope that the Govt will never surrender it until Spain remunerates us for past injuries. In fact I should not be at all surprised if the Govt went on to take possession of the Floridas. And it is more than probable that the Seminoles if defeated by Gaines, will fly for shelter within the Spanish lines, and *Gaines in the eagerness of pursuit* may cross after them and be afterwards unwilling to retrace his steps. These are mere conjectures. Certain it is that by the Treaty of '95 the U. States have a right to demand of Spain to beat down the hostile spirit of the Indians within her boundaries, and if she does not do so, she commits the first infraction of the Treaty." John Tyler to Dr. Henry Curtis, January 19, 1818, John Tyler Papers, LC.

27. Jefferson to Madison, March 3, 1819, in Ford, ed., *Writings*, X, 124–25.

28. J. Adams, IV, 197–98, 221–22, and V, 327. Wiltse, p. 177, expresses the same opinion.

29. Abernethy, *Formative Period in Alabama*, p. 49.

30. Richmond *Enquirer*, July 28, July 31, and December 15, 1818; Macon to Bartlett Yancey, February 7, 1819, Bartlett Yancey Papers, UNC Lib.

31. William Lee Ball to the Freeholders of the Congressional District of the Counties of Northumberland, Lancaster, Richmond, Westmoreland, King George, and Stafford, Richmond *Enquirer*, March 23, 1819.

32. Bibb to Charles Tait, September 19, 1818, Charles Tait Papers, Alabama Dept. of Archives and History. Bibb, admittedly, was a friend of Crawford, but at the date of this letter it is unlikely that Bibb was aware of Crawford's attitude or of the effect of the Seminole campaign on politics in Washington.

33. Sellers, "Banking and Politics in Jackson's Tennessee, 1817–1827," pp. 63–64.

34. *Annals of Cong.*, 14th Cong. 2d sess., 954, 955.

35. J. Adams, IV, 223.

36. *Annals of Cong.*, 14th Cong., 2d sess., 963–69.

37. *Ibid.*, pp. 969–86. Though Williams was shortly to make himself the outstanding spokesman in Congress of the Secretary of

the Treasury, William H. Crawford, this move cannot be considered the opening gun in the long feud between Crawford and the Secretary of War, John C. Calhoun, because Calhoun was not offered the War Department until October, 1817: Wiltse, p. 139. Crawford himself, as late as July, 1817, expected the War Department to be offered to Lowndes or D. R. Williams before Calhoun: Crawford to Charles Tait, July 12, 1817, Charles Tait Papers, Alabama Dept. of Archives and History. Thus Williams' crusade over the next decade for a reduction in the standing army stemmed originally from his own political conservatism.

38. *Annals of Cong.*, 14th Cong., 2d sess., 986–95, 1020.

39. *Annals of Cong.*, 15th Cong., 1st sess., 423–26, 438–40, 443.

40. J. Adams V, 237–38, 314, and VI, 115; Wiltse, p. 225; *Annals of Cong.*, 16th Cong., 2d sess., 743, 1059, 1061–63.

41. John Quincy Adams noted that Williams was a personal enemy of Calhoun and a Crawford partisan as early as 1819. J. Adams, V, 326.

42. *Annals of Cong.*, 16th Cong., 2d sess., 449; *American State Papers*, II, 188–98.

43. *Annals of Cong.*, 16th Cong., 2d sess., 715–34.

44. *Ibid.*, pp. 441, 688–89. On the military committee were: Smyth, Solomon Van Rensselaer (N.Y. Fed.), Robert Moore (Pa.), John Russ (Conn.), Joshua Cushman (Mass.), and the conservatives Cocke of Tennessee and Burton of North Carolina.

45. *Ibid.*, pp. 744–45.

46. *Ibid.*, pp. 767–94, 810–21.

47. *Ibid.*, pp. 823–41, 865–72, 891–901, 925–30.

48. *Ibid.*, pp. 261, 364–65, 367–79, 901, 937.

49. *Ibid.*, pp. 1041–42, 1192, 1215.

50. *Messages and Papers of the Presidents*, II, 18; Monroe to Madison, November 24, 1817, Monroe, VI, 32–33.

51. Other members included: James Tallmadge (N.Y.), Samuel D. Ingham (Pa.), Henry Storrs (N.Y. Fed.), Clifton Clagett (N. H.), George Robertson (Ky.), and William Lewis (Va.).

52. *Annals of Cong.*, 15th Cong., 1st sess., 451–60.

53. Madison to Henry St. George Tucker, December 23, 1817. Madison, *Letters*, III, 53–54.

54. Richmond *Enquirer*, December 27, 1817. "John Hampden" was a favorite pseudonym of both Spencer Roane and Benjamin Watkins Leigh.

55. Macon to Bartlett Yancey, March 8, April 15, 1818, Bartlett Yancey Papers, UNC Lib.

56. *Annals of Cong.*, 15th Cong., 1st sess., 1114–16.

57. *Ibid.*, pp. 1139–51, 1151–64, 1201–17, 1224–35.

58. *Ibid.*, p. 1249.

59. *Ibid.*, pp. 1361–62.

60. Richmond *Enquirer*, April 28, 1818. See also John Tyler to his constituents, *Enquirer*, April 21, 1818.

61. *Annals of Cong.*, 15th Cong., 1st sess., 1385–89, 1678–79.

62. *Annals of Cong.*, 15th Cong., 2d sess., 451–53, 456–57, 460, 471.

63. *Ibid.*, pp. 494–514.

64. *Ibid.*, p. 171. The military affairs committee was dominated by Easterners rather than Old Republicans: John Williams (Tenn.), Abner Lacock (Pa.), Isaac Tichenor (Vt.), Walter Taylor (Ind.), and Clement Storer (N.H.).

65. *Annals of Cong.*, 16th Cong., 1st sess., 1641–49.

66. *Ibid.*, pp. 655, 2244.

67. Moore, pp. 332–36; Harrison, pp. 486–87.

68. *Annals of Cong.*, 15th Cong., 1st sess., 1762–63.

69. Richmond *Enquirer*, September 8, 1818; *Norfolk and Portsmouth Herald*, September 7, 1818.

70. Tyler to Dr. Henry Curtis, December 18, 1818, John Tyler Papers, LC.

71. *Ibid.*, January 18, 1819, John Tyler Papers, LC.

72. *Annals of Cong.*, 15th Cong., 2d sess., 552–73, 598, 1140.

73. Rothbard, pp. 11–13; Dangerfield, pp. 180–84.

74. *Annals of Cong.*, 15th Cong., 2d sess., 1240–50.

75. *Ibid.*, p. 1311.

76. *Ibid.*, pp. 1404–06.

77. Burwell to Caesar A. Rodney, February 20, 1819, Simon Gratz Collection, Hist. Soc. of Penn.; *Anals of Cong.*, 15th Cong., 2d sess., 1411–13.

78. *Annals of Cong.*, 15th Cong., 1st sess., 1726–31, 1740–43, 387.

79. *Annals of Cong.*, 16th Cong., 1st sess., 1663–69, 1913.

80. *Ibid.*, pp. 1950, 1952–63.

81. *Ibid.*, pp. 2054–80.

82. *Ibid.*, pp. 2115–35.

83. *Ibid.*, pp. 2155–56.

84. The standard explanation for the reversal of the South on the tariff between 1816 and 1820 is that Southerners had concluded

that "slave labor was not adaptable to manufactures" and they were committed to an agrarian economy; see Taussig, p. 73, and Stanwood, I, 262. But even if the South had supported the tariff in 1816 through a desire to create her own manufactures, it seems unlikely that this experiment would have proved impractical as early as 1820. A more reasonable assumption is that the postwar nationalism was wearing off by 1820, and the South was becoming more conscious of her own economic interests, particularly under the impetus of the Missouri debate.

85. *Annals of Cong.*, 16th Cong., 1st sess., 656–72.

86. *Annals of Cong.*, 15th Cong., 1st sess., 907–13.

87. *Ibid.*, pp. 918–35, 962–72.

88. *Ibid.*, pp. 1020–27.

89. *Annals of Cong.*, 15th Cong., 2d sess., 1165–66, 1214–15; Moore, pp. 52–53.

90. *Annals of Cong.*, 15th Cong., 2d ses., 1434–35.

91. Dangerfield, p. 218.

92. *Annals of Cong.*, 16th Cong., 1st sess., 223–26.

93. Randolph to Dr. John Brockenbrough, February 24, 1820. Quoted by Garland, II, 133.

94. Moore, p. 105; *Annals of Cong.*, 16th Cong., 1st sess., 270; Richmond *Enquirer*, February 10, 12, and 15, 1820.

95. *Annals of Cong.*, 16th Cong., 1st sess., 424–28.

96. Macon to Bolling Hall, February 13, 1820, Bolling Hall Papers, Alabama Dept. of Archives and History.

97. *Annals of Cong.*, 16th Cong., 1st sess., 1586–88.

98. Richmond *Enquirer*, March 10, 1820; J. Adams, V, 4; Randolph to Henry Middleton Rutledge, March 20, 1820, John Randolph Papers, Duke Univ. Lib.

99. Richmond *Enquirer*, February 10 and March 7, 1820.

100. W. Plumer, Jr., p. 10.

101. Tucker to James Barbour, February, 11, 1820, James Barbour Papers, NYPL.

102. Hay to Monroe, February 17 and 18, 1820, Monroe Papers, LC.

103. Macon to Bartlett Yancey, April 19, 1820, Bartlett Yancey Papers, UNC Lib.

104. Thomas Settle to Bartlett Yancey, April 8, 1820. *Ibid.* This letter is the best document on the subject because the action of the North Carolina delegation was not reported in the newspapers.

105. *Annals of Cong.*, 16th Cong., 2d sess., 10, 26, 41, 116.

106. *Ibid.*, pp. 453–55, 508–95 *passim.*, 669–70.

107. *Ibid.*, pp. 1116–17.

108. *Ibid.*, pp. 390, 1238–40; Hugh Nelson to Dr. Charles Everett, February 26, 1821, Hugh Nelson Papers, LC.

109. Richmond *Enquirer*, June 11, 15, 18, and 22, 1819; Jefferson to Roane, September 6, 1819, in Ford, ed., *Writings*, X, 140–43; see also Madison to Spencer Roane, September 2, 1819, Madison, *Writings*, VIII, 447–53.

110. J. Taylor, *Construction Construed*, p. 234.

111. Jefferson to Archibald Thweat, January 18, 1820, in Ford, ed., *Writings*, X, 184.

112. Richmond *Enquirer*, May 25 and 29, June 1, 5, and 8, 1821; Jefferson to Johnson, June 12, 1823, in Ford, ed., *Writings*, X, 229n.

113. Garnett to Randolph, [December, 1819], Randolph-Garnett Transcripts, LC.

114. Jefferson to Edward Livingston, April 4, 1824, in Ford, ed., *Writings*, X, 300; J. Adams, V, 456.

115. J. Adams, V, 281.

Notes to Chapter VIII: The Radicals

1. Story to Jeremiah Mason, February 21, 1822; quoted in W. C. Ford, ed., *Writings of John Quincy Adams* (New York, 1917), VII, 207n.

2. See speech of John Taylor in the Senate, April 22, 1824. *Annals of Cong.*, 18th Cong., 1st sess., 558–65.

3. Van Buren to Charles E. Dudley, January 10, 1822, in Bonney, I, 382-84. Ammon, "James Monroe and the Era of Good Feelings," pp. 387–398, claims Monroe actively pursued a policy of conciliation, hoping to eliminate all political parties.

4. Remini, p. 15.

5. The earliest extant letter of Randolph to Van Buren, *ca.* 1822, Van Buren Papers, evidences a close friendship. Their mutual friend, a New York Federalist, Harmannus Bleecker furnished Van Buren with a letter of introduction which "dissipated" Randolph's "preposession against him." Randolph to Bleecker, December 29, 1821, Randolph-Bleecker Letterbook, UVA Lib. See also Van Buren, p. 429.

6. Van Buren, p. 126.

7. Ritchie to Van Buren, July 2, 1838, "Unpublished Letters of Thomas Ritchie," p. 229.

8. Wiltse, pp. 236–37.

9. Wiltse, pp. 252–53, assumes that the attack was strictly a maneuver by the Crawford-Clay-Clinton alliance.

10. Jefferson to Nathaniel Macon, August 19, 1821. Jefferson, in Ford, ed., *Writings*, X, 193.

11. *Annals of Cong.*, 17th Cong., 1st sess., 625, 785–87, 1565–66. On the committee were William Eustis (Mass.), Soloman Van Renssalaer (N.Y. Fed.), John Cocke (Tenn.), Burwell Bassett (Va.), William Darlington (Pa.), John S. Smith (Ky.), and John Mattocks (Vt.).

12. *Ibid.*, pp. 1587–89.

13. *Ibid.*, pp. 1591–94, 1594–98, 1608.

14. *Ibid.*, pp. 1608–12.

15. *Ibid.*, pp. 1612, 1615–16.

16. *Ibid.*, p. 1094. Other members were Lewis Williams (N.C.), William Smith (Va.), Thomas Whipple (N.H.), Albert Tracy (N.Y.), George Holcombe (N.J.), and Thomas Ross (Ohio).

17. *Ibid.*, pp. 1551–59.

18. *Ibid.*, pp. 1722–23, 1740, 1782.

19. *Ibid.*, pp. 533, 751–55, 759–65.

20. Richmond *Enquirer*, December 25, 1819; Wayland, pp. 58–59.

21. *Annals of Cong.*, 17th Cong., 1st sess., 766, 770–84.

22. *Ibid.*, pp. 1036, 1039.

23. See speeches of Alexander Smyth of Virginia, *ibid.*, pp. 792–803; Rollin Mallary of Vermont, pp. 955–56; James Blair of South Carolina, pp. 978–81; Thomas Mitchell of South Carolina, p. 1023; John Phillips of Pennsylvania, pp. 1029–30; and James Buchanan of Pennsylvania, p. 1282.

24. *Ibid.*, p. 1298. Identifiable as Old Republicans in the Seventeenth Congress are: Mark Alexander (Va.), William S. Archer (Va.), William Lee Ball (Va.), Burwell Bassett (Va.), Hutchins Gordon Burton (N.C.), Newton Cannon (Tenn.), John Cocke (Tenn.), Henry W. Connor (N.C.), Weldon Nathaniel Edwards (N.C.), John Floyd (Va.), Robert S. Garnett (Va.), Thomas Hall (N.C.), Charles Hooks (N.C.), James Jones (Va.), William McCoy (Va.), Hugh Nelson (Va.), James Overstreet (S.C.), John Randolph (Va.), John Rhea (Tenn.), Alexander Smyth (Va.), Andrew Stevenson (Va.), George Tucker (Va.), Starling Tucker (S.C.),

and Lewis Williams (N.C.). This list includes only those Southern conservatives who entered Congress prior to 1820.

25. *Ibid.*, pp. 1503–08, 1510–13, 1514.

26. *Ibid.*, pp. 50, 58, 748.

27. *Ibid.*, pp. 439, 1690–93, 1734. The seven opponents in the Senate were: John Gaillard (S.C.), William Smith (S.C.), Montfort Stokes (N.C.), Nathaniel Macon (N.C.), William R. King (Ala.), James Pleasants (Va.), and Thomas Hart Benton (Mo.).

28. *Messages and Papers of the Presidents*, II, 142–43.

29. *Annals of Cong.*, 17th Cong., 1st sess., 1874–75.

30. Roane to Monroe, July 1, 1822. Roane, "Letters," p. 180.

31. *Annals of Cong.*, 17th Cong., 2d sess., 84–92; Van Buren, p. 117; Remini, pp. 30–31.

32. *Annals of Cong.*, 17th Cong., 2d sess., 1063, 1074–75.

33. *Annals of Cong.*, 18th Cong., 1st sess., 829–30, 990–98.

34. *Ibid.*, pp. 1005–13.

35. *Ibid.*, p. 1041.

36. *Ibid.*, pp. 1264–82.

37. Macon to Bartlett Yancey, December 26, 1824, Bartlett Yancey Papers, UNC Lib.; *Annals of Cong.*, 18th Cong., 1st sess., 1296–1311.

38. *Annals of Cong.*, 18th Cong., 1st sess., 1311–17.

39. *Ibid.*, pp. 1332–43, 1344–61, 1468–69.

40. *Ibid.*, pp. 558–65.

41. *Ibid.*, pp. 568, 570–71; Jackson to Monroe, July 26, 1822, Jackson Papers, LC.

42. Bassett to St. George Tucker, January 31, 1824, Tucker-Coleman Papers, Colonial Williamsburg.

43. *Annals of Cong.*, 17th Cong., 2d sess., 544–46, 758–60.

44. *Ibid.*, pp. 783–88.

45. *Ibid.*, pp. 936–58.

46. *Ibid.*, pp. 760–67.

47. *Annals of Cong.*, 18th Cong., 1st sess., 795. On the day before the election Lewis Williams predicted that many Crawford men would vote for Clay: Williams to Bartlett Yancey, November 30, 1823, Bartlett Yancey Papers, UNC Lib. Moreover, some Northern Radicals, including Van Buren, hoped to persuade Clay to accept second place on the caucus ticket: Remini, pp. 48–49.

48. Dangerfield, p. 292; *Messages and Papers of the Presidents*, II, 216; *Annals of Cong.*, 18th Cong., 1st sess., 959–65.

49. *Annals of Cong.*, 18th Cong., 1st sess., 1480, 1625–27, 1658.

50. *Ibid.*, pp. 1495–97.

51. *Ibid.*, p. 2429.

52. *Ibid.*, pp. 676–88.

53. *Ibid.*, pp. 743–44.

54. Dangerfield, p. 320.

55. Crawford to Charles Tait, February 22, 1815, Charles Tait Papers, Alabama Dept. of Archives and History; Crawford to Caesar A. Rodney, March 27, 1820, Miscellaneous Collection, William L. Clements Lib., Univ. of Michigan.

56. Macon to Bartlett Yancey, December 19, 1823, Bartlett Yancey Papers, UNC Lib.

57. Remini, p. 36, stresses the similarity in political principles between the two as the reason for Van Buren's choice of Crawford, but Van Buren's own statement in his *Autobiography*, p. 131 ("His friends seemed more anxious to preserve the unity of the Republican Party, and on that account I imbibed an early inclination to give him the preference."), indicates a primary concern with party rather than with principle.

58. Samuel Smith to Mrs. M. B. Mansfield, July 25, 1823, Carter-Smith Papers, UVA Lib.

59. Bruce, I, 488; Ambler, *Ritchie,* pp. 86–87; Richmond *Enquirer*, January 26, 1822.

60. Richmond *Enquirer*, January–February, 1823, *passim.*

61. Richmond *Enquirer*, May 20, 1823; Bassett to St. George Tucker, February 13, 1824, Tucker-Coleman Papers, Colonial Williamsburg; Randolph to Garnett, January 27, 1824, Randolph-Garnett Transcripts, LC: Richmond *Enquirer*, May 25, 1824.

62. Macon to Bolling Hall, March 5, 1822, Bolling Hall Papers, Alabama Dept. of Arch. and Hist.; Macon to Bartlett Yancey, March 17, 1822, Bartlett Yancey Papers, UNC Lib.; Mangum to Thomas Ruffin, January 20, 1824, Ruffin, I, 287–88; Mangum to Seth Jones, February 11, 1824, Mangum, I, 116.

63. McFarland, pp. 140–41, 165–66.

64. Wiltse, p. 237.

65. Calhoun to John Ewing Calhoun, July 1, 1822, Calhoun, II, 204.

66. Malone, *Thomas Cooper,* pp. 294–99; John Taylor to Bolling Hall, January 23, 1824; D. R. Williams to Bolling Hall, January 26, 1824, Bolling Hall Papers, Alabama Dept. of Arch. and Hist.

67. Macon to Bartlett Yancey, February 7, 1824, Bartlett Yancey Papers, UNC Lib.

68. Remini, pp. 47–48; Thomas W. Cobb to Charles Tait, February 2, 1824, Charles Tait Papers, Alabama Dept. of Arch. and Hist.; Mangum to Seth Jones, February 11, 1824, Mangum, I, 114–17; *National Intelligencer*, February 16, 1824.

69. Remini, pp. 48–49.

70. Gallatin to Badollet, July 29, 1824; Badollet and Gallatin, pp. 264–68.

71. Shipp, p. 174; Troup to Macon, June, 15, 1824, Nathaniel Macon Papers, Duke Univ. Lib.

72. Remini, p. 66.

73. Ambler, *Sectionalism in Virginia*, pp. 98–99; Macon to Bartlett Yancey, December 26, 1824, Bartlett Yancey Papers, UNC Lib.

Notes to Chapter IX: The Jacksonians

1. *Norfolk and Portsmouth Herald,* February 4, 1825.

2. Richmond *Enquirer*, January 28, 1823; J. Adams, VI, 285.

3. Stevenson to Barbour, March 28, 1825, Barbour Papers, UVA Lib. A similar neutrality was expressed by Nathaniel Macon, Macon to Judge Charles Tait, February 23, 1825, Macon Papers, Duke Univ. Lib.

4. Gallatin to Badollet, July 29, 1824, Badollet and Gallatin, pp. 265–66.

5. Betsy Coles to Andrew Stevenson, February 3, 1825, Andrew Stevenson Papers, LC.

6. Mangum to Bartlett Yancey, January 15, 1826, Bartlett Yancey Papers, UNC Lib.

7. *Messages and Papers of the Presidents*, II, 299–317.

8. Macon to Bartlett Yancey, December 8, 1825, Bartlett Yancey Papers, UNC Lib.; Jefferson to Giles, December 26, 1825, in Ford, ed., *Writings*, XII, 427.

9. Anderson, *William Branch Giles*, pp. 217–18; Richmond *Enquirer*, December 8, 1825.

10. The only Virginia conservatives who had served in the House prior to 1820 were: Mark Alexander, William S. Archer, Burwell Bassett, John Floyd, Robert S. Garnett, William McCoy, and Andrew Stevenson.

11. Williams and his brother, John, of Tennessee, were per-

sonal and political enemies of Jackson. See John Williams to James Barbour, September 1, 1825, Barbour Papers, UVA Lib. Another North Carolina Old Republican, Hutchins Gordon Burton, who was elected governor in 1824 in opposition to the Jacksonian "Peoples' Ticket," also supported the Adams Administration, as did John Hunter Bryan and John Long, who were former Radicals, but not strict conservatives. Hoffmann, p. 6.

12. Remini, pp. 95–96; Dangerfield, p. 347; Randolph to Tazewell, February 21, 1826, Littleton Waller Tazewell Papers, Virginia State Library.

13. *Register of Debates*, 19th Cong., 1st sess., II, part i, 142; *Messages and Papers of the Presidents*, II, 327.

14. *Reg. of Debates*, 19th Cong., 1st sess., II, part i, 390–401.

15. Macon to Bartlett Yancey, November 3, 1827, Bartlett Yancey Papers, UNC Lib.; Tazewell to Randolph, February 26, 1826, Tazewell Papers, Virginia State Library; *Reg. of Debates*, 19th Cong. 1st sess., II, part i, 150; part ii, 2514.

16. Macon to Bartlett Yancey, April 16, 1826, Bartlett Yancey Papers, UNC Lib.

17. *Ibid.*, November 3, 1826.

18. Macon to Jackson, January 17, 1796; February 14, 1800; January 12, 1801; Jackson Papers, LC; Abernethy, *From Frontier to Plantation*, pp. 180–81, 221–22; Jackson to Randolph [1810], Jackson Papers, LC.

19. Van Buren to Phillip Norborne Nicholas, November, 1826, Martin Van Buren Papers, LC.

20. Randolph to Richard Kidder Randolph, January 17, 1825, January 13, 1827, John Randolph Papers, LC.

21. Wild, pp. 234–35.

22. South Carolina *House Journals*, December 15, 1825; South Carolina *Senate Journals*, December 16, 1825; Cook, *David Rogerson Williams*, p. 291.

23. Van Buren, pp. 198–99; Cook, pp. 243–44; Malone, *Thomas Cooper*, pp. 330–31.

24. Phillips, pp. 111–17.

25. *Ibid.*, pp. 100–9.

26. Abernethy, *Formative Period in Alabama*, pp. 118–21, 141–43.

27. J. Adams, VII, 272.

28. Remini, p. 129; Van Buren to Ritchie, January 13, 1827, Van Buren Papers, LC.

29. Tazewell to Ritchie, March or April, 1827; quoted by Ambler, *Thomas Ritchie*, pp. 108–9.

30. Richmond *Enquirer*, April 27, 1827.

31. Stevenson to John Rutherfoord, December 9, 1826, John Rutherfoord Papers, Duke Univ. Lib.; Chitwood, p. 80.

32. Tyler to Barbour, November 20, 1826, Barbour Papers, UVA Lib.

33. Tyler to Dr. Henry Curtis, September 4, 1827, John Tyler Papers, LC; Chitwood, p. 83.

34. Tyler to Dr. Henry Curtis, December 16, 1827, John Tyler Papers, LC.

35. Remini, pp. 150–51.

36. *Ibid.*, pp. 174–77, 183.

37. *Register of Debates*, 20th Cong., 1st sess., 2472; Tyler to Dr. Henry Curtis, April 23, 1828, John Tyler Papers, LC.

38. Bowers, *Party Battles*, p. 41.

39. New York *Post*, February 24, 1829. See also Livermore, pp. 179, 241, 245.

40. B. Hammond, pp. 329–33, 339–40, feels that even the "Kitchen Cabinet" was dominated by businessmen.

41. Jackson to Randolph, December 22, 1831, Jackson Papers, LC.

42. Ritchie to Archibald Ritchie, June 8, 1830, "Unpublished Letters of Thomas Ritchie," pp. 207–9; *Niles' Register*, July 10, 1830; see also Crawford to Van Buren, May 31, 1830, Van Buren Papers, LC, in which Crawford dislikes internal improvements even more than the tariff.

43. Randolph to Richard Kidder Randolph, June 25, 1830, John Randolph Papers, LC.

44. Conger, pp. 424–27; Wild, p. 374.

45. New York *Evening Post*, July 23, 1828; *Niles' Weekly Register*, 35: 274–75.

46. Cook, pp. 245–52.

47. *National Intelligencer*, July 1, 1830; L. P. Saxon to James H. Hammond, July 6, 1830, James H. Hammond Papers, LC; Charleston *City Gazette*, December 3, 1830; Cook, pp. 329–30.

48. Yorkville *Pioneer*, November 4, 1830.

49. Richmond *Enquirer*, April 19, 1832.

50. Ambler, *Life and Diary of John Floyd*, pp. 98–100.

51. *Ibid.*, pp. 136, 199–200.

52. *Ibid.*, pp. 117–18.

53. Calhoun to Bolling Hall, August 8, September 8, 1831, Bolling Hall Papers, Alabama Dept. of Archives and History; Randolph to Levi Woodbury, December 22, 1831, Levi Woodbury Papers, LC.

54. Raleigh *Star*, June 22, 29, 1832; Cole, p. 14; Wiltse, *Calhoun, Nullifier*, p. 129; Harrison, "Martin Van Buren," p. 455; Ritchie to Van Buren, June 25, 1832, Van Buren Papers, LC; Richmond *Whig*, October 26, 1832.

55. Ambler, *Life and Diary of John Floyd*, pp. 198–99; Randolph to Jackson, July 5, 1832, Jackson Papers, LC.

56. Tyler to Floyd, January 16, 1833, John Tyler Papers, LC; Chitwood, pp. 124–25.

57. *Niles' Weekly Register*, 43: 422.

58. Randolph to Jackson, December 6, 1832, Jackson Papers, LC; Van Buren, pp. 425–26.

59. Raleigh *Register*, July 1, August 26, 1834; Raleigh *Star*, September 18, 1834.

60. Abernethy, *From Frontier to Plantation*, pp. 293, 297–99; Sellers, *James K. Polk*, I, 137 ff.

61. Sellers, "Who Were the Southern Whigs?," pp. 335–46.

62. I am in debt for this insight into the nature of Jacksonian Democracy to Meyers' *The Jacksonian Persuasion*.

63. Ambler, *Life and Diary of John Floyd*, pp. 203–4; Ritchie to Rives, January 6, 1833, William Cabell Rives Papers, LC.

64. McFarland, p. 461; Macon to Van Buren, March 2, 1833, Van Buren Papers, LC; Macon to Hall, April 14, 1833, Bolling Hall Papers, Alabama Dept. of Archives and Hist.; Macon to Van Buren, January 24, 1836, Van Buren Papers, LC; Macon to General H. Blount, May 7, 1836, Macon Papers, Duke Univ. Lib.

65. Crawford to Hall, January 17, 1833, Bolling Hall Papers, Alabama Dept. of Archives and Hist.

66. Kendall, p. 559.

Bibliography

Manuscripts

Ambler Family Papers. University of Virginia Library.

Barbour Papers. University of Virginia Library.

William Wyatt Bibb Papers. Alabama Department of Archives and History, Montgomery.

Bryan Family Papers. University of Virginia Library.

Hutchins Gordon Burton Papers. University of North Carolina Library.

William A. Burwell Papers. Library of Congress, Washington.

Carter-Smith Family Papers. University of Virginia Library.

John Clopton Papers. Duke University Library.

Coolidge Family Papers. Massachusetts Historical Society.

Joseph Desha Papers. Library of Congress, Washington.

Edgehill-Randolph Papers. University of Virginia Library.

Weldon Nathaniel Edwards Papers. Duke University Library.

James M. Garnett Papers. Duke University Library.

Francis Walker Gilmer Papers. University of Virginia Library.

Simon Gratz Collection. Historical Society of Pennsylvania, Philadelphia.

Bolling Hall Papers. Alabama Department of Archives and History, Montgomery.

James H. Hammond Papers. Library of Congress, Washington.

Ernest Haywood Papers. University of North Carolina Library.

Andrew Jackson Papers. Library of Congress, Washington.

Thomas Jefferson Papers. University of Virginia Library.

Thomas Jefferson Papers. Library of Congress, Washington.

William Jones Papers. Historical Society of Pennsylvania, Philadelphia.

Richard H. King Papers. North Carolina Department of Archives and History, Raleigh.

Lenoir Family Papers. University of North Carolina Library.

Edward Lloyd Papers. Maryland Historical Society, Baltimore.

George Logan Papers. Historical Society of Pennsylvania, Philadelphia.

Nathaniel Macon Papers. Duke University Library.

James Madison Papers, Library of Congress, Washington.

James Monroe Papers. Library of Congress, Washington.

Hugh Nelson Papers. Library of Congress, Washington.

Wilson Cary Nicholas Papers. University of Virginia Library.

Wilson Cary Nicholas Papers. Library of Congress, Washington.

Joseph H. Nicholson Papers. Library of Congress, Washington.

John Overton Papers (Microfilm). University of North Carolina Library.

Prentis Family Papers. Colonial Williamsburg.

John Randolph Papers. Library of Congress, Washington.

John Randolph Papers. Duke University Library.

John Randolph Papers. University of Virginia Library.

Randolph–Harmannus Bleecker Letterbook. University of Virginia Library.

Randolph-Garnett Letterbook. University of Virginia Library.

Randolph-Garnett Transcripts. Library of Congress, Washington.

Randolph-Josiah Quincy Letters. Library of Congress, Washington.

William Cabell Rives Papers. Library of Congress, Washington.

John Rutherfoord Papers. Duke University Library.

Shippen Family Papers. Library of Congress, Washington.

Richard Stanford Letters. Library of Congress, Washington.

Andrew Stevenson Papers. Library of Congress, Washington.

Charles Tait Papers. Alabama Department of Archives and History, Montgomery.

Creed Taylor Papers. University of Virginia Library.

John Taylor of Caroline Letters. Duke University Library.

Littleton Waller Tazewell Papers. Virginia State Library, Richmond.

Tucker-Coleman Papers. Colonial Williamsburg.

Henry St. George Tucker Letters. Duke University Library.

John Tyler Papers. Library of Congress, Washington.

Martin Van Buren Papers. Library of Congress, Washington.

John Williams Walker Papers. Alabama Department of Archives and History, Montgomery.

William Wirt Papers. Maryland Historical Society, Baltimore.
Levi Woodbury Papers. Library of Congress, Washington.
Thomas Worthington Diary. Library of Congress, Washington.
Bartlett Yancey Papers. University of North Carolina Library.

Newspapers

Baltimore, Maryland, *Niles' Register.*
Charleston, South Carolina, *City Gazette.*
Fredericksburg, Virginia, *Virginia Herald.*
Georgetown, Maryland, *The Spirit of Seventy-six.*
Norfolk, Virginia, *The Norfolk and Portsmouth Herald.*
Philadelphia, Pennsylvania, *The Aurora.*
Raleigh, North Carolina, *Minerva.*
Raleigh, North Carolina, *Register.*
Raleigh, North Carolina, *Star.*
Richmond, Virginia, *The Enquirer.*
Richmond, Virginia, *The Spirit of '76.*
Richmond, Virginia, *Virginia Argus.*
Washington, D.C., *National Intelligencer.*
Washington, D.C., *The Spirit of '76.*

Books, Articles, and Other

Abernethy, Thomas Perkins. Formative Period in Alabama. Montgomery, Ala., 1922.
—— From Frontier to Plantation in Tennessee. Chapel Hill, N.C., 1932.
—— "The Origin of the Whig Party in Tennessee," *Mississippi Valley Historical Review*, XII (March, 1926), 504–22.
—— The South in the New Nation, 1789–1819. Vol. IV of The History of the South, edited by Wendell Holmes Stephenson and E. Merton Coulter. Baton Rouge, La., 1961.
Adams, Henry. History of the United States During the Administrations of Thomas Jefferson and James Madison. 4 vols. New York, 1930.
—— Life of Albert Gallatin. New York, 1943.
—— John Randolph. American Statesmen Series, edited by John T. Morse, Jr. Boston, 1898.

Adams, John Quincy. Memoirs of John Quincy Adams. Edited by Charles Francis Adams. 8 vols. Philadelphia, 1874–77.

Ambler, Charles Henry. Life and Diary of John Floyd. Richmond, Va., 1918.

—— Sectionalism in Virginia, 1776–1861. Chicago, 1910.

—— Thomas Ritchie, A Study in Virginia Politics. Richmond, Va., 1913.

American State Papers, Military Affairs. 7 vols. Washington, D.C., 1832–61.

Ammon, Harry. "James Monroe and the Election of 1808 in Virginia," William and Mary Quarterly, 3d series, XX, No. 1 (January, 1963), 33–56.

—— "James Monroe and the Era of Good Feelings," Virginia Magazine of History and Biography, LXVI (October, 1958), 387–98.

—— "The Jeffersonian Republicans in Virginia: An Interpretation," Virginia Magazine of History and Biography, LXXI (April, 1963), 153–67.

—— The Republican Party in Virginia, 1789–1824. Dissertation. University of Virginia Library, 1948.

—— "The Richmond Junto, 1800–1824," Virginia Magazine of History and Biography, LXI (October, 1953), 395–418.

Anderson, Dice Robbins. "The Insurgents of 1811," American Historical Association Annual Report for 1911, I (1913), 165–76.

—— William Branch Giles. Menasha, Wis., 1914.

Annals of Congress. 43 vols. Washington, D.C., 1834–56.

Auerbach, M. Morton. The Conservative Illusion. New York, 1959.

Badollet, John and Albert Gallatin. The Correspondence of John Badollet and Albert Gallatin. Edited by Gayle Thornbrough. Vol. XX of the Indiana Historical Society Publications. Indianapolis, 1963.

Balinky, Alexander S. "Albert Gallatin, Naval Foe," Pennsylvania Magazine of History and Biography, LXXXII (July, 1958), 293–304.

Beach, Rex. Judge Spencer Roane. Master's thesis. University of Virginia Library, 1941.

—— "Spencer Roane and the Richmond Junto," William and Mary College Quarterly, 2d series, XXII (January, 1942), 1–17.

Bemis, Samuel Flagg. Diplomatic History of the United States. New York, 1955.

Benson, Lee. The Concept of Jacksonian Democracy: New York as a Test Case. Princeton, N.J., 1961.

Binkley, Wilfred E. American Political Parties, Their Natural History. New York, 1943.

Biographical Directory of the American Congress, 1774–1949. Edited by James L. Harrison. Washington, D.C., 1949.

Bonney, Catharina V. R. A Legacy of Historical Gleanings. 2 vols. Albany, N.Y., 1875.

Bowers, Claude G. Jefferson and Hamilton. Boston and New York, 1925.

—— Party Battles of the Jackson Period. Boston and New York, 1922.

Brant, Irving. James Madison, Secretary of State. Indianapolis and New York, 1941.

—— James Madison, President. Indianapolis and New York, 1956.

Brown, Roger H. The Republic in Peril: 1812. New York and London, 1964.

—— "The War Hawks of 1812: An Historical Myth," *Indiana Magazine of History*, LX (June, 1964), 137–51.

Bruce, William Cabell. John Randolph of Roanoke. 2 vols. New York, 1922.

Burt, Alfred L. The United States, Great Britain, and British North America from the Revolution to the Establishment of Peace after the War of 1812. New Haven, Conn., 1940.

Calhoun, John C. Correspondence of John C. Calhoun. Edited by J. Franklin Jameson. Vol. II of the American Historical Association Annual Report, 1899. Washington, D.C., 1900.

Carpenter, Jesse Thomas. The South as a Conscious Minority, 1789–1861. New York, 1930.

Channing, Edward. The Jeffersonian System. Vol. XII of The American Nation: A History, edited by Albert Bushnell Hart (28 vols., New York, 1904–18). New York, 1906.

Chitwood, Oliver Perry. John Tyler, Champion of the Old South. New York, 1939.

Cobban, Alfred. Edmund Burke and the Revolt Against the Eighteenth Century. London, 1960.

Cole, Arthur C. The Whig Party in the South. Washington, D.C., 1914.

Conger, John L. "South Carolina and Early Tariffs," *Mississippi Valley Historical Review*, V (1918–19), 415–33.

Cook, Harvey Toliver. The Life and Legacy of David Rogerson Williams. New York, 1916.

Corbitt, D. L. "Congressional Districts of North Carolina, 1789–1934," *North Carolina Historical Review*, XII (April, 1935), 173–88.

Cox, Isaac Joslin. The West Florida Controversy, 1798–1813. Baltimore, 1918.

Craven, Avery Odelle. "John Taylor and Southern Agriculture," *Journal of Southern History*, IV (1938), 137–47.

——— Soil Exhaustion as a Factor in the Agricultural History of Virginia and Maryland, 1606–1860. Vol. XIII of the University of Illinois Studies in the Social Sciences. Urbana, Ill., 1925.

Cresson, W. P. James Monroe. Chapel Hill, N.C., 1946.

Cunningham, Noble E., Jr. The Jeffersonian Republicans: The Formation of Party Organization, 1789–1801. Chapel Hill, N.C., 1957.

——— The Jeffersonian Republicans in Power: Party Operations, 1801–1809. Chapel Hill, N.C., 1963.

——— "Nathaniel Macon and the Southern Protest Against National Consolidation," *North Carolina Historical Review*, XXXII (July, 1955), 376–84.

——— "Who Were the Quids?" *Mississippi Valley Historical Review*, L (September, 1963), 252–63.

Cynn, P. P. "Philip Pendleton Barbour," *John P. Branch Historical Papers of Randolph-Macon College*, IV (1913), 67–77.

Dangerfield, George. The Era of Good Feelings. New York, 1952.

Dauer, Manning J., and Hans Hammond. "John Taylor: Democrat or Aristocrat?" *Journal of Politics*, VI (November, 1944), 381–403.

Davis, Richard Beale. Intellectual Life in Jefferson's Virginia. Chapel Hill, N.C., 1964.

Dingledine, Raymond. The Political Career of William Cabell Rives. Dissertation. University of Virginia Library, 1947.

Dodd, William E. "Chief Justice Marshall and Virginia, 1813–1821," *American Historical Review*, XII (July, 1907), 776–87.

——— "John Taylor, of Caroline, Prophet of Secession," *John P. Branch Historical Papers of Randolph-Macon College*, II (June, 1908), 214–52.

——— The Life of Nathaniel Macon. Raleigh, N.C., 1903.

Dorfman, Joseph. The Economic Mind in American Civilization, 1606–1865. 2 vols. New York, 1946.

Drell, Bernard. "John Taylor and the Preservation of an Old Social Order," *Virginia Magazine of History and Biography*, XLVI (1938), 285–98.

Duckett, Alvin Laroy. John Forsyth: Political Tactician. Athens, Ga., 1962.

Eaton, Clement. The Growth of Southern Civilization, 1790–1860. The New American Nation Series, edited by Henry Steele Commager and Richard B. Morris. New York, 1961.

Foster, William Omer. James Jackson: Duelist and Militant Statesman. Athens, Ga., 1960.

Gallatin, Albert. The Writings of Albert Gallatin. Edited by Henry Adams. 3 vols. New York, 1879.

Garland, Hugh A. Life of John Randolph of Roanoke. 2 vols. New York, 1860.

Gates, Paul W. The Farmer's Age: Agriculture, 1815–1860. Vol. III of The Economic History of the United States. New York, 1960.

Gilpatrick, Delbert H. Jeffersonian Democracy in North Carolina. New York, 1931.

Goodman, Warren H. "The Origins of the War of 1812: A Survey of Changing Interpretations," Mississippi Valley Historical Review, XXVIII (September, 1941), 171–86.

Goodrich, Carter, ed. Canals and American Economic Development. New York, 1961.

Grampp, William D. "John Taylor: Economist of Southern Agrarians," Southern Economic Journal, XI (January, 1945), 255–268.

Gregorie, Anne King. Thomas Sumter. Columbia, S.C., 1931.

Hacker, Louis M. "Western Land Hunger and the War of 1812," Mississippi Valley Historical Review, X (March, 1924), 365–95.

Hamer, Marguerite B. "John Rhea of Tennessee," East Tennessee Historical Society Publications, No. 4 (January, 1932), 35–44.

Hammond, Bray. Banks and Politics in America from the Revolution to the Civil War. Princeton, N.J., 1957.

Hammond, Jabez D. History of Political Parties in the State of New York. 2 vols. Cooperstown, N.Y., 1845.

Handman, Max Sylvius. "The Sentiment of Nationalism," Political Science Quarterly, XXXVI (1921), 107–14.

Harrison, Joseph Hobson. The Internal Improvement Issue in the Politics of the Union, 1783–1825. Dissertation. University of Virginia Library, 1954.

——— "Martin Van Buren and His Southern Supporters," The Journal of Southern History, XXII (November, 1956), 438–58.

Hartz, Louis. The Liberal Tradition in America. New York, 1955.

Haskins, Charles Homer. "Yazoo Land Companies," *Papers of the American Historical Association,* V (1886), 395–440.

Hatcher, William B. Edward Livingston. University, La., 1940.

Higginbotham, Sanford W. The Keystone in the Democratic Arch: Pennsylvania Politics, 1800–1816. Harrisburg, Pa., 1952.

Hoffman, William S. Andrew Jackson and North Carolina Politics. Vol. XL in The James Sprunt Studies in History and Political Science. Chapel Hill, N.C., 1958.

Hofstadter, Richard. The American Political Tradition and the Men Who Made It. New York, 1951.

Horsman, Reginald. The Causes of the War of 1812. Philadelphia, 1962.

―― "Western War Aims, 1811–1812," *Indiana Magazine of History,* LIII (January, 1957), 1–18.

―― "Who Were the War Hawks?" *Indiana Magazine of History,* LX (June, 1964), 121–36.

Hutton, Hamilton M. Southern Nationalism, 1790 to 1817: A Map Study Based Upon Votes in the House of Representatives. Master's thesis. University of Virginia Library, 1940.

Jefferson, Thomas. Writings of Thomas Jefferson. Edited by Paul Leicester Ford. 12 vols. New York, 1892.

―― Writings of Thomas Jefferson. Edited by Henry Augustus Washington. 9 vols. New York, 1859.

Jennings, Walter Wilson. The American Embargo, 1807–1809. Iowa City, 1921.

Johnson, Allen, and Dumas Malone, eds. Dictionary of American Biography. 20 vols. New York, 1930.

Johnson, Gerald W. John Randolph of Roanoke. New York, 1929.

Jordan, Weymouth T. George Washington Campbell of Tennessee: Western Statesman. No. 17 of the Florida State University Studies. Tallahassee, Fla., 1955.

Kendall, Amos. Autobiography of Amos Kendall. Edited by William Stickney. Boston, 1872.

Kirk, Russell. The Conservative Mind, from Burke to Santayana. Chicago, 1953.

―― Randolph of Roanoke, A Study in Conservative Thought. Chicago, 1951.

Klein, Phillip Shriver. Pennsylvania Politics, 1817–1832. Philadelphia, 1940.

Koch, Adrienne. Jefferson and Madison: The Great Collaboration. New York, 1950.

Kohn, Hans. American Nationalism. New York, 1957.

Latimer, Margaret Kinard. "South Carolina—A Protagonist of the War of 1812," *American Historical Review*, LXI (June, 1956), 914–29.

Little, Lucius Powhattan. Ben Hardin: His Times and Contemporaries. Louisville, Ky., 1887.

Livermore, Shaw. The Twilight of Federalism: The Disintegration of the Federalist Party. Princeton, N.J., 1962.

Long, W. S. "James Barbour," *John P. Branch Historical Papers of Randolph-Macon College*, IV, No. 2 (1914), 34–64.

McFarland, David Miles. Rip Van Winkle: Political Evolution in North Carolina, 1815–1835. Dissertation. University of Pennsylvania Library, 1954.

Macon, Nathaniel. "Some Unpublished Letters of Nathaniel Macon." Edited by John Spencer Bassett. *Trinity College Historical Papers*, VI (1906), 57–65.

—— "Nathaniel Macon Correspondence." Edited by William E. Dodd. *John P. Branch Historical Papers of Randolph-Macon College*, III (June, 1909), 27–93.

Madison, James. Letters and Other Writings of James Madison. Congressional Edition. 4 vols. New York, 1884.

—— The Writings of James Madison. Edited by Gaillard Hunt. 9 vols. New York, 1900–10.

Main, Jackson Turner. The Antifederalists: Critics of the Constitution. Chapel Hill, N.C., 1961.

—— "Sections and Politics in Virginia, 1781–1787," *William and Mary Quarterly*, 3d series, XII (1955), 91–112.

Malone, Dumas. Jefferson and the Ordeal of Liberty. Vol. III of Jefferson and His Time. Boston, 1962.

—— The Public Life of Thomas Cooper, 1783–1839. New Haven, Conn., 1926.

Mangum, Willie Persons. Papers of Willie P. Mangum. Edited by Henry T. Shanks. Publications of the North Carolina Historical Commission. 4 vols. Raleigh, N.C., 1950–1955.

Mayo, Bernard. Henry Clay: Spokesman of the Old West. Boston, 1937.

Mays, David John. Edmund Pendleton. 2 vols. Cambridge, Mass., 1952.

Messages and Papers of the Presidents. Edited by J. D. Richardson. Vols. I and II. Washington, D.C., 1895.

Meyers, Marvin. The Jacksonian Persuasion. Stanford, Calif., 1957.

Miles, Edwin Arthur. Jacksonian Democracy in Mississippi. Chapel Hill, N.C., 1960.

Monroe, James. Writings of James Monroe. Edited by S. M. Hamilton. 7 vols. New York, 1900.

Moore, Glover. The Missouri Controversy, 1819–1821. Lexington, Ky., 1953.

Mudge, Eugene T. The Social Philosophy of John Taylor of Caroline. New York, 1939.

Murray, Paul. The Whig Party in Georgia, 1825–1853. Vol. XXXIX of The James Sprunt Studies in History and Political Science. Chapel Hill, N.C., 1948.

Nettels, Curtis P. The Emergence of a National Economy, 1775–1815. Vol. II of The Economic History of the United States. New York, 1962.

Newsome, Albert Ray. The Presidential Election of 1824 in North Carolina. Chapel Hill, N.C., 1939.

Pancake, John Silas. The General from Baltimore: A Biography of Samuel Smith. Dissertation. University of Virginia Library, 1949.

——— "The 'Invisibles:' A Chapter in the Opposition to President Madison," *Journal of Southern History*, XXI (February, 1955), 17–37.

Perkins, Bradford. Prologue to War: England and the United States, 1805–1812. Berkeley and Los Angeles, 1961.

Pitkin, Timothy. A Statistical View of the Commerce of the United States of America, Its Connection with Agriculture and Manufactures. Hartford, Conn., 1817.

Phillips, Ulrich Bonnell. Georgia and State Rights. Vol. II of the Annual Report of the American Historical Association for the Year 1901. Washington, D.C., 1902.

Plumer, William. Memorandum of Proceedings in the United States Senate. Edited by Everett Somerville Brown. New York, 1923.

Plumer, William, Jr. The Missouri Compromises and Presidential Politics, 1820–1825, from the Letters of William Plumer, Jr., Representative of New Hampshire. Edited by Everett Somerville Brown. Vol. XI of the Publications of the Missouri Historical Society. St. Louis, Mo., 1926.

Potter, David M. "The Historian's Use of Nationalism and Vice Versa," *American Historical Review*, LXVII (July, 1962), 924–50.

Pratt, Julius W. Expansionists of 1812. New York, 1925.

——— "Western War Aims in the War of 1812," *Mississippi Valley Historical Review*, XII (June, 1925), 36–50.

Preyer, Norris Watson. The South's Experiment with Protective Tariffs, 1816–1820. Dissertation. University of Virginia Library, 1954.

Ravenel, Mrs. St. Julien. Life and Times of William Lowndes of South Carolina. Boston and New York, 1901.

Remini, Robert V. Martin Van Buren and the Making of the Democratic Party. New York, 1959.

Risjord, Norman K. "1812: Conservatives, War Hawks, and the Nation's Honor," William and Mary Quarterly, 3d ser., XVIII (April, 1961), 196–210.

—— "The War Hawks and the War of 1812," Indiana Magazine of History, LX (June, 1964), 155–58.

Ritchie, Thomas. "Unpublished Letters of Thomas Ritchie." Edited by Charles Henry Ambler. John P. Branch Historical Papers of Randolph-Macon College, III (June, 1911), 199–252.

Roane, Spencer. "Letters of Spencer Roane, 1788–1822," Bulletin of the New York Public Library, X (1906), 167–80.

—— "Roane Correspondence," John P. Branch Historical Papers of Randolph-Macon College, II (June, 1905), 123–42.

Rogers, George C., Jr. Evolution of a Federalist: William Loughton Smith of Charleston, 1758–1812. Columbia, S.C., 1962.

Rossiter, Clinton. Conservatism in America. New York, 1955.

Rothbard, Murray N. The Panic of 1819: Reactions and Policies. New York and London, 1962.

Ruffin, Thomas. The Papers of Thomas Ruffin. Edited by J. G. deR. Hamilton. 4 vols. Publications of the North Carolina Historical Commission. Raleigh, N.C., 1918.

Russel, Robert R. Economic Aspects of Southern Sectionalism. Urbana, Ill., 1923.

Savelle, Max. "Nationalism and Other Loyalties in the American Revolution," American Historical Review, LXVII (July, 1962), 901–23.

—— Seeds of Liberty. New York, 1948.

Schachner, Nathan. Thomas Jefferson. 2 vols. New York, 1951.

Schaper, William A. "Sectionalism and Representation in South Carolina, A Sociological Study," American Historical Association Annual Report for 1900, Vol. I, pp. 237–463.

Schlesinger, Arthur Meier, Jr. The Age of Jackson. Boston, 1945.

Sears, Alfred Byron. Thomas Worthington: Father of Ohio Statehood. Columbus, Ohio, 1958.

Sears, Louis M. Jefferson and the Embargo. Durham, N.C., 1927.

Sellers, Charles G. "Banking and Politics in Jackson's Tennessee, 1817–1827," *Mississippi Valley Historical Review*, XLI (June, 1954), 61–84.

—— James K. Polk, Jacksonian, 1795–1843. Princeton, N.J., 1957.

—— "Who Were the Southern Whigs?" *American Historical Review*, LIX (January, 1954), 335–46.

Shafer, Boyd C. Nationalism, Myth and Reality. New York, 1955.

Shipp, John Edgar Dawson. Giant Days, or the Life and Times of William Harris Crawford. Americus, Ga., 1909.

Shulim, Joseph I. The Old Dominion and Napoleon Bonaparte. New York, 1952.

Simms, Henry Harrison. Life of John Taylor. Richmond, Va., 1932.

—— The Rise of the Whigs in Virginia. Richmond, Va., 1929.

Smith, Harry K. "Daniel Sheffey," *John P. Branch Historical Papers of Randolph-Macon College*, IV (1916), 364–71.

Smith, James Morton. Freedom's Fetters: The Alien and Sedition Laws and American Civil Liberties. Ithaca, N.Y., 1956.

Snyder, Louis L. The Meaning of Nationalism. New Brunswick, N.J., 1954.

Spaulding, E. Wilder. His Excellency George Clinton. New York, 1938.

Stanwood, Edward. American Tariff Controversies in the Nineteenth Century. 2 vols. New York, 1904.

Steele, John. The Papers of John Steele. Edited by Henry McGilbert Wagstaff. Publications of the North Carolina Historical Commission. 2 vols. Raleigh, N.C., 1924.

Steiner, Bruce E. Benjamin Watkins Leigh. Master's thesis. University of Virginia Library, 1959.

Stokes, William E. Randolph of Roanoke: A Virginia Portrait. Dissertation. University of Virginia Library, 1955.

Styron, Arthur. The Last of the Cocked Hats: James Monroe and the Virginia Dynasty. Norman, Okla., 1945.

Sydnor, Charles S. Development of Southern Sectionalism, 1819–1848. Vol. V of The History of the South, edited by Wendell Holmes Stephenson and E. Merton Coulter. Baton Rouge, La., 1948.

Taggart, Samuel. "Letters of Samuel Taggart, Representative in Congress, 1803–1814," *American Antiquarian Society Proceedings*, New series, Vol. XXXIII, Pts. i, ii, pp. 113–226, 297–438.

Taussig, Frank W. The Tariff History of the United States. New York, 1931.

Taylor, George Rogers. "Agrarian Discontent in the Mississippi Valley Preceding the War of 1812," *Journal of Political Economy*, XXXIX (August, 1931), 471–505.

—— "Prices in the Mississippi Valley Preceding the War of 1812," *Journal of Economic and Business History*, III (1930–31), 148–63.

Taylor, John. Construction Construed and Constitutions Vindicated. Richmond, Va., 1820.

—— "Letters of John Taylor, of Caroline County, Virginia," *John P. Branch Historical Papers of Randolph-Macon College*, II (June, 1908), 253–353.

—— An Inquiry into the Principles and Policy of the Government of the United States. Fredericksburg, Va., 1814.

—— "Letters of John Taylor of Caroline." Edited by Hans Hammond. *Virginia Magazine of History and Biography*, LII (January, 1944), 1–14, 121–34.

Tolles, Frederick B. George Logan of Philadelphia. New York, 1953.

Tucker, George. Life of Thomas Jefferson. 2 vols. Philadelphia, 1837.

United States Department of Commerce. Historical Statistics of the United States, 1789–1945. Washington, D.C., 1949.

Van Buren, Martin. Autobiography of Martin Van Buren. Edited by John C. Fitzpatrick. Vol. II of American Historical Association Annual Report, 1918. Washington, D.C., 1920.

Van Deusen, John George. Economic Basis of Disunion in South Carolina. New York, 1928.

The Virginia Report of 1799–1800 . . . together with the Virginia Resolutions of December 21, 1798. . . . Richmond, Va., 1850.

Walters, Raymond, Jr. Albert Gallatin, Jeffersonian Financier and Diplomat. New York, 1957.

—— Alexander James Dallas. Philadelphia, 1943.

Wayland, Francis Fry. Andrew Stevenson, Democrat and Diplomat, 1785–1857. Philadelphia, 1949.

White, Leonard D. The Jeffersonians, A Study in Administrative History. New York, 1956.

Wickwar, W. Hardy. "Foundations of American Conservatism," *American Political Science Review*, XLI, No. 6 (December, 1947), 1105–17.

Wild, Philip Frederick. South Carolina Politics, 1815–1833. Dissertation. University of Pennsylvania Library, 1949.

Williams, William Appleman. "The Age of Mercantilism: An Interpretation of the American Political Economy, 1763 to 1828," *William and Mary Quarterly*, 3d series, XV (October, 1958), 419–37.

Wiltse, Charles M. John C. Calhoun, Nationalist. Indianapolis and New York, 1944.

Wolfe, John Harold. Jeffersonian Democracy in South Carolina. Vol. XXIV of the James Sprunt Studies in History and Political Science. Chapel Hill, N.C., 1940.

Wright, Benjamin F. "The Philosopher of Jeffersonian Democracy," *American Political Science Review*, XXII (November, 1928), 870–92.

Young, Jeremiah Simeon. A Political and Constitutional Study of the Cumberland Road. Chicago, 1904.

Index